FUNDAMENTALS OF GLOBAL OPERATIONS MANAGEMENT

Second Edition

The Securities & Investment Institute

Mission Statement:

To set standards of professional excellence and integrity for the investment and securities industry, providing qualifications and promoting the highest level of competence to our members, other individuals and firms.

The Securities and Investment Institute is the UK's leading professional and membership body for practitioners in the securities and investment industry, with more than 16,000 members with an increasing number working outside the UK. It is also the major examining body for the industry, with a full range of qualifications aimed at people entering and working in it. More than 30,000 examinations are taken annually in more than 30 countries.

You can contact us through our website *www.sii.org.uk*

Our membership believes that keeping up to date is central to professional development. We are delighted to endorse the Wiley/SII publishing partnership and recommend this series of books to our members and all those who work in the industry.

Ruth Martin
Managing Director

FUNDAMENTALS OF GLOBAL OPERATIONS MANAGEMENT

Second Edition

David Loader

JOHN WILEY & SONS, LTD

Other Wiley Editorial Offices

John Wiley & Sons, Inc., 111 River Street, Hoboken, NJ 07030, USA

Jossey-Bass, 989 Market Street, San Francisco, CA 94103-1741, USA

Wiley-VCH Verlag GmbH, Boschstr. 12, D-69469 Weinheim, Germany

John Wiley & Sons Australia Ltd, 42 McDougall Street, Milton, Queensland 4064, Australia

John Wiley & Sons (Asia) Pte Ltd, 2 Clementi Loop #02-01, Jin Xing Distripark, Singapore 129809

John Wiley & Sons Canada Ltd, 22 Worcester Road, Etobicoke, Ontario, Canada M9W 1L1

Wiley also publishes its books in a variety of electronic formats. Some content that appears
in print may not be available in electronic books.

British Library Cataloguing in Publication Data

A catalogue record for this book is available from the British Library

ISBN-13 978-0-470-02653-3 (PB)
ISBN-10 0-470-02653-7 (PB)

Project management by Originator, Gt Yarmouth, Norfolk (typeset in 12/16pt Trump Mediaeval).

This book is printed on acid-free paper responsibly manufactured from sustainable forestry
in which at least two trees are planted for each one used for paper production.

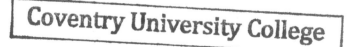

I wish to dedicate this book to the boys and girls, men and women who lost their lives in the terrorist attacks in New York, Washington and Pittsburgh on the 11th September 2001. Many of those totally innocent people worked in the financial services industry and made the ultimate sacrifice whilst simply doing their job.

It matters not whether they were colleagues who we knew: they were our brothers and sisters in a truly global industry. Their loss and the suffering of their loved ones will be felt by every one of us, no matter what part of the industry we work in, for a very long time.

CONTENTS

· ·

Appendices

PREFACE

In this book I hope to be able to take the reader through some of the many, many issues and some of the detail that will be important in a manager or supervisor role. There will be areas of the book that will not cover subjects in great detail and areas of a vast industry that are hardly mentioned. Therefore, there are 'work sessions' that I suggest will enhance the learning process as you carry out your research.

The role and responsibilities of supervising and managing an operations team in global markets should not be underestimated and if you are seeking to take the Securities Institute examinations you will need to work hard on the additional research suggested.

That said, it is – believe me – well worth while as the challenges you will face will be *real* challenges and the satisfaction of successfully establishing your management style and delivering the objectives set for you will be great.

Remember always that you never stop learning, lead by example, listen to others and accept that you are not always right!

I wish you well for the future.

Thanks to the**dsc**.portfolio and Derivative Management Services Ltd.

March 2006

ABOUT THE AUTHOR

David Loader is actively involved in the international financial markets as a director of the Derivatives and Securities Consultancy Ltd, Computer Based Learning Ltd and Derivatives Management Services Ltd. He has over 30 years' experience in the financial services industry, much of the time at senior management level including operations director within major investment banks such as Warburg Securities, SBC Warburg and Warburg Futures & Options Ltd.

David is heavily involved with all three companies of which he is a director, providing a variety of services in training and consultancy to a broad base of clients world-wide. He designs and delivers training courses at all levels on many areas of the financial markets and, in particular, those related to operations. He has been commissioned to deliver programmes to audiences in a variety of countries for industry organisations – such as the Singapore Exchanges, the Stock Exchange of Thailand, the Australian Financial Markets Association and the Malaysian Exchanges. In addition to his work for clients in the UK, he has delivered training and consultancy in centres such as Milan, Prague, Singapore, Hong Kong, Boston, New York, Bermuda, Mumbai, Sydney, Johannesburg, Brussels and Frankfurt.

David is Managing Director of the Derivatives and Securities Consultancy Ltd, an affiliate member of the Securities and Investment Institute, a member of the Institute of Directors (IOD) and also a member of the Guild of International Bankers. Since 1999, David has been involved in CBL, which has been developed as a sister company to DMS Ltd. David is the senior author of CBL's *visUlearn* products, which cover the financial services industry. His practical knowledge of the financial industry is combined with his unique teaching ability, culminating in the innovative *visUlearn* range of multimedia training products.

Chapter

1

....

OPERATIONS
MANAGEMENT

The management of operations in organisations within the financial services industry is a diverse challenge. The complexity of today's financial markets is reflected not only in the provision of the operational support and administration functions within major banks, fund management companies and brokers, but also in private investment, corporate business and the administering of the government in many countries. Trading and investment strategies become ever more innovative as new products are developed to hedge, speculate, arbitrage and invest. With each new product comes the need to administer the transaction, to clear and settle the trades so that the legal ownership is recorded and the relevant payments made. As the complexity of trading and investment increases so the demands on the operational teams that support the business grows. And, yet, it is wrong to assume that the sole function of an operations team is settlement.

Today there are many specialist functions within the overall operations remit. Client services, risk management, regulatory, profit generation and retention, and the marketing/sales of 'operations' products. The deregulation of many financial markets around the world has led to an explosion in transactions not in domestic products but in international products and markets. This move into cross-border trading is followed by cross-border settlement. The latter is infinitely more complex than the trading.

Through the 1970s, 1980s and early 1990s, the changes in the front office environment, particularly the growth of electronic and telephone dealing, growing international investment, the competitive environment created by the deregulation, the increase in the volumes of business and a growing need for greater regulation and protection for the private investor, all impacted significantly on the operations function. Dematerialised settlement saw less paper in the office, computer systems became central to the clearing and settlement process, international securities depositories reduced some of the problems and risk in settling cross-border trades. Industry bodies created guidelines for standard messaging formats, encouraged the use of uniform agreements and advocated facilities such as dematerialised (electronic book-entry non-paper settlement), rolling settlement instead of account settlement and stock lending and borrowing to help reduce the problems of settlement failing to happen on the due date.

However, the real catalyst for the dramatic change in the operations function came with the growth in the use of products like derivatives where an administrative error or the failure to pick up on a dealing error could result in six figure losses, and worse!

Ironically, derivatives were not exactly new instruments, their origins being back in the Middle Ages. What was new was the explosion in growth of financial derivatives, some relatively simple in concept like futures and options, others much more complex and bespoke.

It would be the combination of a dealer and derivative products that would ultimately bring about a complete rethink on the importance of operations, but firms were also conscious of the need for greater technology to be available in the support areas to service the burgeoning business being created in trading and investment. There were also significant changes taking place in the markets themselves and particularly in the use of technology.

The London Stock Exchange (*LSE*) introduced the Talisman system and later CREST (after a debacle over another system, Taurus). The London International Financial Futures and Options Exchange (*LIFFE*) moved from open-outcry to electronic dealing through the LIFFE CONNECT™ system. LIFFE clears through the London Clearing House (*LCH*) its derivative products in what is now a completely electronic process, and both the London Metal Exchange and the International Petroleum Exchange, now part of the Intercontinental Exchange (*ICE*), also use LCH to clear their trades. (In late 2001 LIFFE announced it had accepted an offer from Euronext, the combined derivatives exchanges and bourses of Holland, Belgium and France, and in 2002 became part of that exchange. Subsequently, LCH and Euronext have discussed creating the largest pan-European clearing organisation by linking LCH with Clearnet, the Euronext clearing house.) In Germany the stock exchange and derivative exchange clearing have been merged into a single organisation, Clearstream, that also encompasses one of the first international central securities depositories, Cedel. Subsequently, Euroclear, another major international central securities depository, absorbed SICOVAM, the French depository, and through various shareholdings is closely linked into Clearnet and Euronext. This means that there are two large groupings of exchanges, clearing houses and depositories in Europe and, as a result, the streamlining of the clearing and settlement process is rapidly occurring. Elsewhere, there are more developments such as the Nordic Alliance, Portugal's markets scheduled to be joining Euronext in 2002 and the LSE, having failed to persuade LIFFE to accept its offer, is talking in earnest with the US market, Nasdaq.

So much change is of course both creating short-term problems for operations teams, but generating longer term a more structured and simplified clearing and settlement process. To illustrate some of the slightly confusing situations that exist and will need to be resolved, we have:

- LCH, which is talking about linking into Euronext's Clearnet, is providing central counterparty clearing services to CREST for some LSE transactions; however, the LSE is talking about merging with Nasdaq having seemingly rejected linking to Euronext.
- LIFFE, which has become part of Euronext, is also linked to Nasdaq to trade share futures contracts via *Nasdaq LIFFE Markets* – the first US exchange to list share futures.

The process of rationalisation, links, alliances, take-overs (many exchanges are switching from being mutual memberships to publicly quoted companies) and mergers still has many possibilities and permutations to be played out.

Change is not confined to Europe. In the Far East the stock exchanges and derivative exchanges of both Singapore and Hong Kong have joined to create the Singapore Exchange (SGX) and Hong Kong Exchanges and Clearing (HKEx). In the US the big three derivative markets, the Chicago Board of Trade, Chicago Mercantile and Chicago Board Options Exchange have participated in a joint venture whilst the New York Mercantile Exchange has offered to buy the London Metal Exchange.

There is much more going on and changes will continue to happen around the world for some years to come.

Other influences on the role and structure of operations have occurred – in particular, the impact of this event that occurred in the derivatives market.

In 1995, Nick Leeson, a former back office employee who became a qualified derivatives dealer in the Singapore office of Baring's, changed forever the role and profile of operations.

In the aftermath of the collapse of the bank, it became clear that operations was not only a very critical means of risk control over front office activities, but it was also a major source of risk for a business in its own right.

The need to have independent verification of the trades, positions and financial movements associated with dealing was not simply administration and bookkeeping. Fundamentally, it is the key control, reconciling the actual market situation against the deal records and if it is inefficient, fails or is non-existent the whole business is put at risk.

Today this role is recognised and, thus, from perhaps a humble background, operations is now up there alongside the front office. In many of the more enlightened organisations there is mutual respect for the professionalism of their operations and a realisation that teamwork is not a cliché but a reality for a successful business.

So, the key factors that are changing the role of the operations team are the changes to the regulatory environment in the UK and elsewhere and the recognition of operational risk, as we mentioned earlier. On the one hand, we are looking at more professionalism and qualified personnel in operations teams and, on the other, a crucial role in the risk management of the business. Business skills as well as product knowledge are the requirements of managers and supervisors in today's globalised, diverse and ever expanding financial markets arena. The business skills are to manage budgets, personnel, risk management, and global trading and investment. Above all, the operations manager must be able to manage time and possess coaching and motivational skills. Product knowledge is to ensure that the increasingly integrated use of instruments, the development of systems and critical projects – such as straight through processing – can be managed successfully in the hurly-burly of daily routines.

To a business in the financial markets an inefficient operations function is pure risk. A top operations manager is worth, and today is paid, a significant amount. So, they should be given the diversity of the role. Part business developer, part risk manager, part people manager and relationship manager to internal and external parties, the operations manager's time is unlikely to fall into the leisurely category. Even in 'quiet' market conditions operational functions continue uninterrupted.

Operations is still about routine and administration and record keeping, but today it is much more than this. For the operations manager it is a huge and demanding challenge and one that keeps growing as global financial markets come within the reach of all.

Box 1.1   Work session.

Significant changes have taken place in the industry and are still happening now. What are two significant ones that will or have impacted on your organisation?

Chapter

2

....

MARKETS

Securities markets exist in all the mature and most of the emerging countries. As such they offer investors, speculators and traders not only many opportunities but also a challenge in the settlement and administration of transactions.

The characteristics of different securities products create different clearing, settlement and safekeeping requirements. In recent years, efforts to standardise the clearing and settlement processes have seen some success. The Group of 30 (*G30*), a private sector industry group, was set up in 1978 to look at the workings of the financial markets and to examine the international repercussions of decisions taken which affect the financial sector. It is a non-profit international body with senior representatives of the private and public sectors as well as academics. G30 puts on seminars and symposia and produces papers to debate certain issues. It published recommendations back in the late 1980s covering Securities Settlement and Clearance and Derivatives Practices and Principles. G30 is funded by contributions from foundations, banks, corporations, central banks and individuals. The International Securities Services Association (*ISSA*) is another forum, which was set up in 1979, for operations professionals to exchange information and ideas with regard to the international securities markets. The members, who represent a major share of cross-border investment business, meet regularly to share information, co-operate and, importantly, to explore new ideas and models for improvements in the securities services sector. ISSA carried out a review of the level of compliance with the G30 recommendations, and in 2000 it published a new set of recommendations. Both the original G30 recommendations and the ISSA 2000 recommendations seek to improve the efficiency of the settlement process and to therefore reduce operational risk.

Despite the advances in creating a more uniform settlement process for securities, there are still numerous different practices in place. One key issue is the settlement convention, the date on which transactions would normally be expected to settle in a particular market. Commonly shown as T (Trade day) $+ X$ (Number of days) the convention for equities, bonds, derivatives and money market transactions varies considerably across product and country.

In February 2001 the UK moved from $T + 5$ to $T + 3$ for equity settlement. However, government bond transactions in the UK settle $T + 1$ and corporate bonds $T + 3$, exchange traded derivatives settle $T + 1$ whilst spot foreign exchange deals settle 2 business days later.

There are historical precedents for the settlement convention applicable to certain types of product.

Bearer securities (mainly bonds) can effectively settle immediately as title or ownership passes on the handing over of the security whilst registered securities (mainly equities) take longer as the change of ownership needs to be made by a third party – the Registrar – who maintains the record of the ownership of issued shares on behalf of the company. In traditional, certificated settlement environments this entails the completion of a document – the transfer form – and the forwarding of it with the physical certificate to the registrar. This obviously takes time, but today the impact of electronic markets, dematerialised (paperless) settlement and the use of electronic instructions between clearing house and registrar means that, even with registered securities ownership, details can be updated within a very short time. Exchange-traded derivatives are registered in the sense that there is a record maintained of the holders of the derivative positions, but in this case it is the member firm of the clearing house who may not be the 'actual' owner – i.e., a fund management client of the member broker.

When one considers that the sophistication of users of the financial markets means that frequently a trading strategy or investment decision may involve more than one type of security, the lack of commonality in both characteristic and settlement convention inevitably leads to operational issues.

Consider the example in Box 2.1.

Box 2.1

The fund manager of an international fund with a base currency in US$ adopts the following strategy. Having decided that there is a profit on the BT shares that will generate cash for other investment strategies, but not wishing to lose the exposure to BT shares, the fund manager:

1. Sells 200,000 BT shares that will settle $T + 3$.
2. Buys 200 (representing 200,000 shares) BT call options that will settle $T + 1$.
3. Sells £ and buys US$ spot for settlement in 2 days.

Sterling cash for the settlement of the sterling/dollar foreign exchange (FX) deal and purchase of the option will come from the sale of the shares, but that will be a day after the FX deal is due to settle and 2 days after the option is due to settle.

This is a funding issue for both the client and the broker: the client because they have a mismatch on the cash flow and will need either other cash or a borrowing facility; the broker because, as the party recognised by the clearing house, they are liable to the clearing house for the settlement of the option whether or not the client has the cash available.

This situation would be further complicated if, for some reason, the sale of the shares fails to take place on the settlement date, $T + 3$. Any delay would add to the costs of the strategy unless the circumstances enable some kind of claim to be made against a third party causing the delay.

In Chapter 1 the importance of product knowledge was mentioned. Given the diversity of the instruments available in the financial and commodity markets there is a significant problem for the operations manager. It is important for the manager to have not only a wide knowledge of the key elements of the main markets but to also be able to staff the operation with adequate specialist knowledge. The key question is how much knowledge should the manager have?

It depends on the nature of the business and the structure within the organisation. In a large international bank the structure may be along product lines whereas in a fund management company there may be less segregation of product line within the operations area at least. This leads to, in the first case, specialists in equity, fixed income, derivatives, etc., the latter may also be split between on- and off-exchange. Whereas in the fund management company the need for broad-based product knowledge at the manager level is crucial.

Developing your personal knowledge level and, at the same time, developing the right knowledge level in the team is one of the more challenging tasks the operations manager faces.

We look at the detailed aspects of clearing and settlement in Chapter 5, but let us look at the major securities markets and, in doing so, we can start with the market most people are at least familiar with, the equity market.

EQUITY SECURITIES

Equity markets have seen significant activity in the past decade as interest rates have stabilised in the major economies and the return on equities has grown. The huge activity has not been without problems, with many organisations experiencing problems in keeping their operational functions adequately resourced to deal with the growth in volumes. With the growth in equities being experienced not only in the mature markets but also in the emerging markets, there has been significant pressure put on the managers and teams in operations.

Part of the return on an equity security is of course the dividend, with the capital gain being generated by the increase in the share price. The buoyant market has led to many new issues, rights issues, mergers and takeovers as companies seek to exploit the investors' desire for a home for their money. In some cases the intense activity has created liquidity problems.

Liquidity in a security is an important aspect of the market. The ability to trade – i.e., there being enough participants to meet buying and *vice versa* selling demand – is important, but so is the ability to settle those transactions. As organisations and individuals trade the security every transaction creates a settlement process.

With high and potentially frequent turnover amongst the participants, there is a danger that the settlement processes will not keep pace and, therefore, settlement on the due date does not take place. Quickly, a knock-on effect happens as delayed settlements in turn create delays for other settlements and so on. Liquidity in trading terms can, and often does, create liquidity problems in settlement terms. The successful management of this process is an important one for operations managers and supervisors. We look at various ways in which liquidity issues can be resolved later in the book, but we need to mark this point down as an operational risk.

Equity securities are a source of numerous processes from issuance to distribution of benefits like dividends. Much can happen with a share and many of these events may require a decision to be made either in the front or back office (or both) or by a third party like a client.

The company that issues the shares is sometimes the driver of the processes. For instance, the actual terms of the shares can dictate the subsequent events that impact on the operations area.

Consider the following types of share:

- ordinary share or common stock;
- preference share;
- deferred share;
- designated shares – i.e., 'A' or 'B' shares;
- non-voting and restricted shares.

A company that issues ordinary shares is seeking to raise capital in return for a stake in the company's fortunes. The potential investor will need to decide whether this company represents a reasonable investment. The prospectus that the company issues is therefore of paramount importance as it provides the information on which the investor's judgement is made.

The reason that capital markets exist is to raise capital and provide investment opportunity. Not all investors possess the same requirements in terms of a return on their money. Hence, we have people who are considered 'conservative' in their approach and others who are more 'speculative'. Obviously, there has to be a variety of investment products for these differing views and expectations.

But, just as important are the views of an organisation seeking to raise capital. To issue equity shares raises money but gives away some ownership and control. That may not be desirable or necessary as far as the board of the organisation is concerned.

So, in the capital markets we have two drivers behind the kinds of products available – the issuers of securities and the investors.

From the company point of view, the issue must be attractive to both the company itself and to the potential investor. An investor may be happy to have a stake in a company but does not want the uncertainty of dividend flows. The company can overcome this by issuing not just ordinary shares but preferred shares, giving more certainty to the investor but at the cost of an often fixed liability.

The terms of the issue are therefore extremely important not only to the company and the investor but also to those involved in the settlement process. A dividend may be paid on an ordinary share, but it is more likely to be paid on a preference share, and may be related to a previous period as preference shareholders have the right to their dividend ahead of ordinary shareholders.

Deferred shares are different again, the terms conferring different rights and timings to voting and dividend income.

'A' and 'B' shares will have different voting rights and sometimes different dividend payments.

At the time of issue, the company offers the product and the investor makes the choice. Thereafter, it is down to the operations teams in different organisations and the investor themselves to understand what processes and actions are needed for the product traded.

It becomes clear that information is critically important to the whole trading, investment, settlement, clearing and safe custody process associated with the securities markets and the capital markets.

We need to define the 'capital markets' to understand where securities fit in and to illustrate the complexity of products, investment, participation and support roles.

From Figures 2.1–2.3 we begin to see just how varied the products and participants are. In Figure 2.3, for instance, we see how the fund manager places an order to the broker's desk. From there the order is completed on the exchange, is cleared by the clearing house and, then, for a registered security the ownership change is recorded by the registrar and/or the central securities depository (*CSD*) and the broker's settlement team liaise with the fund manager for the relevant settlement amounts. Some of the settlement process and the custody/safekeeping services will often be managed by a custodian or CSD on behalf of the fund manager. We

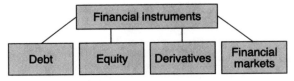

Figure 2.1   Capital markets.

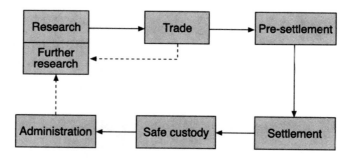

Figure 2.2 Investment cycle.

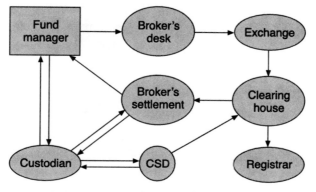

Figure 2.3 Industry relationships.

have already seen how a strategy might involve the equity, derivative and foreign exchange markets. Markets exist to service the requirements of users like corporate entities, investors, traders and hedgers and the many kinds of strategies they utilise.

Markets are either 'real' in the sense that there is a formal structure and location or are colloquially referred to as 'markets'. The foreign exchange market is an example of the latter, the 'market' being counterpart to counterpart or over-the-counter, whereas the London Stock Exchange (*LSE*) is an example of the former, securities trades being dealt within the rules, regulations and facilities of the exchange. It is also important to remember that products traded on an exchange (on-exchange) can also sometimes be traded off-exchange.

Markets also exist where there is a place designated for people to trade face to face, whilst other markets are electronic.

An example of a new market, which is useful to examine, is JIWAY. This is an integrated electronic European stock exchange which is focused on the needs of retail investors; although they are not involved directly, they have to use brokers, financial advisors and other intermediaries to access the market. JIWAY offers real time trading and settlement on major US and European equities. It is owned by the OM Group, Sweden.

From the operations manager's point of view, the source of the trade is as important as the product itself, not least because the settlement convention may differ as a result of being traded on- or off-exchange.

Securities markets are commonly those that are associated with equities and bonds. We have talked about equities and, before moving on to consider the characteristics of bonds, we need to understand some key features of equities (see Table 2.1).

In the Memorandum and Articles of Association of a company is the authorised share capital. This will be made up of designated shares – e.g., 'ordinary 25p shares'. The 25p is the nominal value of the shares and

Table 2.1 UK equities: key features.

Security	Share of ownership
Issued by	Private and public companies
Method of issue	Authorised share capital
Type of issue	Private offering, public offering, placement
Issue document	Prospectus
Traded	On- and off-exchange
Type	Usually registered shares (can be bearer)
Income	Dividend
Unit of trading	One share (can be different – i.e., 50 shares)
Duration	In existence for the life of the corporation – i.e., until the shares are bought back by the company or the company ceases to exist (bankruptcy, takeover, merger, nationalisation)

they cannot be issued for less than that, although of course they can and often are issued at a higher price.

Shares can be issued privately, as is the case with a small company (a company must have at least two shareholders) in which case they are usually 'Limited' (*Ltd*), a term that refers to the liability that the company has (but not the liability of the Directors). If the shares are offered for sale to the general public via a listing on a stock exchange they are usually 'Public Limited Companies' (*PLCs*).

A Prospectus is issued that contains relevant information that enables the potential shareholder to make an assessment of the merits of subscribing for the shares at the price the company is wishing to provide them (the 'offer price').

The Prospectus must be factual, not make misleading or unrealistic projections and must detail the business profile, directors' profiles, any past trading history, projections for the future and the number of shares already in issue and being offered.

The Prospectus will state whether the shares are being offered 'fully paid' or 'partly paid', the former meaning the full value of the shares at the offer price must be paid on application, the latter meaning that a portion of the value is paid on application and the remainder in one or more stages.

Details of the method of applying for shares – the timetable, issuing agents, etc. – must also be included.

An example of a partly paid issue is British Telecom plc that was privatised by the UK government, and in order to encourage private individuals to invest the offer price was split into three separate 'calls'. As a further incentive to the private investor and to encourage long-term investment, bonus shares (shares issued free of charge) were offered to those investors who purchased shares under the original offer and held them for a period of time.

Any 'New Issue' of shares requires an operations team to be aware of the details and, particularly, the critical times such as the closing date for applications, amount of payment, etc.

In some cases there is no offer price and, instead, a tender is made. Tenders are more common in bond issues and require the investor to state how much they will pay for the shares. The highest offers are then successful.

The offer to sell shares is not always matched by the investor take-up and so we have over-subscribed issues, where applications for too many shares are received, and under-subscribed issues, where the opposite has occurred. In the case of the former, details of how such an over-subscription would be dealt with will be included in the Prospectus.

Typically, this will result in a scaling of allocation of shares based on a formula agreed by the company and its issuing agent. This scaling may favour institutions or small shareholders.

To protect against an under-subscription the company may have the issue underwritten. Here, the agent or more likely a syndicate agree to take up any shares not applied for by the public. There will be a fee for this as clearly the underwriters are taking a risk. Market timing and correct pricing of an issue is crucial and many issues have failed or indeed been cancelled as a result of a sudden change in the market sentiment.

The shares we have been talking about here are being offered in the 'Primary' market. To be offered on the stock exchange the offering must meet the criteria of the particular exchange. A full listing on the main market will have many conditions. Growing and new companies in the UK are able to apply for listing in other markets such as the Alternative Investment Market (AIM). The market is under the auspices of the Stock Exchange but the criteria for a listing is less onerous. Thus, a company listed on AIM might be more attractive to a speculative investor who is prepared to take some risk in return for potential growth in the company.

TechMark on the LSE lists innovative technology companies, as these companies have unique requirements. It is a market within a market made up of companies of any size which share a common commitment to technological innovation. In Frankfurt we have the Neuer Markt separate from the main Bourse which lists high growth and technology companies.

Once listed in the Primary market the shares will now trade in the 'Secondary' market. These are not new shares but simply the shares in existence. Trading takes place on either an 'order'-driven market or a 'quote'-driven market. Order-driven markets transact business if and when a matching buy and sell order is in the market. Quote markets have a system whereby market participants, often called 'market makers', make bid and offer prices at which they will buy and sell shares.

When a company has issued shares into a market, any subsequent further issue of shares to raise money is offered to the existing shareholders first. This right, hence the term 'Rights Issue', does not have to be taken up, it will depend on the shareholders' views and means. Rights not taken up can be sold in the market by the shareholder entitled to them or by the company, the shareholder receiving the monetary value.

Rights are offered on a basis – e.g., 2 new shares of every 5

currently held. The rights will be at a discount to the
current share price. If a company is seeking new capital in
a weak situation – i.e., poor performance – the discount
will be greater than a company making a rights issue from
a position of strength.

Other types of actions – rights and other actions are
known as 'Corporate Actions' – can occur with equities.
A company can issue shares free of charge so that the
number of issued shares is increased and the price of the
company's shares in the market will subsequently be
reduced. This is sometimes called a 'Bonus Issue'.

A company can have a share split whereby it has one
million £1 shares and changes them for two million 50p
shares; it could also be involved in a merger or takeover
whereby there will be either an agreement or the takeover
will be called 'hostile' or unwanted.

If a company has surplus cash it might offer to buy back
some or all of its shares.

We can see how intricate the business of trading and
investing in equities can be. We also need to remember
that the processes and conventions in the UK are not
necessarily those of other equity markets around the
world. The size of the equity markets can be seen from
the Table 2.2.

The business carried out on the major global equity
markets is not purely domestic. Today, investors, fund
managers and traders transact business on a global basis,

Table 2.2　Value of business on equity markets 2001.

Market	Location	Main products – indices	Value of business 2001
Nasdaq/ AMEX	US	4,100 household name companies and aspiring household names – Nasdaq Composite Index	$749.049bn
NYSE	US	A cross-section of leading US companies, midsize and small capitalisation companies; also, non-US issuers – Dow Jones	$10.5 trillion
LSE	UK	UK and international companies covering over 60 countries – FTSE 100	£1,909,699.3m
Tokyo Stock Exchange	Japan	2,118 domestic companies and 36 international companies; also, equity and bond futures and options – TOPIX	¥217,026bn
Deutsche Börse	Germany	Domestic companies traded in segments; international companies traded on Xetra Stars; derivatives traded on Eurex – DAX 30	€4,408,752.47m
Euronext	France, Belgium and the Netherlands	1,539 European companies listed; also, bonds, derivatives and commodities – Euronext 100, NEXT 150	€1,668bn
HKEx	China	Equities, bonds, unit trusts, exchange-traded funds and warrants – Hang Seng Index	HK$1,950bn

seeking to achieve growth and to maximise opportunities in the global economies.

With electronic markets and technology aiding dealers, there is no longer any boundaries to trading and investing in equities, save perhaps the regulatory and risk issues and, of course, certain operational constraints that global trading and investing might create such as time-zones, different settlement conventions, etc. We can see this by the diversity of funds and investment trusts that invest in global markets.

The investor, correspondingly, can diversify risk by selecting a particular global fund or by having a portfolio of funds based on different regional markets – i.e., North America, Europe and Asia Pacific. This has to be tempered by the fact that the globalisation of equity trading and investment is allied with a globalisation of business. A simple look at the extent of international ownership of businesses in the UK illustrates this.

However, the important point is that the global economy is just that and, significantly, the global economy is still driven by the US economy. Therefore, any problem with the US economy is likely to impact on other economies around the world. That said, as we saw following the market crash of 1987, the performance of different equity markets varies. Today, of course, we also have a far greater use of derivatives and so the selling pressures in a falling market are not necessarily so marked.

Emerging markets offer huge potential for speculators and investors alike, and yet they do of course carry potentially a far greater risk. The ability of local emerging equity markets to withstand negative pressure – be it domestically or internationally driven – is significantly lower than in a mature market. There is the possibility of political pressure on the markets that may be much greater than in a mature market and, as we saw in Malaysia, there can be direct government intervention in the markets by the changing of laws.

It is worth looking at the example of Malaysia. Essentially, the situation was that Malaysia was concerned that the currency speculators would turn their attention to the ringgit and would force the authorities to use interest rates and other means to try to hold the level of the currency. The impact of volatility in the currency and the 'standard' methods of trying to deal with it were viewed as likely to have a more far-reaching and serious consequence on the economy than the country could stand. The government decided that they would prevent this scenario by introducing an embargo on the currency – despite the International Monetary Fund's (IMF) misgivings – including preventing the removal of realised gains from the country. Thus, if an investor like a UK fund had a profit on a Malaysian portfolio and sold shares in the market to realise the profit and then decided to convert the ringgits to sterling, it would be difficult – if not impossible – to bring that profit back to the UK by selling ringgits for sterling.

The impact of this solution was to negate the currency speculators but to create problems for the international investment community who became reluctant to invest in the securities markets.

Equity markets are measured, of course, by the movement in indices. Almost every equity market has an index or indices based on shares listed on the market and some indices are not based on a single market but have constituents based in many different markets.

Three very well-known indices are the FTSE 100 index in the UK, the Dow Jones in the US and the Nikkei in Japan. As benchmarks they can be viewed with some caution as they may be unrepresentative of the equity market in general. For instance, the Dow Jones index is made up of 30 shares on leading US companies, and the FTSE, on the other hand, is the top 100 UK companies by capitalisation (the value of issued shares at the current share price). Furthermore, the constituents of the FTSE index change on a regular basis as the 'bottom' companies are replaced by companies promoted from outside the top 100.

Over time this, and various mergers and restructures of constituent companies, has changed the FTSE 100 from a broad-based index to one dominated by financials and, until recently, technology companies. It could be said that an investor buying a FTSE 100 index tracker fund is not therefore investing in the fortunes of companies involved in a range of activities, but rather fairly specialist sectors.

In the US the Standard & Poor's 500 offers a broader based index, and therefore benchmark, to the US equity market than the Dow and, perhaps not surprisingly, the main equity derivatives in the US are based on the S&P.

In Europe we have seen the introduction of the so-called *pan-European indices*. These indices, such as the FTSE Eurotop, Morgan Stanley Capital International (*MSCI*) and the Dow STOXX families, represent leading equities from across Europe. For fund managers with European portfolios and/or funds this benchmark and the related derivatives allow better management of the portfolio.

Equity derivatives are important, as the growth in volumes of index and single stock futures and options illustrates. With greater investment in equities, so the need to be able to both hedge and to gain leverage or gearing on investment increases. As derivatives provide the means to both hedge and increase exposure the growth is hardly surprising.

In terms of equities in emerging markets, derivatives again have a part to play, enabling investors and traders to take exposures to the equity markets without involvement in the actual markets. Index products that are listed on mature markets like the Singapore Exchange are based on, for example, the Taiwanese index.

It matters little which international equity market we look at, the same issues arise as those we looked at that relate to the UK equity market. So, we have companies seeking to raise capital, issuing shares, primary and secondary markets, investing, trading, clearing and settlement, etc.

However, equities are not everyone's cup of tea and for investors wanting the peace of mind that comes with a known rather than possible return, other types of security exist. A significant market exists not in purchasing a stake in a company but instead in lending money in return for an income and, usually, the ultimate return of the money lent. This is the *debt market.*

DEBT SECURITIES

Equities are familiar. Most people have heard of a stock exchange and many work for companies whose shares are listed on exchanges. An increasing number – because of privatisations, building societies converting to banks and Internet trading – actually own shares. Most news bulletins tell us how the equity market has performed that day with a single-line statement along the lines of 'the FTSE 100 closed up 220 points at 5623.5'.

The debt markets, however, are not so widely recognised.

There are lots of reasons why this is the case. Some might say they are a more technical market and not for the private investor, others point to lack of volatility (significant movement in price) particularly when interest rates are static.

Strange, then, that debt markets are not only huge, they are also likely to have an impact on each and every one of us and, most likely, that impact will be greater than the equity markets.

Who issues debt or, to put it another way, borrows money and why?

A list would include:

- governments;
- supranationals;
- corporates;
- private companies;
- local authorities.

The reasons for issuing debt can be a matter of choice or necessity.

A company, for instance, might prefer to issue debt to raise capital rather than issue shares which dilutes the ownership and control.

A government cannot issue shares on the country, there is no 'United Kingdom PLC' and yet the government needs capital to pay for services it provides and costs it incurs. The government has tax as a source of income and it also often has investments and reserves; however, it also will have times where it needs to raise additional capital. This borrowing requirement – in the UK it is called the *Public Sector Net Cash Requirement (PSNCR)* – is funded by issuing short-, long- and some-times medium-term instruments, the most familiar of which is likely to be the government bond.

A *bond* is an instrument that often has a fixed duration and a fixed return of interest, and trading in such instru-ments is not surprisingly referred to as the 'fixed income market'. However, there are many types of debt instrument and different types of bond, some of which have variable rates of interest, some have no interest and a very few have no maturity date.

From an operations managers point of view the settlement convention for a government bond or debt instrument is shorter (e.g., $T+1$) than most current equity settlement conventions. But, equally, a corporate bond in the UK would settle $T+3$, the same as an equity.

The income on a bond is the interest or alternatively, where there is no interest paid, the bond will be issued at a discount. The interest on a bond is often called a 'coupon' for the simple reason that most bonds were and are bearer or unregistered securities and the only means of claiming the interest due was to tear a coupon off the bond representing the value of the interest and present it to the issuer's paying agent for payment.

International investment in bonds that were bearer instruments was somewhat of a problem as clearly any loss, or indeed theft, of the bond was a major disaster necessitating either copious amounts of paperwork to obtain duplicate bonds or indeed the total loss of the asset. To some extent these problems were reduced by *Central Securities Depositories (CSDs)* where the bearer securities could be held. The problems with international instruments and the growing cross-border trading were responsible for bringing about a central depository for the bearer securities that were being dealt in internationally. Euroclear and Cedel Bank (later to become Clearstream) became *International Central Securities Depositories* (*ICSDs*).

Raising capital through debt offers an alternative for the investor. The terms of the indenture will provide the investor with details of the debt. This includes not only the maturity of the debt but also the interest or coupon if any, the frequency of payment of the coupon and other material information on specific characteristics of the debt.

For instance, the debt may be convertible – i.e., the bond can be converted either on maturity or during the life of the issue into equity shares instead of having the loan repaid in cash.

The debt may be 'callable' or 'putable' – i.e., the issuer can call or redeem the debt earlier than the maturity or where the investor can put a request or ask the issuer to redeem the debt early. The call or put may be at selected times, can be mandatory or offered as an option, and may refer to specific numbered instruments or on a general first-come-first-served basis.

Debt is issued in much the same way as equity. There is a primary and secondary market, there are offers and placings although the public offering of debt instruments applies primarily to government bonds. In the UK you can purchase government bonds called 'gilts' – an abbreviation of gilt-edged security – the assumption being the government would always honour its debt. Private investors can purchase gilts, along with other national savings products, at the Post Office.

In reality, most debt securities are destined for the 'professionals' who manage portfolios of investments for the major life insurance companies, pensions funds, central government agencies that manage investments for the government, and the providers of retail products to the man or woman in the street.

Debt instruments are commonly referred to as being at the 'long' or 'short' end of the market. This relates to the time to maturity and is also relevant to the yield curve, a term used to describe a view of interest rates over a period of time.

Yield, the return on the investment, is an important factor. The yield on a bond with 30 years to maturity is likely to be different from one that has only say a year to maturity. Equally, the price is different. So too is the yield on a bond compared with the dividend yield on an equity or a cash deposit.

We know that bonds are debt instruments, usually issued for a maturity several years ahead (the benchmark US Treasury Bond is issued with 30 years to maturity) and that fixed income bonds have a coupon payable either annually or semi-annually. Bonds where no interest is paid are called *zero-coupon* bonds and are similar to other debt instruments. Issues with a year or as little as 3 months and sometimes a few days are often referred to as *money market instruments* as the short duration provides them with characteristics similar to cash.

Table 2.3 UK bonds: key features.

Security	Debt
Issued by	Governments, private and public companies, local authorities
Method of issue	Term of indenture
Type of issue	Private offering, public offering, placement
Issue document	Prospectus
Traded	On- and off-exchange
Type	Usually bearer (can be registered)
Income	Interest (coupon) can also be issued at a discount with no interest payment
Unit of trading	£100, £1,000, etc.
Duration	In existence until the maturity date of the bond, unless there are terms that permit the early redemption of the bond

A zero-coupon bond is issued at, for example, £75 and the holder will receive £100 on maturity. The amount of discount is dependent on the projected yield in the market.

Some bonds do not pay a fixed rate of interest but, instead, the interest rate is determined from one period to the next, quarterly, half-yearly, etc. These are called *floating rate bonds* or *notes*, commonly abbreviated to *FRNs*.

International bonds are issued almost exclusively through placements by major banks or syndicates. Sometimes referred to as *Eurobonds*, they are offered by an issuer in a different country or countries, often in a different currency. An example would be a US company issuing the bond in Europe and Asia in British pounds.

Major debt instruments include:

- bonds or loan stock;
- bills;
- notes;
- certificates of deposit;
- commercial paper;
- banker's acceptances;
- asset-backed bonds;
- high-yield bonds.

We need to remind ourselves that most debt instruments have terms or durations until they mature or expire. This duration can be 'short' – 3 months or less – or 'long' – anything up to 30 years or more. Short-term debt, usually 1 year or less, is often referred to as a money market instrument and these include certificates of deposit and Treasury bills. Bonds tend to have a longer time to maturity when they are issued.

The resultant settlement process flows are dictated by the nature of the instrument. These are looked at in more detail in Chapter 5, but the characteristics of securities like bonds and equities are different from those of derivatives and so, therefore, are the processes.

DERIVATIVE MARKETS

Derivatives are instruments that provide both hedging and speculative properties. In general terms, they are products that will or might create a transaction, the terms of which are agreed today but will occur at some time in the future. They could be said to be synthetic versions of the assets on which they are based. Thus, they can give an exposure to an asset or market without the need to participate in the actual underlying asset or market. They also allow an investor to gain that exposure at a fraction of the actual cost or value of the underlying asset.

This *gearing* or *leverage* is a particularly important characteristic, and a failure to have systems, processes and controls over the actual exposure rather than the cost of the derivative is vitally important in risk management.

The names of some derivative products reflect this ability to agree something today to either definitely or possibly happen later, and so we have *futures, forwards, options, swaps*, etc.

Derivatives are traded both on- and off-exchange. *Exchange-traded derivatives (ETDs)* are products created by and traded on exchanges. They are standardised products, called 'contracts' or 'lots', with contract specifications and are traded by members of the relevant exchange either face to face, sometimes called open outcry, or by electronic trading systems.

The contract specification is crucial as it details the essential information on:

- size of the contract and underlying asset on which it is based;
- maturity date;
- the minimum price movement and value;
- settlement convention (cash or physical);
- trading method and times.

Table 2.4 is an example of contract specifications for the LIFFE Long Gilt futures contract.

It may be a surprise to some to learn that derivatives are not new products and in fact can be traced back to the Middle Ages. Originally based on commodities, the derivative industry we know today commenced with establishing of the Chicago Board of Trade in 1848. Growth in the use of derivatives increased sharply in the mid-1970s when financial products were introduced, and in 2000 over 3.5 billion contracts were traded.

The markets are diverse in both products and size, and today it is a truly global industry. It is also misunderstood with many people believing that derivatives pose un-acceptable risk. These detractors would point to various industry events that have resulted in large financial losses, and yet they ignore similar losses made in equities or bonds. Why is this the case?

Derivative problems can be spectacular and therefore make headlines. Just like all financial 'disasters', in the context of frequency of losses versus actual use, derivatives are no more dangerous than any other invest-ment provided adequate controls over their use are in place. Despite this, there will still be those who maintain

Table 2.4 Contract specifications for the LIFFE Long Gilt futures contract.

Unit of trading	£100,000 nominal value notional gilt with 7% coupon
Delivery months	March, June, September, December, such that the nearest three delivery months are available for trading
First notice day	Two business days prior to the first day of the delivery month
Last notice day	First business day after the last trading day
Delivery day	Any business day in delivery month (at seller's choice)
Last trading day	At 11:00, two business days prior to the last business day in the delivery month
Quotation	Per £100 nominal
Minimum price movement (tick size and value)	0.01 (£10)
LIFFE CONNECT™ *trading hours*	08:00–18:00
Trading platforms	LIFFE CONNECT™ central order book applies price/time priority trading algorithm, basis trade facility, block trade facility
Minimum block trade threshold	See block trade facility – contract minimum size thresholds

Source: LIFFE website.

their use is too 'risky' and therefore ignore them, thus potentially and perversely generating risk in their portfolios.

Given that derivatives transfer risks between those who wish to assume risk (speculators) and those who wish to remove risk (hedgers) it is not surprising that the growth in their use over the last 20 years has been spectacular.

The fund manager who is a purchaser of equity stock can hedge the risk of the share price falling by using options, whilst the investor who believes the stock will rise in price can also use options to gain greater exposure to the stock for the available funds than would be the case if they purchased stock.

What is absolutely certain is the need for high-quality operations to process and control derivatives business. Operations managers must be aware of the links between equity, bond, currency or money market activity and the activity in the associated derivatives.

Settlement conventions differ, different clearing houses may be involved, corporate actions in one product may affect the other and the derivative may go to physical delivery of the asset.

Accounting for derivatives may be different than for the underlying asset, and the process for valuing derivatives held in portfolios needs a basis that truly reflects the impact of the use of the derivative on the portfolio. The global extent and diversity of derivative products is illustrated in Table 2.5.

Table 2.5 Exchanges and leading products.

Exchange	Leading products
Chicago Board of Trade	T-Bond T-Note-Futures
Chicago Mercantile Exchange	Eurodollar Future
EUREX	Eurobund Future
EURONEXT	CAC40 Index Future
London Metal Exchange	Aluminium Future
New York Mercantile Exchange	Light Sweet Crude Oil Future
Singapore Exchanges (Derivatives Division)	Eurodollar Future
Sydney Futures Exchange	Australian 3 Year Bond Future
Tokyo Stock Exchange	Japanese Government Bond Future

Operations teams must fully understand the difference in characteristics and settlement conventions of the derivatives traded on- and off-exchange.

Exchange-traded derivatives have settlement processes that are somewhat different from securities. Futures contracts trade on margin, a process whereby the actual value of the futures contract is not settled and, instead, a daily settlement of the change in the value of the contract is paid or received. Only if the futures contract goes to delivery will the value of the underlying be paid or received.

An option contract has a two-stage settlement. The first stage involves the payment by the buyer to the seller of a premium to secure the right to do something. If that right is exercised then a second settlement takes place as the asset is either delivered or received by the buyer.

Over The Counter (OTC) derivatives are not traded on exchanges and do not therefore have standardised contracts. They are traded between two counterparties who determine the terms of the derivative, including how and when any settlement will take place. This ability to bespoke the derivative product is highly attractive and there is a huge market in OTC derivatives. A common product is a swap, where the buyer and seller agree to swap something at set periods or on the occurrence of some trigger event or benchmark. Different participants in the markets heavily use interest rate swaps, currency swaps, commodity swaps and equity swaps.

FOREIGN EXCHANGE AND MONEY MARKETS

Currency exchange movements run into billions per day as the transactions in financial markets, commerce and business are settled. The foreign exchange markets and the markets in financial paper are massive and, like securities and derivatives, are global. The 2001 *Triennial Central Bank Survey of Foreign Exchange and Derivatives Market Activity* published by the Bank for International Settlements in April 2001 (visit *www.bis.org*) measures the average daily turnover in traditional foreign exchange markets as $1.2 trillion. Although this daily global turnover figure is massive, it reflects a 19% decline in activity compared with the last survey in

April 1998. Undoubtedly, the introduction of the Euro is the major contributing factor.

Many organisations will have operations teams dedicated to the clearing and settlement function. Often called 'Treasury Operations', they will deal with instruments such as:

- *Bankers acceptances* – short-term negotiable discount notes, drawn on and accepted by banks which are obliged to pay the face value amount at maturity.
- *Eligible bills* – a bill acceptable to the Bank of England as lender of last resort.
- *Certificates of deposit* – a short- or medium-term interest bearing money market instrument offered by banks. It is a low-risk, low-return investment vehicle.
- *Commercial paper* – an unsecured obligation issued by a bank or corporation to finance short-term credit needs. They usually range in duration from 2 days to 9 months.
- *Treasury bills* – money market instrument issued with a life of less than 1 year issued by the US and UK governments.
- *Domestic and international currencies* – any form of money in circulation. Domestic is the unit of money used in your home country. International currencies are used in countries other than your home country and require exchange to convert them into your domestic currency.
- *Currency futures* – contracts calling for delivery of a specific amount of a foreign currency at a specified

future date in return for a given amount of, say, US dollars.

- *Structured products* – a type of investment product which is made up of two or more products that seek to meet a specific investment objective.

As with securities the various products have different settlement profiles and conventions.

With currencies, for instance, we have both *spot* (2-day) and *forward* transactions as well as currency derivatives, like options and swaps. Many money market trades are off-exchange whilst some derivatives are on-exchange and others off-exchange.

RETAIL AND OTHER PRODUCTS

In today's diverse financial markets there are many products that have been developed as hybrids of 'traditional' instruments.

To meet the specific requirements of clients and investors, banks and investment companies have developed a whole range of bespoke and retail products. For corporate clients we have:

- *Mergers and acquisition services* – divisions of securities houses or merchant banks responsible for advising on takeover activity. Usually work with the corporate finance department and are often kept as a single unit.

- *Structured finance.*
- *Asset-backed securities* – debt obligations that are secured against some type of or specific asset – e.g., property, mortgages.

In the retail sector we have:

- *Life funds* – insurance where the premiums are invested and will provide some level of return on maturity.
- *Insurance* – a promise of financial compensation for a specified potential loss in the future. This promise is in exchange for a monthly or annual premium payment.
- *Pension* – fund set up by an individual, a corporation, labour union, governmental entity or other organisation to pay the pension benefits of retired workers. Pension funds invest billions of dollars annually in the securities markets and are therefore major market players.
- *ISAs* – an individual savings account in the UK which allows tax-efficient investment of up to £7,000 in each tax year. Investment can be made as a lump sum and/ or regular monthly payments and be invested in cash, shares and life insurance, or all three options.
- *Unit trusts* – a vehicle whereby money from a number of investors is pooled together and invested collectively on their behalf. Each owns a unit (or number of them), the value of which depends on the value of those items owned by the trust.

- *Open Ended Investment Companies (OEICs)* – a corporate structure introduced in 1997. It is a form of collective investment vehicle which can expand without limit.
- *Guaranteed fund* – a fixed term investment which guarantees growth or a return of the original investment. It is a relatively conservative investment vehicle.
- *Hedge fund* – a fund used by wealthy private clients and institutions. It operates aggressive investment strategies including short selling, gearing, program trading, swaps, arbitrage and derivatives.

Essentially, these products are combinations of other products. For example, we have pension funds that invest in equities, bonds and money market instruments and we have hedge funds that invest in securities, currencies, derivatives, etc.

Yet, the investment objective of a hedge fund is significantly different from that of a pension fund. As a result there is a different approach to trading the instruments as pension funds take generally longer term investment views, whilst hedge funds take much shorter views of the market.

For the operations manager, the processes, procedures and controls over retail transactions are different from fund management and are very different from principal trading activity.

Operations managers in the offices of a fund manager have to deal with the fund managers/dealers, agent brokers, banks, custodians, trustees and the regulators.

Therefore, to reiterate the point already made, operations is about information and communication. The role of the manager is therefore complex, and it is appropriate to summarise this role and the key issues that need to be addressed and understood.

Other products

Trading in individual shares is still a major part of market activity; however, there is today significant use of products that represent a single order but across many individual securities – for example, basket trades.

Other examples would be a program trade, an index future or an exchange-traded fund. As with all products there are differences between these types of products that determine who will use them and why.

If we look first at a program or basket trade, the rationale for use is about cost and ease of executing an investment strategy. For the operations manager there is an issue about settling such a product. From the trading side there is a single bargain, but the constituents of that bargain will settle as multiple securities. Without their own basket settlement capabilities, any cost reductions will be unlikely to be achieved.

Traded funds offer investors another way to diversify their investments and minimise the impact of market fluctuations.

MARKET AND PRODUCT KNOWLEDGE

There are many changes and developments taking place in markets and exchanges around the world. Keeping track of these changes and applying the necessary procedures and controls are issues the manager needs to address.

The key issues in respect of markets include:

- *The structure of the market* – it is vital for operations managers to understand how each market is structured and the legal aspects under which the market operates. Issues within the structure of the market include the regulation applicable, the membership, and the trading and settlement processes. Managers must be fully aware of their own obligations in respect of the market if they are members directly.
- *The processes for transactions on the market* – this includes the method of trading on the exchange, the access to the exchange and the technology available to process transactions. Managers need to ensure that there are clear communication channels with the market and that they are fully aware of new products and developments in the markets. This is particularly true in relation to how it affects their own business and clients.
- *The processes for clearing and settlement* – the way in which transactions are cleared and settled on an exchange must be an efficient process. There need to

be clear rules laid down in order to deal with trades which fail to settle in the normal course of business.

- *The role of the clearing house* – the relationship between the exchange and the clearing house is very important and has to work well in order to operate an efficient market. The issues which need to be considered in relation to the clearing house are risk management, treasury, collateral management and default policies.

- *The use of markets and products by end-user clients* – users of the markets are either direct or indirect participants, the latter often referred to as 'end-users'. Over the years the sophistication of the end-user has grown significantly, and with technology and outsource services – like fund administration and prime brokerage – available, the extent and diversity of end-user activity has grown. In turn, this has raised issues – and continues to do so – about services offered, risk, multi-currency capabilities, etc.

- *The role of industry associations* – industry associations have a major role to play in the development and operation of the markets. They usually have a great deal of influence over the markets and their practice, as they are driven by the members of the market, but are seen to be an independent body.

- *Issues arising from transacting business in global markets* – this covers the risks of operating in global markets and includes currency risk, operational risk and personnel risk. Global business often necessitates the use of foreign agents and/or the involvement of international group offices, which needs careful consideration and monitoring.

These issues are often complex and, yet, are of great importance in terms of the manager's and supervisor's roles and responsibilities.

The ability of a business to operate safely and effectively in different markets is dependent on operations ability to handle the business efficiently. The service provided by the operations area will be judged not only by the in-house traders, but by the client-focused teams and the clients themselves.

This capability forms part of the overall image and reputation of the organisation.

Managing and supervising an operations team requires adequate managerial knowledge of the markets and products. Team members will be charged with the day-to-day issues of clearing and settlement; however, key issues in respect of markets and products must be understood by managers. These are:

- market structure and membership rules including the liabilities of members;
- products traded;
- structure and characteristics of products;
- clearing mechanisms;
- settlement conventions including conventions applying to underlying assets and associated derivatives;
- structure and role of the clearing house and central securities depositories;
- clearing membership requirements, rules and regulations including default liabilities;
- client documentation;

- understanding the key regulatory and tax issues of the jurisdiction of the market;
- rationale for house and client transactions;
- policy and procedures needed for business on each market and for each product;
- controls needed for business on each market and product.

Without adequate knowledge of the above it will be impossible for the manager or supervisor to effectively manage the operations team.

We therefore need to look at each of these points in greater detail.

Market structure and membership

Exchanges are created or evolve into domestic or international markets. As such, each market is different, even when markets are based in the same geographical or legal jurisdiction.

Exchanges are formed to service a perceived need and are structured and sometimes owned accordingly.

Understanding the structure of the market enables the manager to ascertain the benefits and disadvantages of membership of a particular market. It also helps with the choice of agent to use on a market where, for whatever reason, exchange membership is not deemed appropriate.

Membership of an exchange often allows the manager the opportunity to seek representation on the various committees, etc. the market may have. This ability to hear about the developments that are planned and to influence thinking and strategy can be of immense importance.

The make-up of the membership of a market may be dictated by local regulatory issues. Where this is the case, the manager may need to carefully research the potential counterparts for an agency arrangement or, alternatively, manage the requirements for membership by the organisation, which may include a local presence, adequately resourced and managed.

This research and the ultimate decision will almost certainly be taken in conjunction with the front office as, depending on the anticipated level of business, it may be prudent from a risk and commercial perspective for there to be a single counterparty relationship, at least initially.

There will obviously be different criteria for market memberships. Out of these will come operational issues including processing and risk-related issues.

An example would be where there is a direct system link, such as a transaction matching or registration system. This provides potential advantages in terms of speed and control over transaction processing and monitoring and is also essential for projects like straight through processing (*STP*) mentioned in Chapter 1. Membership of the exchange and/or clearing house might therefore be more beneficial than an agency arrangement for that market.

However, exchange membership creates potential liabilities that may or may not be acceptable, and so operating on a particular market via an agent may be more attractive in some circumstances – e.g., being an exchange member.

Products traded

As we have already noted, understanding the products traded on a market is essentially about the characteristics of the products and the implications for the operational process.

For example, the contract specification for an exchange-traded derivative product or the confirmation and associated documentation for securities and other OTC products, like derivatives, will provide the basic information.

There are, however, other issues surrounding the products that the operations manager needs to be in possession of. These include:

- *The impact on the processes and procedures* – Can the product be incorporated into existing processes and procedures?
- *System requirements to handle the product* – Is the system able to deal with the product or will there be development work needed?
- *Static data control* – Where and how is the information for the static data to be obtained and how is it to be maintained?
- *Regulatory and/or exchange reporting requirements* –

What has to be reported, how is the report made and what is the frequency?

- *Delivery processes* – What is the delivery process, timetable and conditions (cash, physical, exchange for physical)?
- *Impact of corporate actions or other events* – How are different corporate actions dealt with? What are the termination or trigger events? What is the 'calendar' for the product?
- *Control mechanisms for the product* – What are the risk issues that need addressing?
- *Product awareness training for the operations team* – How are the team to be trained?
- *Issues arising from client activity in the product* – settlement, collateral, delivery, close-outs.
- *Funding and collateral issues from activity in products* – cash flow, collateral and margin issues.
- *Changes to product specifications* – How are they notified? What controls are used to ensure changes to static data, etc. are made?
- *Introduction of new products* – information flow, control to action procedure and static data updates, personnel awareness.

All of these must be considered by managers and supervisors and are important for several reasons, including risk management and client service performance. They also have regulatory implications, such as whether they are authorised products for certain types of client.

Product knowledge is fundamental to the ability to design procedures, processes and controls, and thus to the successful management of a securities, treasury or derivatives operations team.

Structure and characteristics of the products

Operations teams will all have different tasks and functions such that an operations manager may be dealing with exchange-traded products or OTC products, or both.

The structure of the products, which will have a major impact on the procedures, processes and controls, varies as do the characteristics.

With the majority of exchange-traded products there are core elements to the structure, such as number of shares or value of instrument, contract size, settlement date, delivery months, tick size and value, etc. It is the variables that create the potential for problems, and yet these are still relatively easy to manage.

The more exotic the product is, the greater the chance of a non-standard settlement feature, and thus the greater the risk potential.

The manager needs to find the right balance between understanding the key features of a product and the routine processing of that product. The key features can be described as:

- exchange traded or OTC;
- settlement convention;

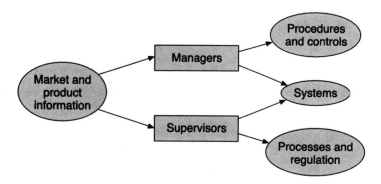

Figure 2.4 Information flow in the operations environment.

- registered or bearer;
- delivery terms and conditions;
- funding and capital adequacy requirements;
- regulatory issues.

Figure 2.4 illustrates how the manager utilises the market and product information to develop controls and procedures, as well as linking this to system development.

At the same time the supervisors will be utilising market and product information for development of suitable processes, again linked to system development.

There is so much change currently taking place in the industry that affects markets and exchanges that the manager needs to organise a continuous and comprehensive supply of information in order to keep up with developments.

To recap, the following list shows some of the major changes that have taken place or are taking place:

- major open-outcry markets switching to electronic trading;
- key derivative and stock exchanges merging;
- derivative and securities clearers expanding product ranges and linking;
- regulation in the UK being centralised into a single regulator;
- 'new' markets – like BrokerTech, JIWAY;
- Internet trading and settlement services.

In the rest of the book we look at specific topics and also set out some exercises in the form of work sessions for you to use. The first work session was detailed in Box 1.1 on p. 8 and another is detailed in Box 2.2. It is suggested that you research the background for the session and then relate that to the comments made in this book.

Box 2.2   Work session.

Consider the impact and implications for the operations manager of the above changes and developments describing how this will apply in the short, medium and long term.

Clearing mechanisms, membership and the clearing house role

The role of the clearing house is based on providing services to the exchange that enable the business transacted on that exchange to be settled efficiently and to varying degrees the associated risk managed. The clearing house achieves this through:

- acting as the counterparty to each trade;
- calculating the settlement amounts due from all clearing members;
- providing the settlement mechanism, including the closing out of liabilities;
- managing risk through the setting and collecting of initial margin deposits;
- providing the mechanism for delivery;
- establishing rules and procedures for clearing members;
- establishing default procedures;
- managing a default fund to provide protection to the exchange and its members in the event of a default by a clearing member.

Understanding the clearing mechanism for each exchange is important from the point of view of the settlement processes, 'give-ups' and timings applicable to delivery. As there are differences to the procedures on each market the manager must ensure that supervisors and team are familiar with the various routings, deadlines, etc.

Securities and derivatives clearing has traditionally been very different. In securities settlement the counterparty relationship at trade time remains through to settlement. Alternatively, with derivatives a central clearing counterparty role operates whereby the clearing house becomes the counterparty to the trade. The clearing and settlement process used in derivatives is based on a margin process rather than the full value settlement traditionally used for securities.

However, a central counterparty process for securities clearing is being and has been introduced in various markets, including London where CREST and the London Clearing House have introduced Equityclear. Similar products have been introduced elsewhere – e.g., by Clearnet on the EURONEXT exchanges.

In respect of derivatives-efficient margin management, this process also requires an understanding of the acceptable collateral, administration costs of utilising collateral and the relevant client money treatment of assets lodged at the clearing house.

Clearing services – such as the London Clearing House's Equityclear, Swapclear and Repoclear products – need to be understood so that the settlement of products through both central clearing and non-central routes can be successfully handled by the team.

It is important to visit the websites of the organisations listed below, as they provide an illustration of the way in which the clearing mechanism works for important clearing organisations:

1. *CREST and the London Clearing House (including Swapclear).*
2. *Clearstream.*
3. *Depository Trust & Clearing Corporation.*

Structure of securities clearing and settlement conventions

Although the majority of securities settle in full within a time scale, most exchange-traded derivatives never go to delivery. It is a key part of the overall clearing and settlement process that delivery should take place on settlement date. Failure to administer the process correctly will result in fines and reputation damage to the firm.

Therefore, the operations manager must concentrate on the processes needed to ensure compliance with the settlement conventions and, when that is not possible, that appropriate escalation procedures and actions monitor, report and control late/failed settlement scenarios. If we bear in mind that the cause of the problems with settlement on due date may be caused by counterparties, then we need relevant documenting of costs and losses for possible claims against the errant counterparty.

There is also the matter of collateral that may be utilised, corporate actions and other events that might affect the derivative product either directly or indirectly.

It is therefore important for the operations manager and team to understand the settlement conventions applying to both securities and derivatives products. The manager needs to ensure he and the team have an adequate knowledge of:

- bond markets;
- equity markets (including exchange-traded funds);
- commodities;
- money markets;
- derivative markets.

An important part of business is client documentation. However, in many organisations client documentation is dealt with by a separate department external to the operations team.

It is nevertheless important for the manager to understand the relevant parts of client documentation, as clearly there will be times where an operational issue arises and the action will be dictated by the contents and terms of the documentation.

This will apply whether the documentation refers to a client of the firm or to an agent the firm is using – i.e., the firm is a client. Equally, it will apply between fund managers and the client, the client and the custodians, fund managers and custodians and trustees.

In most cases standard documentation is used covering various products. Derivatives agreements may be separate and may also differ between on-exchange and off-exchange products.

In many cases standardised documentation is now used, an example being that produced by the *International Swaps and Derivatives Association (ISDA)*. This is an association which is primarily for participants in OTC derivatives markets. It aims to promote the development of prudent risk management practices and is a forum for analysis and discussion of issues and developments in OTC derivatives markets. ISDA sets standards for the efficient conduct of business which includes the development and maintenance of derivatives documentation.

In the case of OTC swap transactions, the confirmations supporting the standard ISDA documentation may be dealt with by the operations team. The manager is there-fore responsible for ensuring adequate procedures, con-trols and expertise are available in the team to handle this.

Compliance issues will be referred to throughout the book.

Regulation, accounting and tax issues

As with client documentation, the bulk of the work related to regulation and tax is likely to be handled else-where in the firm. Nevertheless, there will be issues that impact on the operations function and have implications for the manager.

Ensuring that the firm is complying with the relevant rules and regulations in each market place and juris-diction is a joint effort by the compliance officer and the operations manager.

Regulation is dealt with elsewhere in the book, but as a 'product' it is clear that the manager must have more than a passing knowledge of the subject and also ensure that supervisors and staff understand reasons for, and the importance of, regulation.

Likewise, accounting and tax implications in terms of realised and unrealised profit/losses, hedge trades, utilis-ing collateral, withholding tax, assets delivery arising from derivatives, etc. need to be understood.

Ensuring that the firm meets industry standards and regulatory requirements over valuations and reporting of assets under management, including performance, is also important.

Policy, procedures and controls

Central to the successful management of an operations team is the policy introduced by the manager covering procedures and controls.

The core element of delivery of the policy is the knowledge and understanding of the markets and products that the operations team processes.

The more complex and diverse the business activity, the greater the need for a manager to comprehend the background environment of the transactions. This means understanding the:

- rationale for the types of transactions that take place;
- characteristics of the products used;
- exchange and clearing issues;
- implications in terms of controls, regulation and risk;
- system requirements to handle the transaction and/or product;
- overview of the settlement process.

These headings are, of course, then subject to further sub-headings as the more detailed analysis occurs. These are covered at various stages in the book, and further information and sources of information are provided on the Useful websites page (p. 421).

In this chapter of the book we have looked at the importance of market and product knowledge as part of the manager's role. The ability to successfully manage the operations team stems largely from the respect the personnel have for the manager.

This includes the manager's ability to comprehend the problems and introduce effective solutions, as well as the skill in leaving processing and day-to-day issues to the supervisors whilst clearly being capable of dealing with the higher level issues.

Market and product knowledge is the key to a manager instilling confidence in the team and earning their respect.

Box 2.3   Work session.

Consider the key procedures and controls that will be necessary for a transaction in:

- A UK equity transaction in ordinary shares and an equity option on the same stock.
- A US Treasury bond and associated CBOT Bond futures contract.
- A Eurex equity stock option.
- A London Metal Exchange Copper contract.
- An interest rate swap.

Chapter
3

....

BANKING, BROKING AND INSTITUTIONAL CLIENTS

Within the financial markets the roles of banking, broking and fund management are relatively simple concepts. Today, these functions are often combined in global investment banks, and thus we have multi-product firms as well as specialist or niche firms.

The business profile of each is important to understand for the majority of operations managers, for the simple reason that relationships on a client or principal basis will almost certainly exist between different organisations. It is therefore essential to know how these counterparties operate, what issues they face and how this will impact both positively and negatively.

Banking, investment and merchant, is no longer a business defined along rigid lines. Today, a bank can have a broking capacity, a fund management capacity, a merchant banking arm and a retail banking function. We can see this with the likes of Prudential and Egg, and Standard Life and its mortgage bank. Other examples are Merrill Lynch and its asset management arm and Barclays Bank retail banking and broking business. In fact, the 'specialist' firm is getting difficult to find, with even small private client brokers being linked to larger organisations.

The Internet has also changed the structure in financial markets with many 'broking' firms setting up operations to meet the demands of the 'new' private client!

The global investment bank, as we know it, has evolved from the removal or loosening of the regulatory environment governing participants in the financial markets.

This allowed external or foreign entities to acquire stakes in banks, brokers and fund management companies in both domestic and other countries.

However, global investment banks have not been structured identically. We have organisations that are controlled out of a central hub and these types of firms will inevitably have a high degree of uniform systems, procedures and practices, coupled with client facing services designed to be in a universal corporate style. Controls will be centrally administered and this will apply across the front office and support areas, including operations. Staffing will be 'group-wide' with many different nationalities working in the offices around the world.

Other organisations have adopted a more regional approach allowing much of the management of the firm to be somewhat autonomous with only certain activities, such as systems, centralised. Client services are tailored, local practices recognised and decision making largely left to the managers.

Box 3.1   Scenario 1.

In this scenario the banks will be looking at their global corporate clients, whilst at the same time seeking to provide a localised broking service to key domestic clients. Fund management arms may be driven from the central location or may be at arm's length, working on and building from the strength of name, market awareness, investor profile, etc.

The benefits of uniformity in scenario 1 would be development and ease of distribution of global products and services, cost savings, marketing profile, interchangeability of staff, systems, etc. and central risk control. Downside issues will be the 'global' product versus a 'localised' delivery of the product, referrals for decisions and difficulties in maintaining an even standard across the offices world-wide.

Box 3.2   Scenario 2

In this scenario the benefits are primarily the concentration on developing and servicing local clients in domestic products with an option to offer a global service by networking the various centres of the firm. The individual strengths of the various offices, in theory, are then utilised to provide a strong global product to the client base that wants it.

The downside is the difficulty in actually providing this, as well as significant concerns about the ability to maintain satisfactory levels of risk management when so much decision making and so many procedures are vested in local managers.

It is not possible to say that one or other, or the many variations, is the right way to establish a global business, as clearly each route has its merits and deficiencies. If you are currently employed in such an organisation you will be aware of the kind of problems that occur.

Also, the business profile is key here. If a firm offers Prime Brokerage or Global Clearing in derivatives, for instance, a truly integrated, global, operations function is essential to the successful delivery of the service. Prime Brokerage and Global Clearing in derivatives are both services provided by banks and brokers that offer benefits to the client in the form of reducing the number of counterparties for dealing and/or settlement, enabling efficiencies in cost and administration and providing access to value-added services based on technology, funding, stock lending/borrowing, reporting, etc.

Equally, when we look at fund management companies there is likely to be a situation where the company may administer domestic and international funds from a single location whilst retailing them through sales arms in different locations. Alternatively, funds may be administered and sold in various geographical locations with some kind of central investment policy overlaying the process. Also, with fund management the firm appointed as custodian for the safekeeping of assets, etc. may be appointed by the fund managers or by the client on whose behalf the manager operates.

Quite often a UK-based fund manager may well have offices in, for instance, Boston and Hong Kong, which will service certain local clients and deliver products for the local market. These operations may be significantly smaller than the UK operation.

As far as the settlement and administration processes go, the UK operations manager may have responsibility for these offices and any staff working there.

What are the issues for the operations managers in these scenarios?

Perhaps the first and most important is the lines of reporting and communication. Consider Figure 3.1 which gives a global structure for a firm.

Whatever the specific structure, there is always the need for data to flow back and forth between centres in addition to the data that flow between the centre and its various counterparts. As the figure shows, the three-hub principle allows the operations function to flow around the world, around the clock. In theory, a global client can access any market or transaction and settlement data 24 hours a day from any of its locations.

Figure 3.2 illustrates just some of the potential relationships that an operations team has.

With so many local relationships to manage in addition to the inter-hub relationship, it is not difficult to see just

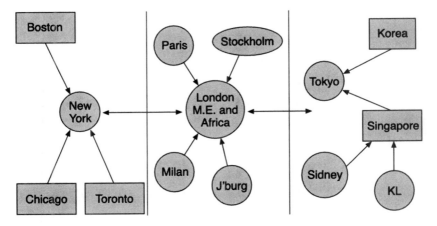

Figure 3.1 Example global structure.

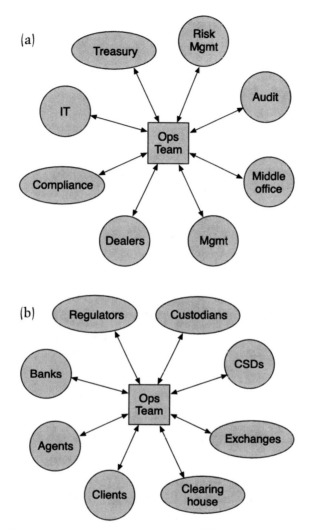

Figure 3.2   Operations (a) internal and (b) external relationships.

how highly skilled the managers and staff need to be to operate within such a structure. As straight through processing, central clearing and dematerialised settlement become the standard in most major markets, the difficulties experienced by firms operating global operations functions will change.

In addition to reliable, fast data flow and effective communication, there are problems, such as risk management, staff competency, the impact different types of client have on workflow processes, etc.

When we look at risk later in Chapter 4 it will be easy to see just how the risk profile of global operations is different from that of operations functions dealing with local markets.

But, what of the smaller organisations that are not 'global' in presence, but nevertheless operate in global markets? What are the problems for operations managers here?

Essentially, they are the same – i.e., communication and data flow through the agents being used to provide access to global markets.

But, obviously the operations profile of a private client broker is going to be quite different from a global investment bank and yet the problems, whilst different in 'size' and style, are very similar for the manager.

Poor systems or lack of competent staff will impact as severely, maybe significantly more severely, in a small broker or fund manager than they possibly would in Morgan Stanley Dean Witter or Deutsche Bank.

As the cost of providing complex systems and resource is high, organisations – such as private client stockbrokers – will often outsource their client settlement, etc. to agents that have the skills and infrastructure to deliver services and manage client assets and money.

Within the exchange-traded derivatives arena, fund managers and small/medium-size clients will utilise global or centralised clearing facilities offered by larger banks to remove the responsibilities of settling obligations with the clearing house of the market and also streamlining the settlement process to a single counterparty.

For major banks, such as UBS, the global clearing services in exchange-traded derivatives is an important business, being as it is a part of a portfolio of services and products offered to their clients by the group.

Managers failing to be aware of developments in the markets, regulation, or clearing and settlement environments are as a big a liability in the global fund manager as they are in a small domestic fund management company.

It is therefore very important for an operations manager to not only understand the business of their own firm and the functions of operations teams within the firm but also how other firms are structured.

The facilities and services on offer to fund management companies through banks, central securities depositories and custodians, if utilised effectively, will save money and reduce risk, both of which are fundamental objectives of operations managers!

This principle therefore also applies to the staff in the operations team, particularly those dealing directly with other firms – be they banks, agents, suppliers or clients.

It makes good sense to not only train staff for the role they undertake internally but also to train them in the other areas of the industry that affect them directly and indirectly.

Suggested further reading and useful websites can be found between pp. 417 and 419.

Box 3.3 Work session.

Consider the clearing, settlement and risk issues for a broker with both fund management and private clients that are operating in international markets.

Chapter

4

. . . .

CONCEPTS OF RISK

Operational risk is a major issue for the operations manager; in this chapter we explore the subject and the way in which operational, market and credit risk impact.

The whole subject of risk is not new, and yet in reality operational risk was certainly not so high on the agenda until high-profile problems and losses, as a result of operational inefficiency started to materialise. For managers, some aspects of operational risk, such as settlement risk, are part of the day-to-day workflow and are managed accordingly. Efficiency in the operations team is therefore an element of the management of one part of operational risk, at least, in that efficient settlement reduces settlement risk. However, we also need to remember that our performance levels may not be reflected in the performance of agents and counterparties we deal with, so we are exposed to a counterparty risk element of operational risk. There are other examples of risk which we will look at in a moment, but it is clear that operational risk is in two parts, that which we generate and control and that which is generated from external sources and needs controlling. For instance, errors and inefficiency in trade input for principal trading are internally generated problems, whereas inefficiency in a custody provider is externally generated. One may be tempted to think that the external risk issues are more difficult to deal with, but this may not be the case. Dealing with internal resource issues can be more demanding than using service level agreements to raise the performance of an external counterparty. The subject of operational risk raises several key issues. These include:

- the approach to risk;
- the sources of risk;
- the impact of risk;
- measuring risk, including the cost of managing risk;
- introducing controls and procedures;
- why disasters will happen if risk is not managed.

Operational risk and operations risk are not new concepts, as we have said. As soon as the first ever trade took place operational risk came into being, and yet it is only comparatively recently that there has been an acceptance that operational risk exists. Contrast this with market and credit risk, both of which have been recognised since the 1970s. Defining risk is a little subjective, especially when we talk about operational risk. Box 4.1 gives some definitions.

Box 4.1 Definitions.

Market risk can be described as the risk of financial loss due to trading errors, adverse market movements, or breaches of market rules and regulations.

Credit risk can be described as the risk of financial loss due to the likelihood of a failure by a counterparty.

Operational risk is defined by the Risk Management Group of the Basel Committee as "the risk of loss resulting from inadequate or failed internal processes, people and systems or from external events."

Operational risk could also be – and is – described as everything that is not or does not fall into market or credit risk.

The Basel Committee was formed in 1974 by the central-bank governors of the Group of Ten countries; it has approximately 30 technical working groups which meet regularly. It is part of the Bank for International Settlements (*BIS*). Its recommendations do not have any legal force, but are intended to bring about common standards and practices amongst its members' systems. One of its important objectives is to ensure that no foreign banking establishment is without adequate supervision. In 1997 the Committee developed a set of *Core Principles for Effective Banking Supervision* (*www.bis.org*). Further, in 1999 it published the *Core Principles Methodology* to assist implementation and assessment of the principles.

Both market and credit risk have been high on the agenda of regulators and risk managers. An example is perhaps the capital adequacy requirements pertaining to over-the-counter (*OTC*) derivative transactions. The Basel Committee has been looking at the subject for some years now and has – through the *Basel Accord* and the *New Basel Accord* (published January 2001) – provided a proposed framework for the regulatory capital charge for operational risk. In outlining proposals for the development of a capital charge to cover operational risk, the Committee has set out three approaches of increasing sophistication to assessing the operational risk charge. These are the *Basic Indicator Charge*, the *Standardised Approach* and the *Internal Measurement Approach*. These proposals are subject to surveys and data collection by the Committee, and it is important to remain up to date with developments. For this reason I do not propose to put into this chapter details of the accords or papers, given that change is taking place and, instead, suggest the work session in Box 4.2 is undertaken.

Box 4.2   Work session.

There are many papers and other information published by the BIS and these are available on their website *www.bis.org*

From the website, study the proposals and amendments as they are being published and consider how these will impact on your organisation and on the operations team.

Whilst BIS has set out definitions of operational risk I find in my dealings with clients on this matter that there is still the issue of defining operational risk in terms of the day-to-day workflow. What really is operational risk? Well, one reason for the delay in recognising operational risk is that as a category of risk it is probably the most difficult to determine, and even Basel recognises that some of the parameters in their risk assessment overlap with market and credit risk. So, once again, we ask the question: 'What exactly is operational risk?'

As we have seen in the definitions (Box 4.1), some would argue that it is everything that affects a business that is not market or credit risk. Others argue that it is everything and anything to do with the post-transaction clearing and settlement process. In the case of the latter, the risk itself is described as 'operations' rather than operational risk. For the purposes of this book we will consider operational risk as being anything that is not market or credit risk. That said, we may find that the views expressed in this book are not the same views taken by risk managers in different organisations. Also, some organisations have been focusing on operational risk for many years and have refined their assessment of it. There are many different approaches to risk in the industry today, but of course the regulatory requirements concerning risk are vitally important to understand. Both domestic regulators and international organisations will have risk-related regulation and recommendations that firms will adhere to. In addition to the regulatory situation, we also have recommendations from organisations, such as ISSA, that are designed to improve efficiency and reduce settlement, systems and counterparty risk.

Equally, firms will need to have a risk strategy that applies to their particular business and which they are comfortable with. No two firms have identical approaches to risk, although, as noted, some risk management requirement is mandatory. Another key factor is that many view the subject of risk primarily in terms of potential financial loss. As such, operational risk is frequently considered to be unlikely to cause a severe financial loss – and certainly not in one hit. The logic here is that an inappropriate or incorrect deal can result in substantial loss, whereas a settlement problem with the transaction, whilst it may incur costs, is not likely to generate a significant loss.

One is tempted initially to agree with these sentiments as history would tend to suggest that the headline making 'disasters' in the financial services industry are all mainly related to market and/or credit risk. However, delve a little deeper and there may be associated operations issues that contributed to the problem. The contribution may not have been 'physical' in the sense of an error in processing transactions, but rather a failure to carry out the risk management role that operations un-doubtedly have. Basel also recognises this and notes that some risks and loss events previously recorded as credit or market risk may actually sit in operational risk, or indeed in more than one category. It is also worth noting at this point that the current proposed framework for a capital charge ignores systemic risk and, therefore, it has been stated that the charge would need to be calibrated to reflect this.

It is important to consider how the manifestation of operational risk occurs, because in my experience it is not always an up-front or visible scenario. Operational risk can manifest itself in many ways. Sometimes, the operational risk will be such that it is not easily or im-mediately identifiable. In most cases an error on a trans-action can and should be identified quickly and adjusted, so that the loss is quantified. With operations, for in-stance, a problem may be occurring only occasionally and yet is having an unseen, dramatic and damaging effect. For instance, a client is being inconvenienced by occasional late and error-strewn reports and settlement, and as such is losing confidence in the broker/bank as their counterparty. In such a situation it is not inconceiv-able that the client may gradually move their business elsewhere and the counterparty may never be aware that it is the operations team's performance that is to blame.

Equally, we need to consider how to quantify and measure operational risk.

Typical ways of measuring risk relate to the allocating of capital against potential losses based, for instance, on

Value at Risk (VaR), historical losses attributable to risk situations and exposures – for instance, credit ratings. This is not too difficult when we look at market and credit risk measurement and management.

Operational risk, however, is difficult to measure and hard to quantify in terms of likely financial loss. It is therefore difficult to allocate capital to cover such a risk turning into an actual loss.

The establishing of the extent of the market risk associated with trading is not simple, but it is nevertheless possible to measure the exposure given various scenarios and to allocate capital to cover the possible worst case outcome. VaR is one common approach, but it is less easy to apply this when dealing with operational risk; although a *Value at Operational Risk (VaOR)* and other technical methodology has been worked on extensively in the industry to find ways of quantifying operational risk. Nevertheless, despite this progress being made on operational risk models, as more and more organisations seek to quantify the operational risk of their business, there are still many operational risk management processes that rely on subjective assessment and input. It is therefore important that managers begin the process of measuring risk by developing both subjective monitoring of elements that contribute to operational risk sources as well as researching the risk measurement models used in-house or likely to be used.

For the day-to-day risk management process, what would we need to incorporate into operational risk measurement? When we look at quantifying and measuring operational risk we need to first consider what it consists of. At high level, operational risk can be said to comprise:

- settlement risk;
- system risk;
- personnel risk;
- infrastructure risk;
- counterparty risk;
- regulatory risk;
- legal risk;
- reputational risk.

These risks are fully explained later in the chapter.

However, within these headings are many sub-sets of risk that can and often do combine to generate risk situations that go across one or more categories. A significant danger therefore is combinations of risks. These risks make the measuring and managing of operational risk a complex exercise, and indeed it can also result in the situation where the cost of managing the risk is prohibitive. As with all types of risks, there is operational risk that is acceptable as part of the business, provided that the risk is known and understood. There is a danger that the subject of operational risk can be so diverse and so large that it becomes an administrative and costly nightmare. It is therefore important for any organisation and any individual manager with responsibility for operational risk to establish exactly what the objectives are when we talk about measuring and managing operational risk.

One approach for the operations manager to take is to consider risk statements and then analyse them – first, in terms of the particular operational function they are involved with and, then, for other operational areas of the firm and counterparts.

Consider the following statements, which will help us to analyse and define what our risk objectives are:

1. Operational risk exists in all businesses.
2. We can ascertain what operational risk is in the context of our business.
3. We can look at individual components of the risk.
4. We can choose to be:
   o aware of the risk;
   o to be aware of the risk and prioritise managing some of it;
   o to manage the risk out of the business.
5. We may need to adopt a mix and match approach.
6. We may need to demonstrate how we manage operational risk:
   o to clients or potential clients;
   o to third parties such as clearing houses;
   o to regulators.
7. We will have to establish a risk culture within the organisation.
8. We need to analyse risk in conjunction with:
   o other parts of the organisation;
   o external counterparties;
   o across products and markets.
9. We will need to allocate capital in accordance with Basel and internal policy to mitigate against the

impact of the operational risk manifesting itself; totally ignoring operational risk is not an option.

When looking at an operational risk model we need to be able to measure risk in such a way that we can:

- predict the type of risk;
- where, when and how it will arise;
- the frequency with which it might occur;
- the impact.

There are a variety of ways in which this can be done. One example is by carrying out a process of workflow analysis that will show:

- the processes and their duration;
- the complexity, ranking (in terms of primary, secondary) and the extent of automation of these processes;
- the deadlines associated with the processes;
- the level of resource available for the process;
- the level of management needed;
- the scope to absorb additional workload and/or delays to the processing.

Workflow analysis is discussed at various times in the book, but from the above we can see that operational risk measurement is both possible as well as a continuous process. However, when the concept of operational risk needs to be explained to the staff and their buy-in sought to implement change (as, indeed, when the business managers are approached to get their buy-in to the cost of establishing effective operational risk management) the manager will probably encounter resistance. This is not surprising, and it occurs all the time anyway simply because change does not sit comfortably with many people. One possible way to overcome this is to relate the argument to an everyday scenario such as: 'Operational risk may not appear to be an important issue and it may never create a major problem, so why all the fuss? But, then, you could leave your house unlocked all day and never get burgled. Do you want to take the risk?'

Having established that operational risk exists and needs to be quantified and measured, we need to identify the risk in more detail. We will do this later in the chapter, but, first, let us look at where the risk might come from. Sources of operational risk can be both obvious and sometimes not so obvious.

Here are just a few potential sources:

- lack of product knowledge;
- poor system reliability;
- inadequate levels of staffing;
- inefficient counterparties;
- diverse and unpredictable business levels;
- overseas clients;
- lack of critical skill sets;
- fraud and criminal activities;
- poor communication and poor internal relationships.

Then, we need to consider the type and frequency of risk. Each of these sources is very different, and so are the types of risk and the frequency with which they might occur.

For instance, lack of product knowledge could be as a result of:

- turnover of staff;
- loss of experienced personnel;
- new products being traded;
- non-availability of information;
- lack of training.

It may be a major problem or it may only be relevant if and when a particular type of product is traded. Bear in mind also that other risks may become associated, such as regulatory risk and reputational risk. For example, a clearing member of a clearing house will usually have to demonstrate the competency of the staff, systems and processes. If problems occur within the members operations function because of the introduction of a new type of product, the clearing house may feel that the member is failing to meet the standards required and any prolonged problem or subsequent repetition may result in the clearing status being withdrawn. The significance of that should not need explaining.

A problem might manifest itself as an error caused because we were not aware of something like a corporate action, expiry date of a derivative or maturity of a bond, or because we were unaware of problems with settlement in the jurisdiction where the product was traded. Some of the problems may be quite obvious, others more obscure. Individually, the problem might be easily identified and managed, but a combination of risk problems might create a far more difficult situation to manage.

I think we have established that the role of operations managers and their teams in managing risk is a key one. Throughout the book we look at how to manage the risk, but as managers we will have already worked out that much of what we do in an operational environment or an operations team day in, day out is geared to directly or indirectly managing risk. A major issue that arises is that the personnel involved in the operations team may not be aware of the importance of their role. Perversely, that in itself is a source of risk!

At this stage we can perhaps summarise operational risk. It is a combination of types and sources of risk that may have a different impact in various circumstances. It may result in direct or indirect financial loss. It may occur frequently or occasionally. It may build up gradually until it is a major problem. It is a risk category of immense importance and must be understood in any organisation, large or small. It can be hard to measure, but nevertheless must be addressed so that, at the very least, managers are aware of the risks. Failure to understand and address operational risk will result in significant damage to the business. We know that operational risk comes in a variety of guises and that we can break down operational risk into several headings. Within each heading will be a complex matrix of possibilities and sources of the risk type. Let us look at these in more detail.

Settlement risk

Definition: *The risk of inefficient processes and proce-dures resulting in the failure, delay or incorrect settle-*

ment of transactions and associated actions, such as payments, delivery and corporate actions.

There are many ways in which this type of risk can occur. The simple inefficiencies of the staff involved are an obvious source. So, too, is inadequate or misused systems. However, not all settlement risk is created within the operations team. External influences – such as delays in getting relevant information from front office to operations or problems with systems run on a bureau basis – can be very influential.

Other causes of settlement risk are:

- client transactions;
- deadlines;
- difficult settlement conventions;
- illiquid stocks/bonds/commodities;
- lack of knowledge of the product/processes/procedures associated with the transaction.

System risk

Definition: *The failure of, or absence of, adequate systems to handle the type of business being transacted and security over such systems, as well as a failure by managers, operations staff, IT staff and others to understand the scope and limitations of the systems and the related workflow.*

The reliance on systems in the financial services industry makes system risk a key issue. Straight through processing (*STP*) is a prime example. The advent of STP is removing elements of settlement risk associated with trade input. Electronic markets, internal dealing systems and direct trade input enable the operations team to maximise auto-reconciliation and concentrate on exception management. However, not all organisations have STP, or if they do it is not necessarily fully front to back. Whatever the situation, the managers must recognise that systems generate considerable capacity, provide efficient and cost-effective processing, and that those systems are also a major source of operational risk.

System security is a key issue. The security over the system is paramount. All too often there are serious problems generated by the failure of managers to adequately manage systems. There are a whole host of possible situations including:

- incorrect, missing or erroneously changed static data;
- failure to make change contract specification;
- ignored, lack of or breached security of access to the system or parts of the system;
- 'shared' passwords lead to breach of segregation;
- access to confidential client information gained by front office;
- inadequate or absence of monitoring of client facing technology services;
- lack of or easily breached firewalls;
- lack or absence of control over access to Internet;
- private, illegal or unauthorised access, download, etc.;
- possibility of hackers and/or viruses entering the system.

System capability and reliability is another key area. It is fairly obvious that any system used in any operations environment needs to be able to adequately handle the products traded. Where this is not possible – as might be the case with use of OTC derivatives – controls need to be devised which will mitigate the risk. End-user organisations can have problems verifying margin calls on the systems they use and managers need to address this issue with suitable controls encompassing the reasonableness of the calls. In terms of reliability, there needs to be awareness of:

- the manual process that can/will be implemented;
- the impact this will have on the risk exposure;
- the procedures and controls that will now apply;
- the potential solutions to eradicate the unreliability.

Counterparty and agent risk

Counterparty risk is not confined to creditworthiness. The performance of a counterparty can have a material effect on the operations team. Where it is necessary to use an agent – e.g., an institutional client using a broker or a broker/bank using a clearing agent on an exchange where they do not have clearing membership – there is potential for heightened operational risk. The standards of performance by these agents will inevitably impact upon the processes and performance of our own team. Late settlement, notification or payment are all significant and may have far-reaching implications. The issues that arise are:

- regulatory;
- reputation;
- client money and assets policy;
- increased costs.

Similar kinds of issues arise in respect of clients. We are dependent on the accurate and timely flow of information concerning transactions, payments, booking instructions, etc. If a position is to go to delivery, the broker/bank is dependent on the client meeting the delivery schedule and deadlines, or they may become liable.

In some cases, there may be very limited resource and product knowledge at the client, and the potential for problems is increased. In many cases, the broker/bank may also be dealing with a custodian. Broker/banks also offer a wide range of client services which may include:

- prime brokerage;
- global clearing;
- single currency settlement;
- average pricing;
- custody.

Each of these is placing additional pressures on the operations processing flow and, therefore, whilst it can be said that client services help to reduce counterparty risk (by providing vital assistance to smooth the settlement flow), its provision does create additional sources of risk internally.

Personnel risk

Key issues that arise under this source of risk include:

- fraud;
- defections/loss of senior staff;
- lack of contingency for absence of staff;
- inadequate training and development;
- relationship issues (work and private);
- excessive pressure caused by poor working environment and hours.

Personnel risk has several key issues.

Knowledge and competency

The knowledge and expertise of staff in all areas is crucial to a business's success. However, this expertise needs to be relevant and current in order to meet the demands of an ever-changing financial industry. It is vitally important that a company demonstrates a commitment to staff training programmes and constant staff development. The quality and integrity of managers and supervisors in an operations environment should be considered and, whilst a turnover of staff is to be expected, this turnover should be small and monitored.

Staff turnover

Where personnel turnover is constant in any area of the business, then questions should be raised about the reasons for this and the effect that it is having on the business should be monitored. However, the future effect that it may have cannot easily be measured, but could potentially be disastrous!

Processing

Within personnel risk, there is an element of danger associated with routine and possibly monotonous tasks. Managers and supervisors should monitor this and, where possible, staff should be rotated or cross-trained to avoid this situation. Mistakes can be made and errors may not be detected where staff are not paying full attention to their tasks due to the repetitive nature. As part of STP projects, these types of tasks should be reviewed and, where possible, automated.

Management style

Whilst managers and supervisors need to instil discipline in their staff and their practices, this needs to be carefully managed, so as not to create an atmosphere of fear of making mistakes and a fear of owning up to them. This will lead to covering up and can lead to more errors, which occur due to the cover-up. In reality, there will be mistakes and staff need to be open about admitting to them. Given the pressures, the so-called 'open door' or 'approachable' management style is crucially important in today's operational environment.

Relationships

An element of personnel risk which needs to be controlled and managed properly is the front/back office relationship. There needs to be mutual respect for each other's roles and there should be good communication channels in order to efficiently resolve the problems and errors that occur. However, if the relationship is too close, then that is a potential danger due to the possibility of fraud.

The way in which personnel interact with clients and counterparties is important. Where staff are directly involved with clients and other counterparties, they should be trained in how to deal with them. This ranges from more simple matters, such as the way in which they speak to outside people, to what they should/shouldn't tell them. Choosing the right people with good communication skills for these roles is vital, as primarily they represent the company to the outside world.

The issue of personnel risk is often ignored, yet the efficiency and effectiveness of the operations team, which is key to profitability, is directly related to the manager's ability to develop the right people and the right environment, which, in turn, is at the heart of operational risk management. Lack of attention to personnel risk will, sooner or later, create a major problem, as other risk control measures are dependent upon and assume a 'risk culture' has been established in the team.

Regulatory risk

It is often tempting to ignore regulatory risk under the misguided assumption that compliance and/or audit will protect against any problem. To some extent they do, but operations influences regulatory risk, as it often generates data used in regulatory reporting and also is in the front line in areas such as client money and assets. Recognising regulatory risk as part of operational risk is essential simply because the consequences of not doing so are too great.

Regulatory risk stems from several sources including:

- reporting requirements;
- client money rules;
- money laundering and fraud (insider dealing);
- complex and differing requirements in regulatory jurisdictions;
- reputational impact of a breach of regulation.

Legal risk

As with regulation, it is tempting to say that legal issues are dealt with elsewhere in the organisation. However, there are many instances where operations personnel are either directly or indirectly involved with matters that present an operational risk. These will include ineffective, absence of or incorrect client documentation in respect of:

- OTC derivative transactions;
- the seizing or impounding of assets;
- entering into illegal transactions or relationships, or carrying out actions/instructions that would be considered illegal.

Reputational risk

This is the importance of the way in which your company is perceived to the outside world. It can be damaged in much the same ways we have looked at under personnel risk. It can also be damaged by inadequate controls over the business, which can lead to a bad reputation in the market. Reputational risk is not only confined to client business, it can also affect your relationship with counterparties. This can be damaged if you do not settle efficiently and operate properly with counterparties. You may be at risk from clients and counterparties damaging your reputation and, therefore, you must have strict procedures for operating with third parties and must take action when they put your business reputation at risk.

Infrastructure risk

There is a significant operational risk in having an ineffective or inappropriate infrastructure to handle the business of the firm. As changes impact on the industry as a whole, so the infrastructures within organisations need to change. Procedures, processes, reporting lines, departments/sections, roles and functions can and will need reviewing and adapting. Failure to do this will lead to unnecessary pressures on people and systems, higher error rates, lack of capacity to handle growth and almost certainly higher costs to the business.

Financial risk

Some elements of financial risk could be classified as settlement risk. This might include errors resulting in interest claims or fines for late delivery, for instance. However, financial risk does exist in other forms as part of operational risk. Included in this would be:

- fraud and default;
- ineffective costs management;
- unclaimed and/or unreconciled floor brokerage;
- poor treasury management.

These are areas that are often 'lost' in the overall process of running an operations team. Costs management, for instance, may be an issue when business is slow, but is relaxed when revenues and profits are good. Likewise, significant additional costs or underperformance of returns on invested capital occur if treasury management is neglected or is carried out by inadequately trained personnel. It may not be significant on a day-by-day basis, but the cumulative effect over a year can be very significant.

Disaster risk

This broadly constitutes the inability (or reduced ability) to continue to operate and can cover such areas as:

- inadequate disaster recovery or business continuation plans;
- forcing of a curtailment or reduction in trading levels;
- unacceptable risk situations.

Many organisations have adequate contingency plans for disasters, such as loss of premises. From an operations point of view, there are many possible disaster situations that have nothing to do with the loss of the premises. Some of these would be:

- sudden unavailability of staff;
- prolonged system downtime;
- external factors, such as problems at agents, clearing houses, clients;
- breaches of client confidentiality.

In this chapter of the book we have looked at an overview of operational risk. We have considered what it is, where it comes from and how it occurs.

We have looked at simplistic ways in which this risk can be measured and at some of the key issues that will need to be managed.

Operational risk is a vital element that needs to be considered by any business operating in financial markets and products. It is a large and diverse subject that needs careful assessment, interpretation of its characteristics in relation to each organisation and, above all, managing.

We can therefore conclude that the manager's role in operational risk management is a crucial one. So, what are the key points in terms of managing the risk and fulfilling the role and responsibilities?

First and foremost is the manager's own understanding of the risk issues, the ways in which their organisation is already addressing the risk issues and the general risk culture that currently exists within the organisation and the operations team. Once this assessment is completed, we can look at tools to help the management process and provide the input to the risk management process in the firm. We have already seen how workflow analysis provides the key efficiency indicators and, where possible, the use of benchmarks should also be used. Then, we need to consider the risk awareness of the team and ensure that adequate training is provided to bring the level of awareness and buy-in to the required status.

Procedures, including those related to risk sources and management, need to be documented and constantly reviewed and updated, as the risk environment changes constantly. Particular care must be taken to ensure that the procedures reflect regulatory changes, industry rationalisations, industry best practices and, of course, internal changes to business profiles, structures, etc. Given that we are talking about global operations management, this process needs to be completed for each jurisdiction, market, etc. The operations manager needs their own 'strategy' to monitor the risks, the sources, the controls and the effectiveness of the controls.

Any risk situations that do materialise need to be logged, actions taken and/or referred to the risk manager or group and then monitored. Any financial cost – i.e., claims, losses – also needs to be logged and, if appropriate, re-ported to the risk manager for the loss database (loss database will have been covered in your BIS/Basel work session earlier in this chapter – see Box 4.2). The management information in current use for general purposes can often be adapted and utilised for operational risk management information (*MI*) purposes.

If from the MI data and from other sources – i.e., supervisor's views, etc. – there are significant risk scenarios or sources arising, then the manager must take action. This would include risks generated by system issues, resourcing, working environment, counterparty/agent and the action will range from re-engineering operations teams to replacing a counterparty.

Operational risk management should be very much proactive rather than reactive management. Planning and assessing are key tools in managing the risk before – rather than after – it happens. Of course, the unexpected always will occur and then the speed of and appropriateness of the course of action will be imperative.

Sources of operational risk are diverse. So, in the rest of the book when we look at specific functions, processes and procedures it is logical to do so from the risk point of view as well.

Organisations have different approaches to managing risk. Figures 4.1–4.4 illustrate how the management of risk might be structured.

Figure 4.1 shows the approach of day-to-day risk being managed as part of the workflow and the responsibilities of the supervisors and operations team, with the operations manager overseeing the control and liaising with the risk manager. This approach to operational risks is

Figure 4.1 Operational risk.

replicated through the organisation, covering different departments and/or sections. The risk manager is therefore receiving data and discussing issues and actions with the manager on the basis of exceptions to the risk limits and profiles set for the area concerned.

Figure 4.2 shows the extension of this approach to illustrate the general roles of the operations and risk managers and that of the Board. The Board will react to the reports

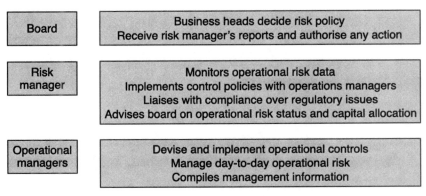

Figure 4.2 Operational risk structure.

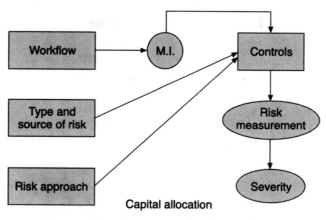

Figure 4.3   Operational risk model 1.

from the risk manager which will include recommendations and requirements for resource, policy changes, etc.

Figure 4.3 shows how the measurement of operational risk might be incorporated into a model. The risk approach and identified sources of risk are mapped into the workflow and resulting management information is used to develop controls. The controls are monitored to give the effectiveness of risk management and to provide historic and predicted potential occurrences of different risks, including the severity – if it were to occur. Against this, capital can be set aside according to the organisation's risk view, policy and any regulatory requirements.

Figure 4.4 shows additional sources of input to the control process, so that any accounting, regulatory or industry best practices, etc. can be incorporated into the risk standard to be used.

Managing operational and operations risk is still in essence about the efficiency and effectiveness of the

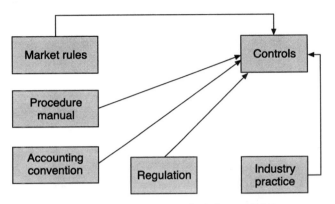

Figure 4.4   Operational risk model 2.

managers, supervisors and staff. Models can show what might happen and predict financial losses, but the people are both a key source of risk and the strongest way to manage it.

There are many articles and books that deal with operations and operational risk as well as papers published by, for instance, ISSA, G30 and BIS (see Useful websites on p. 417). Despite the fact that there are core risks that affect all organisations, the type and degree of impact of operational and operations risk will vary from business to business and organisation to organisation. Consider the types of risk categories that are likely to apply to your organisation and assess the ways in which that risk is identified and managed.

Chapter

5

....

CLEARING AND SETTLEMENT

In this chapter we are going to look at the clearing and settlement processes in some detail, but clearing and settlement takes place after the transaction, although there are, as we will see, certain processes that operations are involved in prior to trades taking place.

Trading in securities – whether in the *exchange-traded* (sometimes referred to as the *regulated* markets) or the *Over The Counter* (*OTC*) markets – generally takes place by telephone or through electronic dealing systems. With most securities, once a trade is executed both parties to the trade enter into a legally binding obligation or agreement that commits them to make a delivery of securities from the seller to the buyer in return for the equivalent value in cash. Derivatives are slightly different, as with some types of products — e.g., purchasing options – the trade is for a right to do something and not an obligation.

There are essentially three stages in clearing and settlement:

- pre-settlement;
- settlement;
- post-settlement.

The first task in the pre-settlement phase is to ensure that both counterparties recognise that the details of a particular trade are consistent. This is achieved by the exchange of confirmations, which enables one counterparty to allow the other to check all the trade details against its records. As settlement cycles are shortening, counterparties need to exchange their confirmations more rapidly. The traditional methods of sending paper contract notes, telex confirmations and transaction confirmations are no longer appropriate and alternative media include *Electronic Trade Confirmation (ETC)* and SWIFT messages.

It is necessary to perform a prompt confirmation-checking routine so that any problems that arise can be resolved as soon as possible (or within pre-determined deadlines set by the market). Trades that are unconfirmed for whatever reason cannot proceed to the settlement stage. It is important to note that the instruction and trade confirm process may be different, so that whilst the transaction cannot proceed to settlement, if uncon-firmed, instructions for settlement can be prepared and sent.

Once the two counterparties have confirmed trade details with each other, the next stage is to pass delivery/receipt instructions to the clearing organisation. The task of the clearing organisation is to:

- match delivery instructions with the corresponding receipt instruction (see Figure 5.1); and
- report the matching results back to the instructing counterparties.

Those instructions which are matched are held by the settlement organisation in a pending file until the due settlement date arrives. No further action is required during this period. The processes of clearing and settle-ment need to be explained as, although there is a blurring of organisations onto multi-functional concerns, the actual process is quite distinct. Broadly, clearing is the

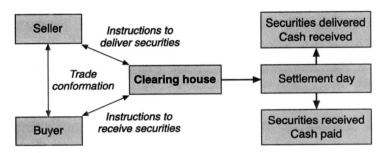

Figure 5.1 The role of the clearing organisation in securities confirmation – settlement overview.

process of recording, matching and confirming transactions, whilst settlement is the exchange of the asset for cash.

It is important to note here that – with an increasing number of electronic trading systems being used in the markets – trade matching is becoming less of an issue as trades are effectively matched at the time of trade. However, this doesn't mean that the dealer has performed the right trade, so internal trade matching to dealer's records/client orders is necessary. Problems arising from unmatched instructions must be resolved and correct instructions submitted to the clearing organisation for further matching. This stage must be completed in time to meet the clearing organisation's processing deadlines.

On settlement day – if there are sufficient assets, cash and securities available for delivery – the trades will settle. The counterparties are advised of their securities and cash movements and, finally, securities ledgers and cash accounting records are updated to reflect these movements.

Box 5.1   Definition.

Settlement is defined as the delivery of an asset in exchange for the equivalent in cash value.

Problems of definition arise with 'exchange' when the mechanics are looked at more closely. For example, there is the risk of non-receipt of funds if settlement is made by cheque. The cheque takes time to clear and might subsequently be dishonoured by the payer. To reduce this risk, the cash element of settlement should be made in such a way that the cash is both *assured* (i.e., guaranteed) and in *same-day funds.*

Furthermore, settlement of securities and cash should take place at the same time and without the possibility of one party to the transaction countermanding the delivery or payment. Settlement should therefore be the *simultaneous and irrevocable* transfer of ownership of the securities in exchange for the agreed cash value, otherwise known as *Delivery Versus Payment (DVP)*. In the markets, settlement periods range from $T+0$ to $T+5$. Most government bonds tend to settle on $T+1$, whilst corporate bonds generally settle on $T+3$. Equities tend to be longer than $T+3$ and higher. Derivatives can be $T+1$ or periodic settlement amounts based on time and/or events that trigger a payment/delivery.

So, which organisations are involved in the clearing and settlement process and how does it impact in terms of different products?

Clearing Houses and Securities Depositories obviously are at the heart of the process and – whilst there are similarities in the ways in which bonds, equities and derivatives settle – there are local variations to be aware of. Let us look at some bond settlement issues first.

International bonds, global bonds and convertible bonds are settled by, for example, two clearing houses, Euroclear and Clearstream. Not only can participants of one clearing house settle trades with another participant of the same clearing house, they can also do so with participants of the other clearing house. This is known as settlement via the (electronic) bridge which exists between Euroclear and Clearstream.

Through their links to each other and to external depositories and central securities depositories (*CSDs*), Euroclear and Clearstream are able to accept instructions to settle the following types of transactions:

- *Internal settlements* – these occur between two counterparties who are both participants of the same clearing house.
- *Bridge settlements* – these occur between two counterparties one of whom is a participant of Euroclear and the other a participant of Clearstream.
- *External settlements* – these occur between a local counterparty and a participant of Euroclear or Clearstream across a range of domestic securities.

Other types of services are offered by these organisations; for instance, Euroclear provides secured financing facilities to eligible participants for the purposes of covering securities settlements, pre-advising receipts of funds and, where appropriate, securities borrowing activities. The facilities are secured with cash and/or securities collateral.

Clearstream provides different types of financing which include:

1. Unconfirmed funds facility.
2. Technical overdraft facility.
3. Tripartite financing agreement.

Details of Clearstream's facilities can be found at its website – see Useful websites on p. 417.

The use of these facilities needs to be assessed from both a convenience and a cost point of view. As part of the overall process of asset management, the manager needs the ability to both ensure compliance with the settlement convention and the maximising of cost controls. Shortening settlement cycles will put further pressure on firms and managers to meet settlement deadlines and so arranging both funding lines and stock sources will become key functions in the operations team.

To help facilitate timely settlement of equity and bond transactions, both clearing houses operate borrowing and lending programmes. In the UK, CREST offers a similar service. These facilities can be automatic, so that a firm short of stock for settlement will automatically be able to borrow securities and effect settlement on the due date. This kind of facility needs to be researched for its cost implications and also in terms of whether it is mandatory or an option. As we have seen, part of the asset management process is the ability to ensure availability of cash and securities on settlement date. We can explore this further.

The prime objective is to ensure that there is sufficient cash available to cover all purchases. Inability to pay for securities when presented by the seller for settlement, will result in a *failed settlement* and an interest claim from the settlement date up to the date on which the purchase finally does settle.

A secondary objective is to make effective use of any cash balances (whether uncommitted funds or funds expected or needed for trade activities) and in so doing enhance the returns and reduce costs. The level of interest received on credit balances and paid on overdrafts and credit facilities can be affected by the timing of the deposit of funds or use of the credit facilities. It is important for the manager to ascertain what, if any, interest is paid on credit balances and charged on debit balances. These returns or charges add to the overall cost of the bargain and – over a year in a high-volume operation if not monitored against alternatives – they can be substantial.

Efficient management of this cash relies on accurate and timely information and communication between operations, treasury, clients and clearing houses. Cash positioning comes under an activity often referred to as cash management. The positioning of cash is part of the cash management process, which includes cash inflows

Table 5.1 An illustration of cash flow movements for the positioning of cash.

Outflow	Inflow
• Call payments on partly paid bonds. • Subscription monies for warrant exercise. • Payments of uncommitted cash balances for money market purposes. • Fees, charges, etc.	• Interest receipts. • Full/partial redemption proceeds. • Receipts of cash to cover anticipated purchases.

and outflows from both transactions and also non-trading events (see Table 5.1).

Efficient cash management therefore seeks to anticipate future cash movements from a variety of sources in order to ensure that cash is in the right place at the right time, to reduce funding costs and to enhance returns on uncommitted cash balances.

Predicting future cash balances is straightforward when sales, purchases and other events take place as expected. This becomes more problematic when trades fail, as it is not usually possible to know the settlement outcome until it has actually taken place. In addition, there will be separate instruction deadlines for transferring sufficient cash to meet the underlying obligation. The issue is further complicated by settlement of derivatives where there is no such situation as a settlement fail and cash must be paid to cover obligations by a set time or default procedures may result. As well as cash there is the issue of securities that need to be delivered, and so securities positioning for sales and therefore deliveries is important. Again, the issue of derivatives arises as settlement of securities for delivery against derivative transaction must take place at the time stipulated by the derivative exchange and clearing house. Any failure to meet this deadline can result in huge fines and/or default.

So, in addition to the cash funding issues for buyers, sellers must ensure that there are sufficient securities available for delivery. If a scenario arises whereby there are – or there are likely to be – insufficient securities available (through previous failed purchases, turnarounds, short selling, etc.), steps must be taken to record the reasons and to deal with this situation. This is covered by what is often known as 'fails control'.

Regular reports are provided from clearing houses or custodian organisations listing all the current securities and cash balances and often will include warnings of any potential or actual restrictions to securities deliveries and cash payments.

Clearly, when a settlement fail occurs or is highly likely to occur, action is needed by the team. It is imperative that clear procedures are developed and understood to ensure that relevant action is undertaken and the action is reported internally and externally as appropriate.

However well the pre-settlement processing has gone, there will be settlement failures and these will not always be the fault of our firm, or indeed the immediate

Table 5.2   Reasons and causes for settlement failure.

Reason	Cause
There are insufficient bonds available for delivery	Selling participant may: • be unable to borrow; • be unable to recall bonds out on loan; • be awaiting receipt of bonds from purchase.
There is insufficient cash	Buying counterparty may: • have cash funding or payment problems; • be awaiting proceeds from a sale.
Trade instructions are unmatched	• One or both counterparty(ies) has/have failed to input correct details. • Both counterparties are in dispute. • Operational error.
Securities are unavailable for delivery	Clearing organisation has blocked deliveries in respect of a corporate event or action.

counterparty to us. For instance, we see in Table 5.2 that a seller to us may be unable to fulfil that settlement. This is because the securities, to fulfil the settlement of this trade, have not been received from the counterparty due to deliver them. There are many reasons for settlement failure (see Table 5.2).

A failed trade will result in one or more of the following situations:

- One failed settlement might prevent other trades from settling either through lack of securities in sufficient quantity or insufficient cash.
- Funding costs and interest claims will occur.
- Resolving failure problems takes up valuable staff resources.
- Organisations who repeatedly cause trades to fail will get a bad reputation in the market, may suffer action by the exchange or clearing house and – on markets where the counterparty is known at the time of trade – a reluctance by firms to deal with the organisation.
- The failure could be related to a derivative delivery requirement.
- Regulatory capital implications.

As well as understanding why a settlement has failed, it is important to have procedures to resolve failed settlements. Depending on the circumstances, the choices are to wait until there are sufficient securities or cash available, or for the seller to try and borrow the securities. If these options are inappropriate, there are two formal courses of action available:

- *Seller is unable to deliver bonds* – the buyer has the right to issue a 'buy-in' notice to the seller whereby the buyer purchases the bonds from another counterparty ('buy-in' agent) who has sufficient bonds to settle the trade. The original trade is then closed out and the difference in cash amounts settled between the seller and buyer. This may be an option for the buyer or a mandatory action initiated by the market/clearing house, but the rules will vary from market to market.

- *Buyer is unable to receive securities* – the seller has the right to close the trade by means of a 'sell-out'. In this case, the seller sells the bonds to another counter-party ('sell-out' agent). The difference in transaction monies plus loss of interest on the sale proceeds is settled between the seller and buyer. Again, this may be mandatory.

However, there are steps that can be taken to reduce the risk of a settlement fail.

In markets with high volumes, the turnover in a particular issue might exceed the total amount of the issue itself or exceed the amount of security 'available' in the market. This can easily occur with bonds, as they are often held to maturity by investors and not traded. This fact, allied to the pressure from derivative products like futures or options where large exposures have been built up and may go to delivery at a single date, can create real problems in the settlement chain. It might be appropriate for a market to settle trades on a net basis rather than a gross (i.e., trade for trade) basis. Depending on volumes, the options are as follows:

- trade for trade;
- bilateral netting;
- multilateral netting;
- continuous net settlement;
- real time gross settlement.

Netting is a process that reduces the risk of a default by creating a single settlement based on the netted credit and debit balances on long and short positions between counterparties (Bilateral Netting). There are issues with netting, not least of which is a legal one concerning enforceability of netting agreements; however, the influential Group of 30 (*G30*) recognised netting as a significant risk reducing tool and have encouraged changes to make its use more easy. In foreign exchange (*FX*) markets CLS Bank is looking to provide a clearing system that will settle transactions in real time, removing the risk of default on one side of a deal.

Box 5.2   Work session.

Research netting and consider the advantages in terms of risk management and operational efficiencies. Also, find out what 'Herstatt Risk' refers to.

One way of quantifying the magnitude of settlement failures is to compare the actual percentage of transactions which settle on time (i.e., on the original contracted settlement date) with a benchmark.

One particular benchmark covering settlement performance has been built by GSCS Benchmarks who state that the purpose of this benchmark is to:

... provide a means of comparing the settlement efficiency of different markets and track the evolution ... over time. The benchmark incorporates the four components which combined together, reflect the overall cost to market participants of failed trades.

Source: GSCS Benchmarks

The funding costs associated with interest charges and lost opportunities to promptly re-invest cash balances can over time amount to a significant financial impact on a business if it is not monitored and dealt with. The direct market participants – such as the dealers, brokers and market makers – will also be obliged to consider the impact of failed settlements on the organisation's requirements under regulation and risk capital. Any need to bring in further capital to cover this area obviously increases the cost to the organisations concerned.

With most types of securities there are corporate actions. A major operations function is dealing with corporate actions. 'Custody' is a term that relates to a number of services that take place before or after settlement. Once settlement (or before settlement in the case of a trade where settlement is outstanding) has occurred, further settlement activity might occur as a result of a change to the security; for instance, a convertible bond or a benefit accruing to the holder of a security that is held – i.e., interest. These types of changes are called 'corporate actions'.

We know that a security has been settled and will be kept in safekeeping for as long as the investor or firm owns the security. A simple example of a corporate action is an interest payment due on a bond or money market instrument. It is imperative to not only know when such a payment is going to be made, but to also ensure that it is received and booked through the accounts correctly.

Table 5.3 shows interest payment rules for a selection of bonds.

Table 5.3   Interest payment rules for bond securities.

Security type	Normal rules
UK Government (Gilts)	Gilts go 'ex' 7 business days before the interest payment date. (An exception is the $3\frac{1}{2}$% War Loan which goes 'ex' 10 business days before the payment day.)
International/Eurobonds (held by Euroclear and Clearstream)	Both Euroclear and Clearstream use a record date to establish which bondholders are entitled to receive the interest payment. The record date is usually the close of business, 1 day before the payment date of the interest.
	After the record date, settlements are processed ex-coupon.
German Bonds	The record date is the close of business, 1 day before the payment date of the interest.
Netherlands	The record date is the close of business, 1 day before the payment date of the interest.
Denmark	The record date is 1 month and 1 day before the payment date of the interest.
Japan	Record date prior to interest payment is:
• Samurai Bonds (Bearer)	• 6 business days in Tokyo
• Samurai Bonds (Reg'd)	• 21 calendar days
• Daimyo Bonds	• 1 business day
• Shogun Bonds (Bearer)	• 1 business day in Tokyo
• Shogun Bonds (Reg'd)	• 21 calendar days
Australian Global Bonds	The record date is 14 days before the payment date of the interest.

Remember that the terms of securities and their related corporate actions can be varied, and it is crucial to keep information such as that shown above closely and constantly monitored. Once the correct beneficiary has been identified, all that remains is for the interest to be paid. In a manual process, the coupon will be detached from the bond certificate before being presented to the issuer's paying agent. The relevant amount of interest, as indicated on the coupon, is paid to the presenter of the coupon. In dematerialised/immobilised scenarios the coupon value is paid to the holder in the book-entry system.

Bond issuers usually make interest payments on either an annual or semi-annual basis, although there are bonds on which interest is paid quarterly. There are different interest conventions for different types of bonds (as shown in Table 5.3).

Fixed rate bonds

In the case of fixed rate bonds, where the amount of interest does not change throughout the life of the bond, the amount of interest and the payment date will be printed on the coupon.

Floating rate notes

Interest rates on Floating Rate Notes (FRNs) fluctuate with movements in the money markets. As the interest rates change, it is not possible to print the amounts on the coupons. For this reason, FRN coupons will differ slightly from fixed rate coupons.

Issuers advise bondholders of the new interest rate and next payment date by advertising the details in news-papers, such as the *Financial Times*, and informing the clearing houses, Euroclear, Clearstream, etc. through their depository banks.

For holders of international bonds/Eurobonds held by Euroclear and Clearstream's depositories, their cash accounts will be credited on the payment date with same-day value (the exception being Yankee Bonds, a dollar bond issued in the US by a non-resident, which pay with next-day value).

If, however, a trade dealt 'cum' (i.e., cumulative, includ-ing the coupon as opposed to 'ex' without or excluding the coupon) does not settle until after the record date, the coupon is paid to the bondholder who held the bonds on the record date – i.e., the seller.

The systems automatically recognise that the rightful recipient of the coupon should have been the buyer and the result is that the seller's cash account is debited and the buyer's cash account is credited with the full coupon payment. In addition to any coupon entitlements, there is also the capital repayment by the issuer to the bond-holder either on maturity, or in some cases earlier. A repayment of capital occurs when there is a partial or full return of the bonds to the issuer in exchange for cash. The terms of any repayments will be included in the original issue prospectus.

There are several instances when this might take place:

- final redemption;
- early redemption (via an issuer's call option);
- early redemption (via a bondholder's put option);
- partial redemption (drawing).

Typically, the depositories will present the bonds for repayment and debit the participants' securities accounts and credit the cash accounts with value on the repayment date. In order to allow sufficient time to surrender the bonds, the depositories will usually block the positions in order to prevent any further bond movements.

With convertible bonds, we have another type of consideration and therefore need to have suitable procedures in place. A bondholder is entitled to convert to another bond or equity as per the terms of the convertible bond, during a conversion period, usually at any time from 90 days after the bond was issued up to the final redemption date. However, any accrued interest is lost on conversion and the price of the bond must allow for the lost interest when calculating the conversion premium. The bondholder instructs the custodian to withdraw the bonds from custody (from the depository bank) and to deliver them to the conversion agent. The conversion agent will execute the conversion in accordance with the terms of the issue and local market practice.

The shares that have resulted from the conversion are subsequently delivered in accordance with the bondholder's original conversion instructions. There may be a delay before the shares are made available to the shareholder or custodian especially if they are in certificated form.

There are also bonds which are issued 'cum-warrant'. These warrants can be split away from the host bond and be exercised at the holder's option into a specified amount of shares at a pre-determined price and at a set time(s) in the future. This 'purchase' or exercise requires the payment of cash to the issuer of the warrant.

The exercise price and the date or period during which the exercise might take place are given in the subscription terms of the warrant. An exercise may take place at a time pre-specified by the issuer:

- on an annual date; *or*
- during a pre-defined period; *or*
- at any time.

In terms of giving instructions to exercise their warrant, the holders do much the same as with conversions except that an additional amount of cash must be paid to the issuer in exchange for the underlying shares.

With other types of conversion, custodians will, for instance, convert the various types of *Depository Receipt* (American, Global, etc.) into the underlying shares and will arrange delivery of these in accordance with the investor's instructions and local market practices.

It is important that adequate procedures are in place to ensure that reconciliation of securities and cash movements takes place.

There are many different situations when securities are received and delivered, and cash is paid and received. These can happen together by transactions being settled on a DVP basis, or separately – i.e., conversion of bonds into equity, partially or in full.

For all transactions and settlement actions – whether securities- or cash-related – market participants will keep accurate records of all movements and positions. This is known as 'reconciliation'. Reconciliation is the front line and defence line for the protection of a business. Reconciling cash movements against transactions, positions and delivery are fundamental controls against rogue dealers, fraud, etc.

Reconciliation can be described as the process by which cash and securities ledger positions are agreed to a third party's records with any differences or imbalances identified, investigated and resolved without delay. Operations managers must ensure the quality and robustness of the reconciliation processes are adequate and that the reconciliation staff understand the processes and how to act on and escalate any discrepancy effectively.

Cash, bank and nostro reconciliations are relatively straightforward to process insofar as the bank statement is compared with the ledger either manually or electronically and any unreconciled items recorded. These outstanding items must be monitored by operations managers and relevant action taken if they are not addressed promptly.

The following basic steps are applied:

1. Compare bank statement with ledger.
2. Identify and record bank statement entries that cannot be identified.
3. Identify and record ledger items for which there is no bank statement entry.
4. Prepare reconciliation sheet or review electronic reconciliation.
5. Identify and refer to operational sections for investigation and correction.

What makes manual cash reconciliations so problematic is the sheer quantity of items that pass over a client's account, especially when the client uses several of the bank's or broker's services. For the fund management company, payments and stock movements will go through the custodian for the fund, often on instructions from the fund management operations team. Reconciliation of these instructions is imperative.

Reconciliation of securities at the depot and cash records are performed by comparing the investor's ledger records with those of the custodian or International Central Securities Depository (*ICSD*). The investor's reconciliation is based on trade date. The custodian's records reflect the actual (settled) position. Not surprisingly, there will be differences and these can include:

- trades pending settlement;
- failed settlements;
- corporate actions;
- securities lending and borrowing positions;

- bond positions blocked for whatever reason by the custodian.

These and any additional differences should be investigated, reported and action taken to resolve them immediately. The following flow could apply:

1. Compare the custodian's balance with the ledger via automated reconciliation or manually ticking off items that match.
2. Identify and record ledger items for which there are no corresponding custodian balances.
3. Identify and record custodian items for which there are no ledger records.
4. Prepare reconciliation and outstanding queries data and management reports.
5. Ensure that outstanding items are investigated and resolved.

As part of the regulatory environment in most jurisdictions in the world, there are specific rules that deal with protecting customers. In the UK, the *Financial Services Authority (FSA)* specify detailed record-keeping requirements requiring routine reporting and reconciliations with the records of customer investments held.

As one might expect, the comprehensive reporting services provided by the custodians, in general, and the ICSDs, in particular, include reports covering all the custody operations events. Examples of these types of reports follow.

- *Preliminary advice/information reports*:
  - FRN coupon fixing;
  - forthcoming redemptions;
  - forthcoming coupon payments;
  - conversion opportunity timings;
  - exercise opportunity timings.
- *Portfolio position reports*:
  - list of securities held;
  - valuation of portfolio in currency of securities/ base currency of investor.

Depending on the nature of the reports, the custodians will communicate by one or other of mail, telex, email, proprietary system or SWIFT messages. What kinds of operational issues and controls arise for the manager?

In the post-trade environment, it is the role of the operations teams to ensure that, for example:

- the trades are verified;
- details are correctly uploaded into the relevant databases;
- dealers sign off their agreement of position balances;
- all trades are correctly processed;
- failed trades are identified and any discrepancies resolved;
- cash balances and securities positions are reconciled and outstanding items chased;
- derivatives margin is reconciled and covered.

As the majority of trades are settled on a 'true' or 'real' DVP basis – i.e., simultaneous and irrevocable – the risk of one-half of the trade settling and the other half failing is eliminated. This is an important control and, therefore, any trades settling free of payment need to be approved by managers. This extra attention must be paid to deliveries on a free of payment basis, especially if this is outside the normal market practice for that particular product. Table 5.4 illustrates some of the main issues and controls required to protect the organisation from risk exposure and potential financial loss.

Supporting these control activities will be the Internal Audit team. Their role includes:

- Ensuring the adequacy of Management Information Systems.
- Reconciliation control where there are differences in valuation methodologies or systems used by the front office and operations department.
- Increasing the depth and frequency of audits where weaknesses and significant issues are brought to light or significant changes have been made to:

  1. product lines;
  2. modelling methodologies;
  3. risk oversight processes;
  4. internal controls; or
  5. the overall risk profile of the organisation.

- Facilitating the development of adequate controls by being brought into the product development cycle at the earliest possible stage.
- Evaluation of the independence and overall effectiveness of the organisation's risk management functions.

Table 5.4 Illustration of the issues which arise from operational activities and the suggested controls.

Activity	Operational issue	Controls
Trade verification	• Trade date • Settlement date • Price tolerances • Approved products • Settlement instructions	• Reference to market settlement conventions • Pre-specified price limits • Dealer authorities and limits • Reference to counterparty/client standing instructions
New products New clients	• Details of clients and products must be correct and current • Unnoticed/incorrect information will have an adverse impact on any dealings • There are regulatory implications associated with clients	Full details of product should be obtained and checked before release into the database
Position agreement (dealer's 'blotter')	Trade dealt and dealing positions should agree with the dealer's own records	Daily reconciliation of blotter with settlement's records. Any discrepancies should be resolved by close of business
Trade confirmation	Trade details must be in agreement with those of the counterparty (the confirmation, once agreed, becomes a legally binding contract)	There are various ways to generate and transmit confirmations. All outgoing confirmations should be ticked off against the trade, and incoming confirmations checked and discrepancies dealt with on trade date.

Table 5.4 Illustration of the issues which arise from operational activities and the suggested controls (*cont.*).

Activity	Operational issue	Controls
Trade instructions	Clearing systems can only settle those trades which have been submitted by both counterparties and matched.	Unmatched trade reports should be reviewed and appropriate action taken before settlement date.
Cash funding	There should be sufficient cash available to cover all requirements. This is a predictive activity which considers previous fails and future needs.	Cash predictions should be made daily in sufficient time to meet treasury/ bank/clearing system deadlines.
Securities balances	There should be sufficient balances 'available for delivery', otherwise there will be failed settlements to deal with.	Use of securities borrowing will reduce the incidence of failed sales. (Uncommitted positions should be considered for lending purposes.)
Review settlement results	Settlement fails cause funding inefficiencies and further delivery problems. There will also be concerns of exposure to counterparty risk and regulatory requirements to increase financial resources – i.e., extra capital	• Reports should be prepared by product type, counterparty and dealer for analysis. • Failed trades should be chased, and buy-ins and sell-outs used where appropriate.

(*cont.*)

Table 5.4   Illustration of the issues which arise from operational activities and the suggested controls (*cont.*).

Activity	Operational issue	Controls
Product lending and borrowing activities	Issues cover: a loan/borrow initiation b collateral receipt c repricing outstanding loans and collateral d income collection and corporate actions activities e interaction with other operational units (dealers, settlements, etc.).	Activities must be covered by a standard lending agreement and adequately margined collateral. Outstanding positions should be monitored and reported to associated departments.
Nostro reconciliation	Key control ensuring that cash ledger positions agree with bank statements.	• Unreconciled positions should be investigated and resolved. • Reports should be prepared for review by management.
Depot reconciliation	Key control ensuring that securities positions agree with depository statements allowing for settlement fails, securities loans and borrows and any other relevant activities.	• Unreconciled positions should be investigated and resolved. • Reports should be prepared for review by management.
Corporate actions	Information on corporate actions should be obtained and verified in time to allow the client/dealer to make a decision within the issuer's deadlines.	Extra care is required through use of diary systems and constant verification of event processes and deadlines.

Table 5.4 Illustration of the issues which arise from operational activities and the suggested controls *(cont.)*.

Activity	Operational issue	Controls
	Failure to instruct on time exposes the organisation to financial loss.	
Income collection	• Income on registered securities will be paid to the beneficiary, and income on bearer securities will be claimed from the issuer. • The correct amount of income considers tax situations and trades dealt cum- and ex-dividend.	Reports will indicate which cash payments will need to be claimed from the market or paid direct. Any claims for income or WHT reclaims should be prepared and chased.

Now let us look at equities and equity derivatives and consider the clearing and settlement issues for these products. As we know, when an investor purchases an equity instrument they are buying partial ownership in the issuing company. An investor's amount of ownership in a company is determined by the number of shares owned by the investor in proportion to the total number of shares outstanding.

An equity instrument may offer the following *rights* to investors:

• The right to vote in company matters.
• The right to have access to company books and records (accounting and record keeping).

- The pre-emptive right (or right of first refusal). This means that if the company issues new securities, the current holders may have the right to purchase additional shares to maintain their proportional ownership of the company. This offer to the original holder is generally given before the offer is made to the public.
- The right to share in the company's profits through dividend payments.

The different classes of equity instruments each have different rights attached to them. If you recall, there are:

- ordinary shares;
- preference shares;
- redeemable shares;
- convertible preference shares;
- 'A' or non-voting shares;
- deferred shares.

In overseas markets there may be similar products, but with different terminology. For example:

- USA – Common Stock/Preferred Stock.
- France – Action Ordinaire (Ordinary Share).
- Germany – Stamm-Aktie (Ordinary Share).
- Japan – Futsu Kabushiki (Ordinary Share).

Ordinary shares represent partial ownership in a corporation. Typically, the shareholders will:

- have the right to vote in the election of the board of directors;
- have the pre-emptive right to purchase any additional shares sold by the company;

- receive a dividend, but only if the directors decide to issue a dividend;
- generally, receive a declared dividend only after preferred shareholders have been paid.

In addition, if the company is liquidated, (un)secured creditors, bondholders and preferred shareholders have a prior claim to the company's assets before the common shareholders.

Preference shares also represent ownership in a corporation. Characteristically, shareholders will:

- generally, have no voting rights.
- generally, receive dividends before the ordinary shareholders.

The dividend is frequently fixed as a percentage of the share's stated value. However, the dividend is not guaranteed. If the company does not post strong earnings, the directors can omit the preferred dividend.

A cumulative feature may be attached to a preference share, which states that all dividends in arrears must be paid to holders at some point in time prior to any dividends paid to common shareholders.

Participating preference shares may benefit from an increased level of dividends if the company does well. Redeemable preference shares have a fixed repayment date and may be entitled to more than their nominal capital amount (i.e., face value).

Preference shareholders generally have priority over ordinary shareholders to the company's assets in the event of bankruptcy or liquidation.

In addition, some issues have features such as:

- a 'callable' feature which stipulates that the issuer may, at a time or times as is in the provisions of the issue, call an issue for redemption;
- a feature making the shares 'convertible' to common shares.

There are some companies that issue shares with restricted or no voting rights. These shares are entitled to receive dividends and, in the event of a liquidation, they rank alongside the ordinary shareholders. Deferred shares usually do not qualify for a dividend until the company's profits have reached a pre-set level, or until a particular date. So, we have the basic characteristics of equities and the manager will need to devise procedures to reflect those differences. We can take this further in terms of specific situations, such as when shares are first issued.

We know that when a corporate entity offers its shares to the public for the first time, it is said to be 'going public'. This 'Offer for Sale' or Initial Public Offering (IPO) will be underwritten by investment banks or brokers. A prospectus containing information on the issuer, the terms of the issue, the management structure and any other important aspects of the issuer is prepared. The issue itself will either be placed amongst clients of the brokers (institutional investors) or advertised to the general public through the publication of mini-prospectuses and application forms in the financial press and elsewhere.

Any shares which are not bought by the public will be taken up by the underwriters (underwriters agree to take up any shares not applied for) who will take the shares onto their own books or sell them on to their own clients. On the other hand, issues that are initially over-subscribed will be distributed on a scaled-down basis. One of the consequences of an over-subscription is that the share price will rise to a premium over the issue price. Transactions in shares are processed in much the same way as with debt instruments – i.e., trade confirmation followed by instruction matching and final settlement. There are, however, some differences both in terms of methodology and performance.

As shares are becoming increasingly immobilised or de-materialised, this enables shares to be delivered by book entry rather than by physical transfer. Whilst this is helping to overcome problems with equity settlement, it is a fact that equities currently have longer settlement periods compared with debt and derivative products.

As with debt market instruments, equities transactions will also be settled and held through third-party organisations. In some markets, the clearing house will be independent from the depository, or one and the same entity. Today, many clearing houses and depositories deal with a cross-section of products including bonds, shares, warrants, convertible bonds and unit trust shares.

In the UK, CREST and the London Clearing House (*LCH*) have from February 2001 provided settlement of equities on $T + 3$ and a Central Clearing Counterparty facility (EquityClear). This is a similar arrangement to that used for exchange-traded derivatives and is also in use on Euronext – the combined Belgian, Dutch and French securities and derivatives markets – through the clearing house Clearnet.

We know, from looking at bonds earlier in the chapter, that there are various types of corporate action. With equities there are various benefits that are distributed. A benefit distribution is a distribution made by a company to its shareholders in the form of cash, securities or a combination of both in cases where an entitlement is a fraction of a share. Distributions are usually made in proportion to the investor's holding as at the record date. The prime example would be a cash benefit, such as a dividend, to shareholders on a regular basis. This would be typically on a semi-annual or quarterly basis. As the dividends are paid from profits, the amount of cash paid will change from payment to payment.

As the majority of equities are in registered form, it is theoretically straightforward for the issuing company to identify the beneficiaries. If the shares are in bearer form rather than registered securities, the issuer will require some form of proof before making a payment; this proof, as with bearer bonds, is in the form of a coupon which is detached from the share certificate.

A problem arises for a 'cum-dividend' purchaser, whose

name is not recorded on the company's share register in time to receive the dividend.

In order to establish correct entitlement, it is important to understand how some key dates come into play. These dates are:

- record date;
- pay date;
- ex-date (ex-dividend date).

The record date is the date upon which the issuer or the Registrar closes its books for the purpose of capturing the names of the legal owners to whom the distribution will be paid. All legal owners will participate in the distribution, whether or not they are the beneficial owners. In other words, the issuer will pay the 'registered holder', even if the shares have been sold. As they will need to be re-registered in the new owner's name, it follows that until such time as re-registration is performed, the seller is still the legal owner and therefore the initial recipient of any benefits. Clearly, it is important that there are procedures in place to ensure that entitlements such as dividend benefits are claimed if the shares were not registered in time. As certificated securities are traded, the buyer (the new beneficial owner), or their fiduciary agent (broker, bank custodian), should submit the physical shares to the Registrar (or Transfer Agent), appointed by the issuing corporation to handle such transactions. The Registrar will cancel the old certificate(s) and issue new ones. The new beneficial owner (or its nominee) has now become the new legal owner.

With dematerialised and book-entry settlement common in major markets, this process is completely automated; so, the operations manager must ensure that staff are clear on the procedures for both automated and residual certificated settlement processes. A list of owners will be supplied to the issuer's paying agent in order that they may disburse income payments to shareholders of record on the pay date. The pay date is the date on which the issuer or its agent pays the distribution to the owners of record. The distribution of income payments to clients should take place on time – i.e., on the pay date.

Note: the Paying Agent may be a financial institution or company treasurer who is named as the organisation or person responsible for disbursing payments to share/ bondholders on behalf of the issuer.

The ex-dividend date (ex-date or xd) is the date upon which the security begins to trade without the declared benefit; for example, in the *Financial Times* we will see *xd* after the share price. Investors who purchase securities 'cum' of the entitlement are entitled to receive any benefits that the issuer decides to distribute. In most cases the trade, once settled, will be processed by the Registrar who then substitutes the seller's name with the buyer's. Although the settlement should occur before record date, it is quite possible for a re-registration on such a purchase to be late. In this case the seller would receive the benefit, although they are not entitled to receive it.

In order to bypass this situation, the local stock exchange

will determine a date (known as an ex-dividend date) after which any purchaser will buy without entitlement to the particular benefit. Instead, the seller retains the benefit. This ensures that there should, in the majority of cases, be no need to initiate a benefit claim. Once the pay date has passed, everything reverts to normal.

A *capital repayment* is a partial repayment of a company's issued capital. The company pays each shareholder a proportion of the value of the shares at the current market price. Whilst the number of shares issued remains the same, the nominal value of each share is reduced by the amount of the capital repayment per share. Other benefits may be in the form of shares rather than cash. An example would be a rights issue.

A *rights issue* is a further issue of shares offered by a company to its existing shareholders and in proportion to their existing shareholdings as at a record date.

Shareholders are offered the right to subscribe for new shares on or before a pre-determined date in a ratio to their holdings at a price below the current market price. The custodian's first task is to provide all the clients who have a shareholding with full details of the issue including dates and payment amounts.

We can flag here another key issue for managers to consider in respect of any corporate action, and that is where and how is information on these benefits obtained? Typically, the information can be provided by one or more of the following:

- company/issuers, announcement via the press and/or exchange;
- information service suppliers – i.e., Reuters;
- custodians;
- specialist data providers;
- internal databases – i.e., coupon payment dates, expected dividend announcements.

Time is an important issue because decisions need to be made, as we can see from the following options open to a shareholder.

Returning to rights issues, with a rights issue there are several options available to the shareholder:

- nil-paid rights can be traded for cash;
- rights can be accepted and paid for by making a cash payment (known as a call payment);
- nil-paid rights can be allowed to lapse – i.e., neither traded nor accepted;
- sufficient rights can be sold and, with the proceeds, the remaining rights taken up.

Unlike a rights issue – which requires a shareholder's decision – a capitalisation or bonus issue is mandatory. A capitalisation is the free issue of shares to existing shareholders in proportion to the shareholders' balances as at record date. In this case, the client does not need to give any instructions; however, they should be informed of the issue by the global custodian, as the number of shares will change and so will the price of the shares. Initially, the market value remains unaltered.

Scrip dividends are a method companies use to distribute profits in the form of shares instead of cash. The shareholder is offered the basic benefit of receiving cash or given the option to receive shares. Entitlement to scrip dividends is based on shareholdings on the register as at record date. The number of shares offered takes into account the amount of dividend payable and the underlying market price of the shares.

The custodian must also ensure that the client's instructions are obtained and passed on. Although the company will usually pay the cash dividend in the absence of any instructions to the contrary, it is important to check the terms of the issue in case the basic offer is for scrip. In most cases, it is possible to issue standing instructions for future scrip dividends.

Other kinds of corporate actions or events that the manager must take into account in the workflow include the following:

- A *stock situation* is any event that changes the nature or description of a company's securities. Stock situations are either optional, where the shareholder has a choice, or mandatory, where the shareholder is required to accept the company's decision for the change.
- A *take-over*, for instance, is a situation in which a bidding company wishes to obtain a controlling interest in a target company. It is optional for the investor to the extent that he can accept or decline the offer within the deadline specified by the bidder.

If, in the terms of the offer, the bidder agrees to take over 100% of the company on condition that there is, say, a 75% acceptance level, then the remaining shares are compulsorily acquired – i.e., the situation becomes non-optional for those shareholders who did not accept the offer.

- A *warrant subscription* is optional and gives the holders of warrants the right to 'exercise' the warrant in exchange for equity by making a subscription payment to the issuing company. If they are not exercised by the last possible date, the warrants expire worthless.

- *Pari passu lines of a security* can cause many problems for the global custodian and investor alike. A company might issue securities which are identical to existing securities already in circulation except that, for a predetermined period of time, the new securities do not qualify for a particular dividend or are subject to some other type of restriction. Once this period is over, the two lines of securities are merged and become *pari passu*; they rank equal in all respects. Until the two lines of securities become *pari passu*, they are given separate security codes and, in addition, will trade at different prices. Both global custodian and investor must be aware of these differences and reflect the holdings accurately in the safekeeping records.

- An investor of a company which goes into *liquidation* will be in the situation where the security is not only worthless but also un-negotiable. The security will be suspended in the relevant stock exchange(s) until such time as the liquidator is able to repay amounts due to the various classes of creditor. Once there is no more cash that can be retrieved for the creditors, the company is wound up and the certificates cancelled. This process can take years to resolve and the global custodian must ensure that any information is passed to the client and that all expected liquidation payments are collected and paid to the client.

- *Proxy voting* has been defined as 'the exercise of the voting right(s) of an investor in shares, bonds and similar instruments through a third party, based on a legally valid authorisation and in conformity with the investor's instructions.' Depending on the country in which the 'proxy' is being exercised, the 'third party' can be:
  - a bank, or a person designated by the company; *or*
  - another shareholder.

  Proxy voting generally takes place at shareholders' meetings of companies (annual general meetings and extraordinary general meetings) for the purpose of approving or rejecting certain pre-advised resolutions. Proxy voting can be subject to more or less stringent restrictions depending on national legislation and company by-laws. In each case, therefore, the legal aspects must be carefully examined.

- With *equity derivatives* and, in particular, stock options the impact of corporate actions can be significant. With a rights issue, for instance, the strike/exercise price may be changed – so, too, may the number of shares per contract. Developing procedures for information about corporate actions in underlying assets to be simultaneously and automatically passed to the operations team dealing with the derivatives products is vital.

Allied to this is the need to have operations staff trained to adequate competency in both derivatives and securities, and a successful manager will ensure that this happens.

What about the issues for managers in, say, a global custodian? Here, there is the problem of collating sufficient information to allow the client to make a decision where appropriate and ensuring that the results of the corporate action or event are correctly received, recorded and accounted for.

Operational issues and controls for equities are generally similar to those required for debt securities. In terms of trade capture from the dealing or fund management desks, counterparty trade confirmation, trade instruction/matching within a third-party clearing environment and final settlement, there should be no differences.

The areas where there will be differences include the following.

- Poorer settlement performance, especially where certificated settlement is concerned and in emerging markets.
- Greater variety and complexity of corporate actions types:
  - Issues associated with registered securities:
  - use of nominee names;
  - street names;
  - pooled and segregated holdings;
  - timing issues for share re-registration.

- Less sophisticated or developed securities depository systems in some jurisdictions.
- Greater use of physical delivery and custody systems.

As we saw earlier in the chapter, there are times when settlement of securities might fail. One possible way of avoiding that situation is for a seller to borrow stock to effect the settlement on time. Stock lending and borrowing facilities are therefore important for different types of organisation, but equally they require very clearly defined procedures and careful monitoring of exposures.

Securities lending is the lending of equities and bonds by, or on behalf of, an investor to counterparties who are authorised to borrow securities in return for a fee.

Securities lending provides liquidity to the market by utilising securities that otherwise would be 'side-lined' by being held in safekeeping.

The G30, an industry body, recognised the importance of securities lending in their Recommendation No. 8 (published in the late 1980s – *www.issanet.org*), which stated that:

Securities lending and borrowing should be encouraged as a method of expediting the settlement of securities transactions. Existing regulatory and taxation barriers that inhibit the practice of lending and borrowing securities should be removed.

Securities lending and borrowing is now widely accepted and permitted. Legal title to the securities passes from the lender to the borrower, but the beneficial ownership is retained by the lender. This means that the lender continues to receive income and retains the right to sell the securities in the stock market. The lender, however, does lose the right to vote. Income will not be paid direct to the lender, as his name will have been removed from the company's register; instead, the income is claimed from and paid by the borrower.

Market participants need to borrow securities for a variety of reasons, including:

- to cover short positions (where participants sell securities which they do not hold);
- to support derivatives activities (where participants may be subjected to an options exercise);
- to cover settlement fails (where participants do not have sufficient securities to settle a delivery).

Market participants are happy to lend securities to earn fee income. This has two benefits:

- Fee income enhances the investment performance of the securities portfolio.
- As securities lending decreases the size of the portfolio, there is a corresponding reduction in safekeeping charges.

Global custodians take advantage of securities lending and borrowing by acting as intermediaries in the process. The global custodians benefit by:

- retaining a share of the fee income whilst running a discretionary lending programme for their client; and/or

- charging a transaction fee for every movement across their client's securities account where the custodian is unaware of the reasons for the securities movements.

As a global custodian holds sizeable quantities of any particular issue, it is able to play an important role by providing liquidity to the market. Furthermore, lenders and borrowers benefit from increased operational reliability and reduced risk by using the global custodian's services such as:

- clearance;
- payment;
- settlement;
- collateral pledging;
- valuation (mark-to-market).

Chapter 6 (on custody) explores the role and services in greater detail.

There is risk in lending stock. The lender is primarily concerned with the safe return of his securities by the borrower and that there are adequate means of recompense in the event that the securities are not returned.

There are four situations, each of which could place the lender at a disadvantage:

1. The most serious situation is where a *borrower defaults* with no chance of the lender retrieving the securities.

2. Timing differences between delivery of the loaned securities and the corresponding receipt of sufficient collateral.
3. The late/delayed return of securities due to settlement and securities liquidity problems experienced by the borrower.
4. Settlement inefficiencies or a systemic collapse within the local market itself.

Various countermeasures are taken in order to reduce the risk associated with each of the above situations. We can start by considering a default by a borrower.

Securities are delivered by the lender on a 'free of payment' basis to the borrower. For his part, the borrower covers the loan by delivering collateral to the lender.

Clearly, it is of utmost importance that the collateral should be of such quality and quantity that it must be readily exchangeable into cash in the event that the borrower defaults. With this type of liquid collateral the lender is able to replace the missing securities. So, the manager needs to be aware of the implications of using cash and non-cash collateral in lending and borrowing situations. The manager needs to know what is efficient, what is the risk policy – as this determines what is accepted – and also what is market practice in different jurisdictions. We look at some of these issues in more detail over the next pages.

As far as collateral quantity requirement is concerned, the borrower must obviously deliver collateral with a market value which exceeds the market value of the loaned securities (the outstanding loans) by a pre-determined margin.

This margin allows for any variation in the value of outstanding loans. The securities out on loan are 'marked-to-market' (priced at the current market value) at least daily using the previous business day's closing prices and sometimes intra-day in fast-moving markets. Any resulting shortfall in the amount of collateral is made good by the borrower. Conversely, any excess collateral is returned to the borrower. Managing this process needs effective records, exposure assessments, collateral valuations and effective procedures calling for increased collateral. When a volatile market develops and we have daylight exposure there is a real risk to the business.

Daylight exposure is the intra-day settlement risk that loan securities may be delivered before the collateral is received. If the borrower should then default during the intervening period, the lender would be unsecured. The reverse is also true for a loan return.

The example given in Box 5.3 illustrates the problem.

Box 5.3 An example of daylight exposure.

A lender who delivers securities to the borrower at 10:00, but does not receive the collateral until 15:00 has a daylight exposure of 5 hours.

There is a particular problem when the parties to a loan transaction and the domicile of the securities are all in different time zones. For example:

- lender in London;
- borrower in New York;
- securities in Tokyo.

Loan transaction for value Wednesday; securities delivered on Wednesday (Tokyo time zone).

Collateral due for delivery value Wednesday: collateral delivered Wednesday (New York time zone).

In the lender's time zone, there is an exposure of at least 14 hours – i.e., from the time the securities are delivered (before close of business in Tokyo) to the receipt of collateral (after start of business in New York).

We have established that delays in settlement can be caused by the usual settlement failure types:

- insufficient securities to satisfy the total delivery;
- lender or borrower gives late or incorrect delivery/ receipt instructions.

For a market maker with a net 'short' trading position, these delays will have an impact on the settlement process unless there is a reliable source of stock lending.

Investors will always want to invest in countries where there are opportunities for capital gain and income growth and with scant attention to the efficient operation of the settlements systems. Emerging markets are a prime example of this. Securities lending does, however, depend on the ability to deliver securities without delays and complications. For this reason, securities lending is primarily undertaken in the established markets with reliable and robust settlement processes. Any stock lending and borrowing in emerging markets needs careful consideration by the operations manager. The ability to mitigate some of the risk through the use of collateral may not be sufficient and any direct stock lending arrangement may also be concerned with the credit rating of the borrower. With discretionary lending programmes run by, for instance, custodians, the default risk is theirs. To ensure that collateral is of the acceptable quality and liquidity, the following types of collateral would be generally acceptable.

Cash – where the lender places the cash out into the money markets and agrees to pay interest (a rebate) to the borrower at a rate lower than the market rate. The difference in rates reflects the lending fee payable to the lender.

Advantages of accepting cash as collateral:

- Acceptance of cash collateral allows the securities to move on a DVP basis and thus eliminates the risk that the securities delivery and collateral receipt do not occur simultaneously.
- Cash is regarded as the safest form of collateral in domestic markets, including the USA where it is used in the majority of cases.

Disadvantages of accepting cash as collateral:

- Operational issues – many institutional lenders are not prepared or able to undertake the extra administrative burden of reinvesting the cash.
- The tax and regulatory situations in such countries as the UK and Germany make the use of cash impractical.
- There are the added problems of foreign currencies which require 1 or 2 days' notice prior to placing funds.

- There is an exposure to adverse exchange rates when using foreign currencies.

Collateral in the form of other securities can be acceptable in certain circumstances. The market value of the collateral must also be margined and easily realisable into cash in the event of borrower default. Commonly acceptable types of securities used as collateral are:

- *Certificates of Deposit* (*CDs*). CDs are certificates which give ownership of a deposit at a bank – there is an established market for CDs.
- *Treasury Bills*. Again, there is an established market for Treasury Bills.

The advantages of using CDs as collateral are:

- Considered to be of high quality and 'near-cash', they are guaranteed by the banks on which they are drawn. The lender is able to specify the creditworthiness of the banks by only accepting paper with a rating of, say, 'A' or better.
- CDs are in bearer form and therefore straightforward to sell should the need arise.
- Movements of CDs in the UK take place almost exclusively by book-entry within the Central Money-markets Office operated by the Bank of England through CREST.

The disadvantages of CDs as collateral are:

- The nominal amount of CDs tends to be in shapes or sizes of £1,000,000 or $1,000,000, and this makes it difficult to ensure that the margined collateral value matches the value of outstanding loans.

- CDs have a limited lifespan, and borrowers must ensure that CDs are substituted as old CDs mature.

Other forms of high-quality securities are sovereign and government bonds (UK Gilts, US Treasury Bonds, German Bunds and French OATs) which also benefit from high credit ratings and ease of sale.

Equities are used, but the issuer creditworthiness and the high-risk nature of the security type itself are not generally acceptable to lenders. In addition, long settlement periods can delay the time from borrower default to receipt of the collateral sale proceeds.

Another popular method of providing collateral cover is a letter of credit issued by a bank. But, their use is under threat as the cost of a letter of credit is making borrowing against them unprofitable.

Advantages of taking letters of credit as collateral:

- Lender does not need to reinvest or revalue the letter of credit.
- Daylight exposure (see Box 5.3) is eliminated if receipt of a letter of credit is pre-advised to the lender before the securities are released to the borrower.
- Face amount of letter of credit is more than adequate to cover the margined value of the outstanding loans, and this results in less collateral movement to maintain the margin levels.

Disadvantages of taking a letter of credit as collateral are:

- Credit risk of bank that issued the letter of credit.
- (For the borrower) the high cost of obtaining a letter of credit from the bank.

Any activity in lending and borrowing needs to be covered by an agreement – in this case a Stock Lending Agreement (SLA). In order to protect the interests of the lending parties, the borrowing parties and the intermediaries, agreement forms are drawn up to clearly define the rights, duties and liabilities of those concerned.

An agreement will contain references to, *inter alia*, the topics given in Table 5.5.

The extent to which the global custodian is involved in the stock lending and borrowing activity of an organisation depends on the type of service offered. Direct lending will suit the bigger investors who are able to offer portfolios with large and varied holdings. They are therefore able to earn higher fees by going direct to the market. Large life funds hold significant amounts of securities and would be 'natural' lenders; however, they must abide by the trust deeds and other conditions, so will not always be involved in lending.

The key points are:

- Investor negotiates loan agreements and recalls/ returns with the intermediaries or borrowers.
- Investor controls the movement of collateral and ensures that margins are maintained.

Table 5.5 Clarification of the terms contained in stock lending agreements.

Agreement topic	Comments
Interpretation	Definitions of the terms used in the agreement.
Rights and title	Includes reference to the protection of lender's entitlements.
Collateral	Loans should be secured with collateral.
Equivalent securities	Securities and collateral should be returned in an equivalent form to the original deliveries.
Lender's and borrower's warranties	Statement that both parties are permitted to undertake the lending/borrowing activities.
Default	Remedies available in the event that one or other party defaults on its obligations.
Arbitration and Jurisdiction	How and where disputes will be submitted for resolution and under which governing law.

- The investor assumes the counterparty risk of the intermediary.
- The global custodian delivers and receives securities on a 'free of payment' basis on instructions taken from the investor.

The risks for the investor are that they assume all risks associated with stock lending including:

- *Intra-day exposure* – the investor must ensure that securities are not released until adequate margined securities are under his control (directly in-house or indirectly through a global custodian or settlement agent).

- *Settlement risk* – the investor must ensure that deliveries of securities for loans are made on time. Deliveries of securities 'free of payment' demand a higher level of authorisation and control than deliveries made on a DVP basis. The investor must be able to identify the situations where securities on loan are required to settle a sale transaction and to initiate timely recalls.
- *Market risk* – collateral should be revalued more frequently in volatile markets.
- *Legal risk* – the investor is responsible for arranging and monitoring the effectiveness of the SLAs.

The rewards are:

- *Fee income* – the investor receives the full amount of the fees.
- *Exposure* – the investor is free to choose the intermediaries and not be part of a direct queuing system.

Non-discretionary lending differs from direct lending insofar as the global custodian takes a more involved role in the process.

The key points are:

- The custodian seeks approval from the client for each loan request.
- The custodian receives collateral from the borrowers and ensures that the margins are adequate.

- A fee is charged by the custodian for this service.
- The client assumes the risk of the borrowers.

The extra advantage for the client is:

- The custodian ensures that the collateral is matched to the movement of securities.
- The custodian is better placed to initiate timely loan recalls to cover the client's sales.

The disadvantage is that the client's relationship with the intermediaries might suffer now that they approach the custodian for loan requests and returns.

Discretionary programmes tend to suit the small-/medium-sized lenders whose individual holdings are not always large and varied enough to attract borrowers.

The stock lending is delegated entirely to the custodian in the following key ways:

- The custodian actively seeks to place securities out on loan with the intermediaries.
- The custodian takes collateral and monitors the margins.
- A portion of the risk of the borrower is transferred from the client to the custodian.
- Depending on the level of risk assumed by the custodian, anything from 50% to 60% of the fee income is retained by the custodian.

The advantages for the investor are:

- The service is totally linked into the custodian's settlement systems, thus ensuring that the risk of settlement failure through late recalls is almost eliminated.
- The investor benefits from being a part of substantially larger holdings which may be more attractive to potential borrowers.

The disadvantages for the investor are:

- Depending on the method of loan allocation adopted by the custodian, the investor's assets may not be fully utilised.
- The investor receives only a portion of the fee income. However, this will be offset by reductions in transaction charges and safekeeping fees.

There is an issue which affects the ability of an investor to participate in securities lending on an equitable basis. This presents the global custodian with the problem of ensuring that loans, and fee income, are allocated fairly. To cope with this, global custodians use sophisticated algorithms to allocate loans and fee accruals fairly. As stated earlier, the lender loses legal ownership and the voting rights associated with the securities, but retains the benefits of ownership. It is important to appreciate that the lender is treated as if he had not lent the securities; any shortfalls are made good by the borrower who, as temporary legal owner of the securities, will receive the benefits in the first instance. It is the responsibility of the intermediary or global custodian to ensure that the lender is not disadvantaged through securities lending activities.

This part focuses on the expectations of the securities lender and the actions which they must take in order to satisfy the lender's requirements. Therefore, the manager must ensure that the impact of corporate actions on any stock lending or borrowing situation is identified and dealt with. Any inadequate procedures or competency in the operations team will lead to potential significant financial losses and loss of reputation.

We can recap on why companies create corporate actions, for instance:

- *Rights issues* – raise cash in order to:
  - finance acquisitions;
  - expand business;
  - reduce borrowings;
  - stay afloat.
- *Convertibles* – lower interest payments.
- *Warrants* – future cash inflow at no cost.
- *Capitalisation issues*:
  - convert reserves into share capital;
  - increase marketability by reducing price.
- *Repayment of share capital* – return surplus cash to shareholders.

We also know that the main types of corporate action fall into two key categories; those which are *optional* in nature and those which are *mandatory*. How does this impact in terms of lenders and borrowers? Lenders retain the right to participate in all dividends, interest payments and other benefits on securities that are on loan. The one exception is that the lender loses the right to vote. It is therefore essential that lenders are able to focus on two areas by having certainty in the knowledge that incoming corporate action information is sufficient to ensure that they can make an informed decision and assurances that all decisions are dealt with in accordance with their instructions.

If securities are on loan over the record date, the issuing company will pay the dividend to the party at the end of the borrowing chain. The lender will therefore be paid an amount of cash in lieu of the actual dividend. In other words, the borrower manufactures a dividend payment in order to make the lender whole. The rules regarding overseas securities require manufactured dividends to be paid under a deduction of the *Withholding Tax* (WHT) applicable to the country of issue of the securities.

The lending intermediary's prime role is to ensure that the lender is 'made whole' and this can be achieved in the following ways by:

- gathering information from numerous sources;
- comparing information from one source with another to ensure consistency;
- rearranging the information (including any translations) into a form from which the lender can make a decision;
- ensuring that all expected instructions are received from the lenders;

- giving accurate and timely instructions to the correct destination;
- informing the lender of the corporate action results.

The need for the intermediaries to receive the lender's instructions in advance of the issuing company's own deadlines can cause problems with the lender. The lender might wish to delay a decision until the last possible moment – sometimes past the intermediary's deadline. Nevertheless, the intermediary should, in this situation, attempt to comply with the instructions on a 'best efforts' basis.

As we have already noted, information on impending events is obtained from a variety of sources – e.g., the issuing companies, central securities depositories, exchanges, the press and information vendors. The way in which the investor receives information depends very much on the nature of the event itself and the manner in which the investor chooses to hold the securities in safekeeping. We also know that all corporate actions have deadlines, especially those which require a decision (the optional events). Unfortunately, differing world-wide standards do not make the task of monitoring corporate actions any easier. For this reason, it is important for the intermediaries and/or their agents to ensure that the information received is accurate and that any instructions are given in the form and within the deadlines specified by the company. Failure to settle situations – such as market purchases and sales on time – will result in delays and inconvenience. There might be occasions when penalty interest is payable and both counterparties will be exposed to an element of risk whilst the trade remains unsettled. Remember also that the obligation to settle the trades remains until such time as the delivery of securities (together with the underlying cash payment) takes place. Remember also that with an optional corporate action, failure to give and act upon accurate and timely instructions will usually result in a loss of entitlement to the benefit. The defaulting party will have to purchase securities (if securities were to be the benefit) in the market and pay the extra costs.

Let's consider some of the actions that are needed:

- *Voting rights* – lenders who wish to exercise their right to vote must arrange for the loans to be recalled in sufficient time to comply with local voting rules. These rules might call for the re-registration of the securities into the lender's (or their appointed nominee) name or might necessitate the blocking of the shares until the annual (or extraordinary) general meeting has taken place. Sufficient time should be allowed for this to happen.
- *Corporate actions* – it is the responsibility of the borrower to ensure that the lender is made whole with respect to corporate actions. The borrower can either unwind the loan, returning the securities to the lender, or can take up any entitlements on behalf of the lender – making any extra cash payments as and when required.
- *Implications for collateral* – there are two points to note with respect to collateral. The amount of collateral pledged may have to increase or decrease in order to maintain the required (margined) levels of cover.

This applies equally to collateral that is taken in the form of cash or other securities (whether in the same currency or different currencies). If other securities are used, there will come a time when corporate actions will affect the collateral itself. In this case, the collateral can either be substituted or treated in much the same way as the loaned securities.

So, clearing and settlement is varied, and the challenge for the operations manager is to deal with the process flows. In the initial phases it is the trade confirmation process, settlement instructions and the management of the cash and securities positions prior to and over the settlement date. Additionally, there will need to be in place adequate procedures and controls to ensure that issues like settlement fails, corporate actions, stock lending and borrowing and collateral are efficiently and safely handled. Some of the key areas to focus on will be information source and records – i.e., positions, actions, etc., terms of lending agreements, recording and valuing of collateral and loaned securities, and taking necessary action to adjust the level of collateral and/or rebate and the way in which the decisions on optional corporate actions are received and instructions passed within the time constraints that exist.

Operations teams are obviously structured differently in organisations, but Figures 5.2 and 5.3 give a generic overview of the structures for (a) derivatives and (b) securities business.

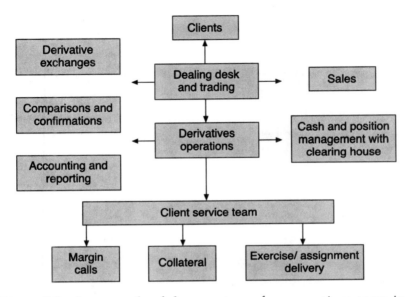

Figure 5.2   An example of the structure of an operations team in a derivatives business.

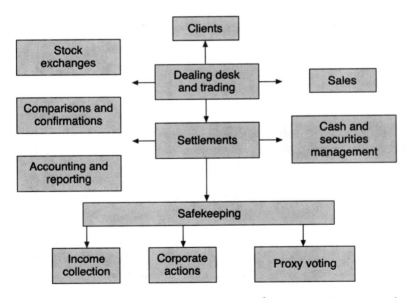

Figure 5.3   An example of the structure of an operations team in a securities business.

THE ROLE OF
THE CLEARING HOUSE

The role of the clearing house is to act as a counterparty to both sides of the trade, thereby breaking the direct counterparty relationship between the two trading counterparties. It is fundamental to the integrity and credibility of the market for which it operates, as its purpose is to guarantee the performance of each and every transaction.

By assuming the legal responsibility for the trade, the clearing house removes any risk on each other that the two original counterparties might have had.

There are two main types of clearing houses; those that are a division of the exchange itself and indistinguishable from the exchange that owns them, and those that are more independent of the exchange with their own financial backing. In most cases, for these independent clearing houses, the members of the markets provide the financial backing.

The LCH.Clearnet (*LCH*) and the Options Clearing Corporation (*OCC*) in Chicago are unique amongst clearing houses as they clear for more than one exchange. This is advantageous for the broker having a clearing member of Euronext.liffe available – LME and IPE in London, for example – because it means only one point of settlement for all of their trading in these markets.

Clearing houses must be financially robust in order to sustain a default in the market(s) for which they operate.

The financial standing of the clearing house is a very important consideration for brokers when they are contemplating becoming clearing members of an exchange. It is also an important issue for companies researching the potential of trading in the market, as they need to know that their trades will be efficiently settled and that their positions will be secure in the event of another unrelated party causing a default in the market.

The FSA has designated LCH.Clearnet as a Recognised Clearing House and regulate LCH.Clearnet. This gives the members and users of the market comfort that it is a properly organised and approved clearing house.

Novation

The process of creating the trade in the name of the clearing house as counterparty to each member is called *novation*. In this process the clearing house becomes buyer to every seller of each transaction and seller to every buyer of each transaction. At this point, the clearing member has no counterparty risk in the market for their trade other than with the clearing house. All open positions are only held with the clearing house and it becomes irrelevant which market member the trader dealt with originally. Once this process is completed, the clearing house is in a position to effect settlement of the two transactions.

The concept of margining, collateral and treasury management

Derivatives have a characteristic that is important in terms of their flexibility and usefulness. That characteristic is that the full value represented by the derivative is not usually settled until or unless delivery takes place.

This makes them very effective tools for investors and traders, but also represents a possible risk. That risk is that the full value will not ultimately be settled. We mentioned earlier that the clearing house has a role as the risk manager for activity between members, and one way in which it manages that risk is to establish margin requirements on positions until all obligations have been met.

Margin

Initial margin

The deposit which the clearing house calls to cover margin requirements is called *initial margin* and is returnable to the clearing member once the position is closed.

The amount for each product will vary, as it is geared to the current volatility of the particular product. The margin will be sufficient to cover an approximate 3–5% movement in the price of the contract on a day, but can and often is changed to reflect the current situation. If this occurs during the day, it is called *intra-day margin*. This will only occur when there is a very large movement up or down in the price of the contract.

When you buy or sell a futures contract you do not pay the full value of the contract, only the margin requirement. This deposit is held by the clearing house throughout the time that the position is maintained. The clearing house must have some kind of insurance that any delivery obligations could be fulfilled.

Options on futures positions are margined in the same way as futures contacts with initial and variation margin requirements.

Long premium paid option positions are not charged initial margin because once the premium has been paid for the option, on $T + 1$, then there is no further risk to the clearing house. The worst that can happen is that the option can expire at 0.

If a long option is exercised then the clearing house will call margin to cover the delivery obligations. Short option positions are margined, as there is a risk of the writer being unable financially to fulfil their delivery obligations. This margin requirement is typically calculated using Standard Portfolio Analysis of Risk (*SPAN*) or a similar exchange margin method – such as Theoretical Inter-Market Margining System (*TIMS*), as explained below.

Interest

It varies from clearing house to clearing house whether interest is paid to members on cash deposited to cover their initial margin requirements.

At LCH, interest is paid on cash balances using rates which are actually set by the clearing house. These rates are known as the London Deposit Rates (*LDRs*) and they are derived from bid rates for overnight funds quoted by selected money brokers and major banks for each currency. The highest and lowest rates are discounted to calculate the average.

Many brokerage houses use LDRs – plus 1% or minus $\frac{1}{2}$% – as a basis of rates charged or paid to their clients.

An explanation of delta

The delta of an option can be described as the speed with which an option's premium moves, in respect to the changes in the underlying security price. As time value decreases, this also affects the delta of an option. A deep in-the-money option has a delta of 1, a far out-of-the-money option a delta of 0 and an at-the-money option a delta of 0.5.

SPAN uses the delta value of options to convert them to equivalent futures when calculating the inter-month spread charge, because gains in one month may not exactly offset losses in another and there is a risk for the clearing house.

Intra-day margin

As we have already said, in times of very large movements up or down in the price of a contract, the clearing house or exchange will recalculate the initial margin requirement. An additional amount may be required per contract for all open contracts that are affected. It is unlikely that all contracts are affected because the news that caused the volatility may concern, for example, a foreign economy, which has a knock-on effect for domestic bonds. If the clearing house believes that the situation is only temporary and that conditions will quickly return to a more stable environment, then they will leave the initial margin requirement at its original level for the next day, only calling the intra-day margin as a one-off payment. More likely, however, the initial margin level will be changed as a result of volatile conditions. The intra-day margin call is made to cover the increased risk since the original initial margin was paid in the morning, and then the new increased initial margin rate is called from the next day onwards.

Intra-day margins can be called from the clearing members by the clearing house at any time, as determined in their rules. The clearing members must pay the required amount to the clearing house; however, depending on the time of day that the call is made, it may be difficult for the clearing member to receive the funds from their clients. They must endeavour to receive the funds and at the very least must contact the client and let them know that additional funds are due. In this respect, it is necessary that the clearing member is able to recalculate margin requirements during the day on their own systems, so that they may see accurately which clients are affected and reconcile the amounts that are due.

Spot month margin

This is an additional rate of margin which is charged by the clearing house to cover the risk that they incur between the last trading day of a contract and its ultimate delivery. It covers the risk of a default during the delivery process. There are no offsets allowed for spread positions. The clearing house on settlement day +1 releases initial and spot month margins, once they are satisfied that delivery has been effected correctly.

Margin methods

The method for calculating margin also varies from clearing house to clearing house. It may be different for futures and traded options. However, in 1988 the Chicago Mercantile Exchange (CME) devised a method known as SPAN, which we explained a little earlier. This risk-based margining system is now used by many exchanges for the calculation of the initial margin on futures and options. Most exchanges that have adopted SPAN have 'tweaked' it for their own particular use, and therefore there are different versions in use. For example, Euronext.liffe use London SPAN.

SPAN looks at a set of 16 possible changes in market conditions within the boundaries of the risk parameters set by the clearing house, which is known as the risk array. The profit or loss for one long position in each futures and options contract is worked out under each scenario, for valuing positions. By combining all of the individual arrays, London SPAN determines the scanning risk, which is the worst possible loss for the portfolio.

Each position in the member's portfolio is calculated and totalled across the same underlying contract. The final result is the largest potential loss for the portfolio, which is charged as initial margin.

London SPAN uses pricing models to calculate the option prices. The Binomial model is used for equity and index options but the Black-76 model is used for options, which are priced off the future.

The parameters are set using both the historic and implied volatility of the contract, and in agreement with the exchange.

Margin offsets

Where investors in a market employ particular trading strategies, then the clearing house may allow certain reductions in the margin requirements to reflect the reduced risk of the position. In the US markets, for example, a 'hedge' rate of initial margin is quoted, which can be applied to positions that are a hedge. This is a position where the opposite side reduces the risk of one side of the position.

Movements in the market would have a negative impact on one side but a positive impact on the other side. This would be a significantly lower initial margin rate than a 'spec' rate, which carries the full risk of the position, as there is no balancing side to offset any of the risk.

London SPAN calculates an inter-month spread charge to compensate for the basis risk incurred, because futures prices do not correlate exactly across contract months. This is calculated for futures and, using the delta value for options to convert them to equivalent futures. Where a spread exists but does not have equal and opposite sides, then spread margin is only charged on the number of contracts that are equal. The remaining contracts are charged margin at the full rate.

The inter-month spread charge calculation is:

Number of spreads × Inter-month spread charge rate

Additionally, certain different contracts can be offset across portfolios, where the clearing house can justify it on risk grounds.

Delta spreads are used in the calculation:

Weighted futures price risk × Spread credit rate
× Number of spreads
× Delta spread ratio

In order to calculate the total initial margin requirement, the following rule is applied:

Scanning risk + Inter-month spread charge
+ Spot month charge
− Inter-commodity charge

Note: delta is also a term used in options where it is the rate of change of price of the option in response to a change in the price of the underlying asset.

Variation margin

For most types of futures contracts, the clearing organisation pays and collects the profit or loss that is accruing on the open futures positions as the price moves up or down each day. This movement generates pay-and-receive situations for the members with the open positions. The clearing organisation will call in and pay out this net amount to each clearing member daily. This amount is known as Variation Margin (*VM*).

For other types of futures contracts, usually known as forwards, the VM is calculated each day, but any profits accrued are not paid out until the settlement date of the contract. This applies even if the position is closed out in the exchange early on in its life. The profit will stay with the clearing house until the settlement (delivery) date. Any profit that is accrued can be used to offset initial margin requirements, but it does not attract interest, as it is unrealised. All losses that occur must be settled on a daily basis. This is true of contracts traded on the London Metal Exchange and the Swedish markets.

An example calculation of VM is given in Box 5.4.

Box 5.4   Calculation of variation margin.

- The client buys 1 Sep Long Gilt Future at 109.13 on June 1st.
- The client sells the position at 109.42 on June 8th.
- The contract size is £100,000 nominal value with a minimum price fluctuation of 1 pence per £100 nominal. This gives a tick size of £10.

Date	Trade price	Net position	Closing price	Daily price movement	Sett. date	Daily settlement
1/06	109.13	+1	109.09	−4 ticks	2/06	£40 loss
2/06		+1	109.28	+19 ticks	3/06	£190 profit
3/06		+1	109.28	No change	4/06	No movement
4/06		+1	109.35	+7 ticks	5/06	£70 profit
5/06		+1	109.40	+5 ticks	8/06	£50 profit
8/06	109.42	0		+2 ticks	9/06	£20 profit
Total				**+29 ticks**		**£290 profit**

The profit on the trade was 29 ticks or points, which is the difference between the buying and selling price:

Each tick = £10   therefore, 29 × £10 = £290

The initial margin of £500 per contract would be called from the clearing house on 13/1 and held until 20/1 when it would be returned.

It must be remembered that VM must always be settled in cash.

This is because the broker must always settle with the clearing organisation in the currency of the contract. Clients without cash in place to cover VM may incur harsh debit interest penalties.

Tick size

The tick size of a contract is not always worked out in the same way – for examples see Box 5.5.

Box 5.5   Examples.

Chicago Mercantile Exchange Standard & Poor's 500 Index Future

- The contract size or trading unit is S & P Index × \$250.
- The price is quoted in index points and the minimum price fluctuation is 0.10 index points. This gives a tick size of \$25 (\$250 divided by 10).

Euronext.liffe Short Sterling Interest Rate Contract

The tick size is the value of a 1-point movement in the contract price. This price is arrived at by multiplying the notional contract size by the length of time of the notional time deposit underlying the contract in years multiplied by the minimum tick size movement of 0.01%:

$$£500,000 \times \frac{3}{12} \times 0.01\% = £12.50$$

The tick size of the Short Sterling Future therefore = £12.50.

Collateral

Initial margin obligations at the clearing house can be covered in various ways. Collateral in the form of cash in the currencies of the contracts traded is most commonly used. In addition, Bank Guarantees, Government Treasury Bonds and Bills, CDs and certain Equities are also accepted – at LCH.Clearnet, for example. Each clearing house or exchange will publish the collateral that they accept. LCH.Clearnet has quite a wide range, but some markets only accept cash in their domestic currency.

It is possible to use a combination of cash and physical collateral in some markets. For 10-Year Japanese Government Bond Futures in the Tokyo Stock Exchange (*TSE*), however, only a maximum of 2% of the margin requirement may be covered using collateral and the remaining 1% must be cash.

The collateral that the broker will accept from a client is usually negotiable. There may, however, be restrictions about where it must be held and also an arrangement fee. In some cases, the client may have to check with their trustees about whether they have any additional restrictions. By physically transferring the collateral into the name of the clearing member or clearing house, the client loses 'beneficial ownership' of the collateral. Therefore, there is a credit risk with the clearing member or wherever the collateral is held, as it is shown as their assets and may be seized in the event of a default by the organisation, even though the client is not involved in the default situation.

Acceptable collateral

Most of the clearing houses for exchanges publish lists of acceptable collateral.

It must be understood that these are lists of collateral accepted from the clearing member. The clearing member may or may not be prepared to accept the same collateral from a client. Even where it does agree, it may levy additional charges to cover the administration costs.

Margining to a client

It is relatively easy to understand the concept of VM. It is possible for the client to calculate the amounts themselves, in order to verify what their clearing broker is charging or paying them. Depending on the complexity of the position, it would be easily possible for the clients to work it out for themselves using a pen, paper and a calculator, so long as they know the necessary variables, such as the tick size and value.

Initial margin is much harder to explain. For futures contracts where an initial margin rate is published by the clearing house, it can be easily calculated and verified by clients, but only if the position is very simple and no off-sets have been given under a portfolio margining system.

The biggest problem can occur if the client wants to trade a particular strategy and needs to know how much the initial margin will be approximately, so that they can work out the financing costs. It may be possible for some clearing brokers to run test accounts for clients where such positions could be input and the margining run using the last available arrays. This would give the approximate cost, but can be very time-consuming for the broker's staff to accomplish and would not be part of a regular service to the client.

Although risk-based margining systems are very efficient and result in the client paying a lower overall initial margin, clients can find it very difficult to understand and generally have to take the clearing broker's word for it that the amount required is correct. In order for the client to accurately verify the initial margin required, they need to be able to receive the risk arrays from the clearing house or exchange and then have a system which is able to correctly compute this. Some clearing houses publish their risk arrays openly, and clients are able to obtain the information easily. A charge is usually made for this service though. Other exchanges do not openly publish the arrays, except to their clearing members. Additional problems occur for clients who have a port-folio of global market positions such that it becomes almost impossible for clients to perform margining them-selves.

For larger volume clients, a solution may be for them to use a recognised futures system for their own processing and accounting. Systems such as Rolfe & Nolan's are available on a bureau basis, so clients only pay for the use that they make of the system. These systems should have all of the margining capabilities already established.

Single currency margining and settlement

For clients trading in various different markets around the world and having numerous currencies to move, the settlement process can be quite cumbersome. Therefore, many clearing brokers offer a service known as 'single currency margining'.

This involves the deposit of one currency, which is equal to, or more than, the total amount of currencies due. In order to calculate this, each currency is notionally con-verted to the base currency chosen by the client as the preferred settlement currency. Interest would normally be received on the currency deposited and would be charged on the currencies that are in debit. Both the clearing broker and the client – as the amount due in the settlement currency is only calculated once over-night, using the end-of-day foreign exchange (FX) rates – incur an intra-day FX risk. Therefore, if this service is offered to many clients it needs careful control by operations management to ensure that FX risks are properly managed. Even major currencies need to be monitored, so that the management team is aware of exposure to each currency. Additional problems can be incurred with some of the minor global currencies, as these are not always readily available for use. It may be useful for the clearing broker to have an agreement for single currency margining that stipulates which currencies are included under normal use and what should happen for the exceptional currencies.

Although no formal charge is made for this service, clearing brokers recoup their expenses through the interest rates that are paid and received. They need to be relatively competitive in order to make the service viable, but they are designed to cover at least all of the financing costs that the broker incurs on behalf of the client. From the client's point of view, it makes the settlement process much more efficient and, in particular, reduces bank charges and administration for foreign transactions.

Treasury management

The efficient management of the margin calls is essential for several reasons.

As we have said, margin and the collateral used to cover it are vital to controlling risk.

From a regulatory point of view, the efficient management of margin calls enforces disciplines on the operations team. For instance, the client's clearing broker must make good the non-receipt of collateral from a client from its own funds.

We have already mentioned that the clearing houses have different rules about how margin is calculated and what is acceptable as cover. With a variety of acceptable collateral the clearing broker has to carefully assess the most efficient means of meeting the margin call at each exchange or with the clearing broker's agent used on an exchange.

In addition to these issues, the clearing broker will also find that for certain exchanges the clearing house will margin the members on a net basis – i.e., offset the long and short positions in the client account. The broker, of course, will charge the client the full rate for the positions they have, thus creating a potential excess of collateral.

If this excess is cash, the ability to effectively perform the treasury management function can provide important additional revenue.

However, an effective treasury management function is dependent on accurate and timely information about the margin calls from clearing houses/agents, the acceptable collateral, the margin calls for clients and the way in which the calls are to be covered, as well as what excess funds might be available.

The client side of the process is particularly important as the broker may be, or need to be by commercial considerations, prepared to accept collateral from the client that cannot be used at a clearing house or agent and which cannot be transferred to the broker. In this situation the clearing broker must use their own means of covering the margin and pass on a funding charge to the client. The client would need to consider the merits of paying this charge in relation to the interest gained on cash utilised elsewhere.

Interest rate calculations

The disciplines associated with treasury management also include the constant monitoring of interest rates and the setting of the rate that the client will receive. If this is not performed accurately and in a timely manner, it is quite possible over the course of a year to reduce possible income and even, with clients that have complicated positions, to have lost money.

A simple example is where excess funds on deposit were receiving say $5\frac{1}{4}\%$ and the client was being paid $4\frac{3}{4}\%$. The rate for the deposits falls to 5%, but the operations area is not told to change the client rate.

Or, where the client is using Japanese yen to cover positions on Euronext.liffe and, say, the TSE.

Let's assume Euronext.liffe pays its clients interest on yen and the TSE does not, but it is administratively difficult for the clearing broker to separate out the two balances and pay interest accordingly.

The issue becomes more of a problem where the client has margin calls in say US dollars, euros and Australian dollars, but is covering the margin call with sterling.

The client may be charged a debit interest on the 'overdrawn' currencies and receive credit interest on the sterling. The funding costs must be carefully monitored so that the respective debit and credit rates applied to the client accounts are correct in relation to any credit rates and funding costs incurred by the broker.

From the client's point of view, margin and treasury management implications in respect of costs to the fund, cash utilisation, foreign exchange risk, etc. may well become extremely important as their use of derivatives grows.

In terms of control, the client will need to check the interest calculated and posted to the client accounts on a monthly basis. It is very important to check the accuracy of the interest rates charged and paid by the broker.

OTC derivatives

Introduction

OTC derivatives constitute a large market, estimated by the International Swaps and Derivatives Association

(ISDA) as being in trillions of US dollars in value. The combined OTC and exchange-traded markets can be reasonably said to be the largest market in the world.

How do OTC derivatives differ from exchange-traded products?

We have seen how exchange-traded products are standardised into contracts, such as futures or options, and that they are actively traded in the secondary market – i.e., someone who buys a futures contract can sell it in the market to someone else.

However, standardisation of the contracts does cause some problems when it comes to their use as hedging instruments, as the amount of an asset to be hedged is often different from the size of the derivative contract, which is of course fixed by the standardisation process.

Also, the hedger may want to hedge the position for, say, 12 months and the asset may be a combination of different classes of the asset (Box 5.6).

Box 5.6   Example.

A fund manager has a portfolio of UK equity shares in a combination of FTSE 100 stocks and smaller companies and wants to hedge the portfolio for 12 months. The value of the portfolio is £2,425,000 and the FTSE 100 Index Future is currently trading at 5823.5.

If the fund manager decides to use the FTSE 100 Index Future, there are some problems.

First, the most liquid contract will be the nearest maturity, a maximum of 3 months away. Therefore, the futures position will need to be 'rolled' over through different maturities in the course of the 12-month period.

Second, the FTSE 100 Index Future is based on the 100 stock index and will therefore move in price according to the movement in the 100 stocks and will not therefore take into account the change in value of the smaller companies not in the index. The hedge correlation is therefore not right.

Third, the number of contracts required to hedge the portfolio would be:

$$\frac{\text{Portfolio}}{£10} \times \text{Index point} = \frac{2,425,000}{£10} \times 5823.5$$

$$\frac{2,425,000}{58,235} = 41.64 \text{ contracts}$$

You cannot trade 41.64 contracts, so the fund manager must trade either 41 or 42 contracts. In either case the portfolio is not precisely hedged.

It is because of these kinds of issues that hedgers often look to arrange an OTC deal with a counterparty – usually a bank if it is a financial product – that can be tailored to meet the precise hedging requirement.

On the other hand, the fund manager knows that there is a counterparty risk in an OTC transaction, there is no clearing house guarantee, possibly a capital adequacy issue as a result and that the position cannot usually be traded out of if the fund manager changes his mind.

Therefore, both OTC derivatives and Exchange-Traded Derivatives (*ETDs*) can and often are used by the same organisation, and the choice will depend on the strategy, risk appetite, liquidity, cost and ability to close the position if desired.

Table 5.6 OTC derivatives and ETDs.

Characteristic	Derivative product	
	OTC	**ETD**
Contract terms	Tailored, negotiated, flexible and confidential	Standardised quantity, grade, maturity
Delivery	Negotiable dates and very often go to delivery	Defined delivery dates and terms, but majority of contracts are closed out before delivery
Liquidity	Negotiated, so can take time and can be limited by available counter-parties	Usually, very good for main contracts
Credit risk	Risk is with counterparty although some OTC products are now cleared by clearing houses. Collateral is also used to reduce the risk	Clearing house becomes counterparty to all trades and manages risk through daily revaluations and margin calls

With the terms of OTC derivatives being totally nego-tiated, the operations function is different from that of ETD products.

Instead of standardised settlement processes and pro-cedures – like daily variation margin calls – we have periodic or event-driven settlement.

We can illustrate this, as we look at some of the products traded OTC in more detail.

Products

Forward rate agreements

A forward rate agreement (*FRA*) is an agreement to pay or receive, on an agreed future date, the difference between a fixed interest rate at the outset and a reference interest rate prevailing at a given date for an agreed period.

FRAs are transacted between buyers who agree to the fixed rate and sellers who agree to the floating rate or benchmark.

The benchmark rate will be, for instance, the London Inter Bank Offered Rate (*LIBOR*) and the settlement is calculated using a formula (Box 5.7).

Box 5.7   Example of calculation of settlement.

Suppose a manufacturer needs to borrow £5m in 1 month's time and needs the loan for a period of 3 months. Concerned about interest rates rising, the manufacturer decides to buy a FRA that will fix the effective borrowing rate today, as they have no wish to borrow the money now when it is not needed. The terms of the FRA are that the fixed rate is 7.25% and the benchmark is LIBOR. It will start in 1 month's time and finish 3 months later and would be known as a 'one versus four' FRA.

In 1 month's time the calculation of the settlement of the FRA can take place. The prevailing LIBOR at 11:00 a.m. is used and let us assume this was 7.5%.

The formula used to calculate settlement is:

$$\frac{NPA \times (FR - LIBOR) \times \dfrac{\text{Days in } FRA \text{ period}}{\text{Days in year}}}{1 + \left(LIBOR \times \dfrac{\text{Days in } FRA \text{ period}}{\text{Days in year}} \right)}$$

where NPA = Notional principal amount;

         FR = Fixed rate.

Calculation:

$$\frac{£5,000,000 \times (0.0725 - 0.075) \times \dfrac{91}{365}}{1 + \left(0.075 \times \dfrac{91}{365}\right)} = £3,059.23$$

The LIBOR rate was higher than the fixed rate, so the buyer (the manufacturer) receives this amount from the seller.

There is no exchange of the £5m, the manufacturer will borrow the money from a lending source and the money received from the FRA will offset the higher borrowing costs of around 7.5%.

Had the LIBOR been lower than the fixed rate, the manufacturer would have paid the difference to the seller, but of course would borrow the money at a lower rate.

The manufacturer 'locked' in a rate of 7.25% for their planned future borrowing.

As far as settlement is concerned, the amount due is known on the settlement date, the date at which the FRA period starts (1 month's time) and the calculation period is known (3 months).

Unlike most transactions which settle on maturity a FRA can be settled at the beginning of the calculation period. The amount is present values or discounted to reflect the interest that would accrue if the amount paid was deposited to the end of the FRA period.

Swaps

Swaps are products that – as their name implies – involve the swapping of something.

This can be, for instance, interest rates – i.e., an interest rate swap (*IRS*), see Box 5.8 – currencies, equity benchmarks against an interest rate or commodities.

Box 5.8 Example of interest rate swaps.

An IRS would be an agreement to swap or exchange, over an agreed period, two payment streams each calculated using a different type of interest rate and based on the same notional principal amount.

The exchange of cash flows originating from, say, a fixed rate and a floating rate would be called a 'plain vanilla' or 'vanilla' IRS.

By using swaps, a company can fix interest rates in advance for a specific period – typically, 3 to 10 years (Box 5.9).

Box 5.9 Example of fixed rate.

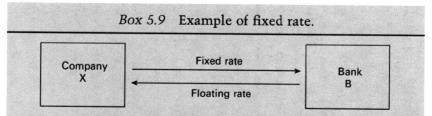

During the life of the above swap (known as the *term*) there will be an exchange of the netted payment flows at *payment date*, calculated at what is known as *reset dates* – i.e., semi-annually, annually and valued against the benchmark rate(s).

The payments cannot be netted at each reset date if the payment dates are different – i.e., the fixed is paid annually and the floating semi-annually.

The IRS will be transacted to start at a forward date and will run for the agreed period. The start date is known as the *effective date* and the end date is known as the *termination date*.

The floating rate is reset at the effective date for the next period and then at reset dates for the next period throughout the term of the swap.

Suppose Company X currently pays a floating rate of interest – say, LIBOR +0.4% – for a loan of $10m over 5 years. Concerned that rates will rise the treasurer wants to change the payment flow to a fixed rate, but is unable to alter the terms of the loan.

Company X approaches Bank B and agrees a 5-year IRS, the terms of which are that Company X will pay 6.3% fixed, paid annually on an ACT/360 basis, and receive LIBOR semi-annually on an ACT/360 basis.

At the beginning of the swap, LIBOR is 6%. At the end of the first 6 months, the floating rate payment is:

$$\$10,000,000 \times 6.00\% \times \frac{181}{360} = 301,667$$

which is paid by Bank B to Company X.

Note: there is no netted payment against the fixed rate flow for the period as the terms state that settlement is made annually.

At the beginning of the next 6 months, LIBOR is 6.25% and after the 6 months the payments are:

$$\text{Floating:} \quad \$10,000,000 \times 6.25\% \times \frac{184}{360} = 319,444$$

(due by Bank B to Company X), and:

$$\text{Fixed:} \quad \$10,000,000 \times 6.30\% \times \frac{365}{360} = 638,750$$

(due from Company X to Bank B).

This time the settlement can be netted so that Company X pays $319,306 to Bank B.

In this IRS, Company X has a risk as their view on interest rates over the next 5 years may be wrong and rates might actually fall, not rise. By agreeing to pay a fixed rate, in this case 6.3%, their cost of borrowing may be much higher than it would have been if they had entered into the swap.

As an alternative strategy the treasurer may have entered into a *swaption*.

This is an option to enter into a swap. Like all options it gives the treasurer the right, but not an obligation, to enter into the swap at some stage. As this is an OTC transaction the precise terms of the swaption and the cost of buying it will be negotiated.

Box 5.10 Example of currency swap.

A currency swap is an exchange of a series of cash flows in one currency for a series of cash flows in another currency, at agreed intervals over an agreed period and based on interest rates.

It is possible to have a combination of fixed and floating rates in two currencies in a currency swap:

- fixed interest in one currency to floating rate in another currency;
- fixed interest in one currency to fixed interest in another;
- floating rate in one currency to floating interest in another.

In a single currency interest rate swap, as illustrated above, there is no exchange of the principal amount; however, with a currency swap there is usually an exchange of the principal amounts at the beginning and end of the term at a rate agreed at the beginning.

Remember this is an OTC transaction, so a currency swap can have an exchange of principal at the beginning or end, or not at all.

If, say, a UK company wants to expand business in the US by providing an influx of capital and it can borrow money cheaper in the UK, where it is well known to its bankers, it can enter into a currency swap whereby:

- It can borrow British pounds (GBP) on a floating rate basis from its bank and swap the GBP for dollars with the swap counterparty. It will agree to pay a fixed rate of interest on the dollars and receive a floating rate of interest on the GBP, which it uses to pay the interest on the original GBP loan from its bank.
- It agrees to exchange the principal amounts at the beginning at an FX rate that is agreed, and will therefore need to fund the

> repayment of the loan – which is a totally separate transaction from the swap – from its own resources.
>
> The dollars are given to the US business and the subsequent income stream pays the interest on the dollars, which is paid to the swap counterparty. As we have said, the GBP interest received from the swap counterparty pays the interest on the loan.
>
> During the term of the swap, which will correspond to the loan duration, the payment streams will be settled on reset dates. They are not netted because they are in different currencies.

This type of swap has achieved for the company protection against FX movements during the period of the swap and protects against interest rate movement in the UK market rate during the period of its borrowing.

OTC options

OTC options are often called 'exotic' because, unlike the standardised exchange-traded product, they possess additional characteristics that change the relatively simple call and put outcomes. As the terms are negotiated, they are of course very flexible.

Common OTC options include:

- *Calls and puts* with specific amounts and duration – e.g., a £1m, 2-year call option on the FTSE 100 index at a strike of 5005.2 (exchange-traded FTSE 100 index options on Euronext.liffe are listed with 9-month duration and a fixed unit of trading and strike prices).

- *Interest Rate Guarantee (IRG)*, which is an option on a FRA.
- *Swaption*, which is an option on a swap.
- *European, American and Bermudan*-style options, which have different exercise characteristics – i.e., expiry at any time or at specific times.
- *Asian or average rate or average price options*, which use a different benchmark from the price of the underlying asset on expiry to determine if they are in or out of the money – e.g., the average price of the underlying over the last month.
- *Barrier options*, which is a general term for a family of options that are either cancelled, or activated if the underlying price reaches a pre-determined level. They are also known as *knock-out, knock-in* or *trigger* options.
- *Caps and floors*, which are a series of 'rollover' rates agreed whereby the difference in rates is paid, if applicable, at the time of the rollover.
- *Collars*, which operate like ordinary options, but have limits on the level at which the customer can deal at a better market rate than the underlying, in exchange for a lower premium.

We also have *putable* and *callable* swaps, which allow the fixed rate receiver and fixed rate payer, respectively, to terminate the swap early. They are traded as European, American and Bermudan styles of exercise right.

Other products traded OTC are, for instance, forwards and warrants, structured products and credit derivatives.

Settlement of OTC products

The settlement of OTC derivatives is determined by the terms of the product as agreed by the two counterparties. There are, however, relatively standard settlement characteristics for particular products, as we have already seen.

Settlement events are triggered by such things as the:

- effective date, reset date and payment date for swaps;
- settlement date and calculation period for FRAs;
- premium convention, exercise date and trigger events for options;
- maturity of all products.

We also know that most products settle at the end of a period or on maturity, with the exception of FRAs and IRGs, where the settlement takes place by a discounted present value.

Key to the settlement of OTC products is the terms of the transaction.

Unlike ETDs where the terms are stipulated, each OTC trade is effectively a new set of terms, even though the product may be the same – i.e., a swap or option.

OTC derivatives have documentation that helps to ensure that the terms of the derivative trade are agreed.

In the past this was a major obstacle to the use of OTC derivatives, as each trade had a separate agreement. This had to be vetted by the legal department and, consequently, delays and disputes caused considerable problems.

ISDA has greatly helped to resolve the problems by developing standard documents for use by counterparties in OTC derivatives. The British Bankers Association also developed standard documentation for FRAs.

The standard documentation, known as a 'Master Agreement', can be supplemented with schedules, annexes and appendices that allow specific issues to be covered.

ISDA master documents cover provisions for numerous aspects that are relevant and may need enforcing during the term of the agreement. These include:

- contract currency;
- multi-branch facilities;
- payment provisions;
- default procedures;
- termination events;
- warranties, covenants and representations;
- tax indemnities;
- notices;
- assignment;
- legal jurisdiction;
- waiver of immunities.

Also produced is what is known as a *confirmation*.

This is provided as a detail of the trade terms, rather than the general terms, under which business is being transacted between the two counterparties.

The confirmation therefore lists key details for the operations teams as well as enabling the trade details to be reconciled. Confirmations should be issued by the operations team as quickly as possible, so that the trade details can be reconciled. Equally, receipt of a confirmation from the counterparty, or a signed copy of a confirmation sent to the counterparty should be chased, as the confirmation cannot be legally enforced unless both parties have acknowledged the details are the same as agreed.

Typically, two banks participating in a trade will send each other confirmations, whilst a bank and a client trade will result in a confirmation from the bank to the client, which the client will sign and return.

The role of the confirmation/documentation team in the context of OTC settlement is therefore vital.

The post-trade environment

There are many processes in the post-trade environment that are common to all transactions. These include:

- trade capture and verification;
- position keeping;
- profit/loss analysis;
- confirmations and documentation;
- settlement;
- customer services;
- reconciliation;
- collateral management;
- risk management.

Trade capture and verification require considerable details to be input to the system. From a risk and control point of view the system must be capable of handling certain key information about a trade, such as:

- title of instrument traded;
- buy or sell (FRAs, options), pay or receive (swaps);
- currency or currencies;
- amount or number of contracts (option), notional amount (FRAs, swaps);
- exchange rate, price, rate of premium (two rates in the case of a fixed/fixed rate currency swap);
- floating rate basis/bases;
- exchange rate agreed for conversions of principal (currency swap);
- strike price or rate (options);
- trigger level (barrier option);
- trade date and time;
- underlying asset (option, equity swap, etc.);
- effective date;
- period (FRA);
- settlement date(s);
- maturity date;
- expiry date (option);
- exercise styles and dates;
- day/year calculation bases (swaps);
- physical/cash settled (options);
- special conditions – e.g., for Asian options;
- trader;
- counterparty;
- deal method – e.g., screen, telephone.

This list is not exhaustive and certain types of products, as they may have specific terms, will need additional information. In such cases, where the full details cannot be recorded in the system, then adequate manual processes and checks must be employed.

Certain transactions, such as swaptions, require both the option details and the swap underlying the option to be entered.

Details of the settlement instructions, including netting if agreed, will also be input to the system, so too will information such as the reference sources for fixings and, possibly, the documentation (ISDA, FRABBA) and governing law.

It is important that all these data are in the system, so that key reports and information can be supplied to operations, dealers (positions and p/l), risk managers, general ledgers, reconciliation systems, etc.

Event calendar

The information will also help to provide an event calendar that will enable operations to track the settlement events that will be occurring – e.g., resets, expiry, settlement dates.

Some events are mandatory and/or automatic. This would include those related to:

- barrier options;
- swaps;

- caps, collars and floors;
- FRAs.

Others may require an instruction and/or decision by the dealer or client, and this includes:

- option exercise – however, some options are automatically exercised on expiry if they are in-the-money;
- termination (callable, putable swaps).

Communication/Information

Clearly, the efficient settlement of OTC products requires a high degree of skill in managing the flow of information at, and immediately after, trading and then during the term of the transaction.

Central to this is the confirmation.

For a FRA, a confirmation will typically be sent via SWIFT and would contain information such as that given in Table 5.7.

An IRS confirmation for a fixed/floating transaction would contain information such as that given in Table 5.8.

There are other pieces of information that can or will be added to this, such as frequency being modified following convention.

Table 5.7   Information relating to a FRA confirmation.

Confirmation from Mega Bank	To: InterBank Inc.
Buyer: *Mega Bank*	
Transaction date	19/06/2005
Effective date	21/06/2005
Terms	ISDA
Currency/Amount	GBP 3,000,000
Fixing	19/09/2005
Settlement	21/09/2005
Maturity date	21/12/2005
Contract period	91 days
Contract rate	5.79% p.a. on an actual/360 basis

Table 5.8   Information relating to an IRS confirmation.

Confirmation from Mega Bank	To: Interbank Inc.
Interest rate swaps	
Transaction date	19/06/2005
Effective date	21/06/2005
Maturity date	21/12/2005
Terms	ISDA
Currency/Amount	USD 5,000,000
We pay	5.76%
Frequency	Annual
Calculation basis	Actual/365
We receive	6-month LIBOR
Frequency	Semi-annual
Calculation basis	Actual/360

Other settlement issues

OTC products are heavily used, and the number of organisations using them increases all the time. With some of the products being quite complex in their structure and certainly different in terms of the settlement process, the relationship with counterparties and clients, in particular, is important.

There will be many queries related to transactions, settlement, etc., and it is important that the operations teams within the two parties to the trade work closely together to resolve any problems quickly.

Reconciliation is also a key issue, and the reconciliation of the nostro accounts, in particular, is important to ensure payments and receipts have been made. Any failure to receive expected payments may indicate a potential default.

It is also important to mark to market OTC positions for profit/loss and to reconcile the positions against the dealers' records for exposure, limits and risk control management.

The treasury management – including funding lines, cash flow management, etc. – is crucial and so too is the reconciliation.

Collateral is a key risk control and, where collateral has been taken as part of the risk management process, it is vital to monitor that the collateral value is sufficient to cover the exposure risk. The key to whether collateral is required at all is the credit rating of the counterparty and the type of product.

We need to be aware that with an OTC position, if a default should occur, there is no central guarantee provided by a clearing house unless the product is one of those cleared under, for instance, the LCH.Clearnet SwapClear facility.

As a dealer may have the fixed side of a swap 'matched' between two counterparties – e.g., they are receiving fixed from one counterparty and paying a lower fixed rate to the other – if the first counterparty defaults the dealer faces losses as the other counterparty must still be paid and it may cost the dealer more to replace the defaulting swap with another.

The amount of collateral needed will obviously rise or fall during the duration of the product. Making calls and returns is part of the operations role, as is the calculation of any interest due on cash collateral.

Collateral helps to offset replacement cost, and therefore reconciling its value and managing the process generally is vitally important.

As well as the event calendar there are other key static data issues to focus on including the standing settlement instructions, client and product profiles, records of fixings, which need to be maintained in case of queries or for subsequent calculations.

Accounting and regulatory issues

The accounting issues related to derivatives are potentially complex.

Each product and each strategy employed can create

differing accounting entries. The taxation of flows gen-erated by derivatives use can also be different for product and user. There has also been a major change to the accounting requirements in many jurisdictions, and any user of derivatives will need to be quite clear as to how they may be affected before entering into transactions.

The FSA has reporting requirements related to trans-actions including options, and the European Union and Bank for International Settlements (*BIS*) have established guideline limits on risks, which each bank may take. In turn, the local regulator – such as the FSA in the UK – will enforce these limits and may even make them stronger.

SwapClear

The introduction of a central clearing counterparty facility for OTC products including derivatives greatly helps to reduce the capital adequacy requirements asso-ciated with OTC transactions. The LCH.Clearnet (*LCH*) launched SwapClear in September 1999 so that existing members that meet the membership criteria for Swap-Clear can have their OTC transaction cleared under the same principals used for ETDs – i.e., variation margin, initial margin.

By having the OTC transaction cleared by LCH.Clearnet, an independent third party, the requirement to put up capital to cover counterparty risk is removed.

Note: LCH.Clearnet also provides the same type of facility for other products through RepoClear and EquityClear.

SwapsWire

SwapsWire is an electronic dealing system designed for the electronic online negotiation and trading of benchmark swaps and eventually options.

Its objectives will be to provide:

- lower transaction costs;
- fast transfer of deal information in a standard format;
- the facilitation of straight-through-processing (*STP*) in OTC transactions.

One significant advantage is that SwapsWire will provide the evidence of the deal and, thereby, remove the need for a confirmation to be sent. This will dramatically reduce the paperwork and process currently undertaken by OTC operations teams.

Summary

Derivatives are widely used instruments designed to transfer risk whilst at the same time offering opportunities to arbitragers, speculators, fund managers and private clients.

Derivatives are either exchange traded, where they are standardised products, or OTC where they are negotiated and bespoke. Some types of derivative instruments are available in both forms. As versatile products, whether traded on an exchange or OTC they have differing characteristics, uses and of course settlement conventions.

The clearing and settlement process will either be via a clearing house (exchange traded and some types of OTC transactions) or counterparty to counterparty (OTC). The clearing house provides a central guarantee and manages the counterparty risk as well as the settlement and delivery processes. Documentation and events tend to drive the settlement process in OTC transactions.

As with all types of transactions in financial markets, reconciling trade details, positions, cash movements, etc. is absolutely vital. With derivatives, the problems of errors are magnified by the gearing or leverage characteristics so that any unresolved errors and unreconciled trades or positions are potentially going to lead to significant loss.

That said, many millions of derivative transactions take place daily around the world without problems occurring because the user understands the product and the processes involved.

Derivative markets continue to grow steadily, and in some locations spectacularly. New products are constantly being designed and requested and the infrastructure in the industry changes constantly to meet these challenges.

It is important to keep up to date with developments and these websites may be useful:

- *www.issanet.org*
- *www.futuresindustry.org*

- *www.fow.com*
- *www.Euronext.liffe.com*
- *www.isda.org*
- *www.fsa.gov*

In addition, the following reading and information sources are suggested.

Suggested further reading

Clearing and Settlement of Derivatives. Elsevier Butterworth-Heinemann. Available at *www.books.elsevier.com/finance*

Exchange Traded Derivatives Administration and OTC Administration (IAQ workbooks). Securities and Investment Institute. Available at *www.securities-institute.org.uk*

Introductory Level (CD-ROM Understanding the Markets – Derivatives and Commodities). Computer Based Learning. Available at *www.dscportfolio.com*

CHECKLISTS

The following two checklists (Tables 5.9 and 5.10), one on corporate actions the other OTC derivatives, are examples of the type of assessments that will enable the operations manager and team to ensure that all processes, reconciliations and communications relevant to a function have been completed.

Table 5.9 OTC derivatives checklist.

Procedure/Task	✓ or N/A	Sign
Identify type – e.g., credit default, IR, currency		
Verify source and details – e.g., trader		
Identify if physical or cash settled		
Confirm trade date/effective date/expiry date		
Create event timetable – e.g., resets, expiry date, reference entity		
Reconcile position – i.e., calculate total position for product/account/counterparty		
Compile/Send/Receive confirmation		
Notify trader/client of disputes		
Create new security in system (if applicable)		
Identify and document settlement procedure		
Identify payments to be received or paid – i.e., frequency, calculation method		
Reconcile documentation – e.g., ISDA agreements		
Reconcile and record agreed confirmation		
Compile instructions to custodians/counterparty/ agent		
Confirm reference entities and exercise procedures		
Confirm calculation agent		
Reconcile and monitor open positions		
Reconcile trade updates – e.g., exercise/assignment/ result of corporate actions		
Advise trader/counterparty of exercise/assignment/ expiry/termination		
Confirm position successfully closed		

Table 5.10 Corporate actions checklist.

Procedure/Task	✓ or N/A	Sign
Identify event type – e.g., rights, merger, dividend		
Verify source and details		
Identify if mandatory or optional		
Confirm closing date/redemption date		
Create event timetable – e.g., closing date, payment date		
Reconcile position – i.e., calculate total position for entitlement		
Calculate entitlement		
Notify trader/client of entitlement and timetable		
Create new security in system – e.g., XYZ partly paid		
Identify claims to be made – e.g., settlement fails, stock loans		
Identify claims to be received – e.g. settlement fails		
Reconcile issuer documentation – e.g., allotment letter		
Confirm decision – e.g., 'take up rights'		
Instructions to CREST/custodian/issuer's agent		
Confirm instructions actioned		
Confirm receipt of entitlement		
Reconcile entitlement received		
Reconcile account updates – i.e., confirm result of C/A booked to relevant account		
Chase/Deal with claims		
Confirm corporate action successfully closed		

The major problem with OTC derivatives is the diversity of the events and the timetable of process associated with an event – e.g., swap resets, option triggers, etc.

The checklist (Table 5.9) is a generic example of a procedure that any team dealing with OTC derivatives will find helpful in managing what can be a difficult process that can cause both financial and reputation loss if errors occur and is a category of operational risk.

Additional boxes will almost certainly need to be added to reflect internal systems and procedures. It is also useful to have the verification box signed by a manager/supervisor and, where applicable, the trader, as a double-check that nothing has been missed.

The major problem with corporate actions is the diversity of the events and the timetable of process associated with an event.

The timetable (Table 5.10) is also a generic example of a procedure that any team dealing with corporate actions will find helpful in managing what can be a difficult process and one that can cause both financial and reputation loss and is a category of operational risk.

As with the checklist, additional boxes will almost certainly need to be added to reflect internal systems and procedures. It is also useful to have the verification box signed by a manager/supervisor and, where applicable, the trader, as a double-check that, again, nothing has been missed.

To help the process outlined in this chapter we can look at completing the work session presented in Box 5.11.

Box 5.11 Work session.

Think about the process flow from trade to settlement for a product and then consider the controls needed for post-trade situations – like different corporate actions – and identify the likely problems. Look also at the ISSA Recommendations (visit *www.issanet.org*) and consider how these have impacted or will impact and what effect the problems you have identified will have in terms of operational risk.

The process of clearing and settlement does, as we have seen in this chapter, involve custodians in various ways and so in the next chapter we look more closely at the role of the custodian.

Chapter

6

. . . .

CUSTODY

We have already looked at how the role of custodians is important, so we need to understand more about what they do and how that affects the operations teams within the custody provider and the organisations taking the custody services.

With access to sophisticated computer systems and a worldwide network of subcustodians, global custodians are in a position to deliver a variety of services to their clients. These services are often referred to by custodians as either core services or value-added services.

The range of services includes:

- the safekeeping of securities;
- the maintenance of multi-currency securities and funds accounts;
- the settlement of securities trades in domestic and foreign markets, free of or against payment;
- the collection of dividends, interest and principal due for redemption on the due date;
- the exercising or selling of subscription rights and attending to other corporate actions as well as pending fails;
- the reporting of transactions completed and the periodical delivery of hardcopy statements of account;
- contractual or actual settlement date accounting;
- contractual or actual income collection;
- terminal or computer-to-computer links to pass on instructions and retrieve client information from the custodian's database;

- customised multi-currency reporting and perform-ance information;
- securities borrowing and lending;
- assistance with withholding tax claims;
- handling/settlement of derivatives;
- briefings on specific countries – in particular, on emerging markets;
- cash projection and cash management;
- ensuring that physical certificates and associated documentation are in good order.

From a global custodian's perspective, core services are those which are so standardised that there is not a great deal of scope for any particular global custodian to differ-entiate its service from that of another global custodian. Any fundamental changes and improvements will affect the industry as a whole.

Value-added services, on the other hand, provide the global custodians with the opportunity to offer a mark-edly better service to their clients and, in so doing, enhance the global custodian's standing within the market place and improve their fee-earning capabilities.

Settlement is the final transfer of cash from the purchaser to the seller in exchange for the delivery of the securities to the purchaser.

Settlement conventions vary widely from country to country and especially in the following areas:

- *Physical delivery versus book entry transfer of secur-ities*. Prior to the introduction of CREST in the UK, an investor had to physically lodge the share certificate, together with relevant transfer documentation, with a London Stock Exchange processing office prior to settlement.

International/Eurobonds, held in electronic book-entry form by Euroclear and Clearstream, are settled by *Book Entry Transfer (BET)*. The securities accounts of the seller and the buyer are credited and debited respectively. Over 10% of securities markets are still paper-based.

- *Rolling settlement versus fixed settlement dates.* In the majority of world-wide securities markets, trades settle on a rolling basis – i.e., a fixed number of days after trade date – in line with the Group of 30's *(G30)* Recommendation No. 7, which recommended that settlement conventions should be changed from settlement of trades in a period – e.g., in the UK equity trades transacted in a 10-day account period all settled on a single date – to rolling settlement.
- *The length of elapsed time from trade execution to trade settlement.* In the United States, the settlement of equities and corporate bonds occurs within three business days from trade date $(T + 3)$. This was changed in June 1995 from the old $T + 5$ convention.

G30 recommended that settlement of all types of securities should take place on a $T + 3$ basis throughout the world. In theory, all securities transactions should settle on time and in accordance with local market conventions. This would allow investors to make efficient use of their money, whether for funding a purchase or placing/reinvesting sale proceeds.

In reality, the ability to settle securities transactions on time varies from country to country and within security types.

We need to consider why trades fail and how this impacts on the custody services.

Examples are:

- Late/Incorrect settlement instructions from a counterparty to the custodian or clearing agent.
- Seller has insufficient quantity of securities to deliver either as a result of a failed purchase or, for example, a market maker's business decision to go short (i.e., to sell securities that he does not have).
- Purchaser has insufficient funds to pay.
- Certificated securities are not yet available from the registrar from a recent purchase to cover a sale: the registration process can take up to several months to complete. Whilst there are individual market mechanisms, such as buy-ins, to help resolve these failures, the result is that securities administration becomes inefficient, exposure to risk increases and costs rise. Buy-ins permit the purchaser to achieve timely settlement by purchasing the securities from another agent. The securities are delivered and the extra costs passed on to the original seller. In some Far Eastern markets the buy-in process is automatically generated by the market together with financial penalties and, in some

circumstances, suspension of the offending broker's trading licence.

In terms of settlement accounting, global custodians would credit sale proceeds and debit purchase costs on whatever date the trade actually settled. This is known as *Actual Settlement Date Accounting* (ASDA). The application of ASDA works in favour of purchasers as they will have the use of their funds for an extra few days and perhaps have the opportunity either to earn interest or place the funds on deposit for that period.

However, ASDA is a disadvantage to sellers who will be unable to use the funds until received. This can cause a knock-on problem where the expected funds were committed for other purposes on the original settlement date. Overall, ASDA, in poorly performing markets, handicaps the investor by making it difficult to manage cash flow requirements and cash positions effectively.

The global custodians have approached this problem by making a commitment to the investor that funds will be debited or credited for good value (in this case on the original settlement date). This is *Contractual Settlement Date Accounting* (CSDA). It enables the investor to operate in the certain knowledge that the cash accounts will reflect the expected entries and balances.

However, in one or more of the following circumstances the global custodian will protect himself from risk of non-performance of the trade by insisting on variations in its contractual commitments to the investor:

- CSDA is unlikely to be offered in those countries which the global custodians consider to have a sub-standard settlement infrastructure.
- Investors' settlement instructions which have missed a deadline will be considered received the following day by some global custodians. In other words, either the CSDA value will be applied on a later date or ASDA will be applied.
- The global custodian retains the right to reverse cash entries in the event that trades remain unsettled after a particular length of time.
- CSDA on a sale will not be provided if there are insufficient securities to satisfy the delivery.

Whichever accounting practice is used, it is in the global custodian's interests (and the investor's where ASDA is used) to apply pressure on the local stock markets and authorities to improve the settlement environment.

The objective is to pass an accurate and timely instruction from the investor to the Central Securities Depository (CSD) or clearing agent based in the country of the security via the global custodian and subcustodian network (Figure 6.1).

There are numerous ways in which the investor is able to send a settlements instruction to the global custodian.

Manual/Verbal instructions

- Telephone instruction (with call-back from the custodian to the investor) supported by a mailed confirmation from the investor.

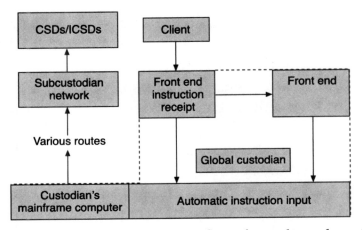

Figure 6.1 Example of information flows from client through to the CSDs via global custodian and subcustodians.

Source: the *dsc*.portfolio.

- Faxed instruction supported by a mailed confirmation from the investor.
- Written instruction duly authorised by one or more officers of the investor.
- Tested telex instructions in which the message is preceded by a series of digits uniquely identifying the instruction initiator to the receiving custodian and confirms to the custodian that the instruction may be acted upon. Usually, investors have the preparation of telexes automated within their systems.

These methods are in many ways inefficient and are not to be encouraged for the following reasons:

- Even though a telephoned instruction is called back correctly, there is no guarantee that the initiator of the instruction had the authority to issue the instruction.

- Control is difficult to maintain in the absence of an effective and robust audit trail of the instructions.
- It is not possible to authenticate with absolute certainty the location from which a faxed instruction was sent.
- Written instructions can easily be delayed, misdirected or lost, and the investor has no means of knowing if the instruction has been received until it is possibly too late to issue a replacement instruction.

All the above methods are to a greater or less extent time-consuming and open to error and misuse.

Electronic instructions

The investor enters instruction details into the global custodian's proprietary software installed in the investor's personal computers (*PCs*). The software converts the instructions into electronic data files which are then transmitted via a modem/telephone link to the global custodian's computer system.

Electronic transmission of instructions is preferable to manual methods for a variety of reasons:

- The software applications and the hardware in which it resides can be protected by both physical and electronic methods, such as siting the PCs in a secure environment in the office and only allowing access to those staff who have authorised system identification numbers and user passwords.
- The preparation of electronic instructions is faster and more accurate.

- More effective controls can be established with full audit trails generated by the software.
- Data files can be retained by using the archiving capabilities of the software, thus dispensing with the need to retain large quantities of paper files.

There are three main methods by which the global custodian is able to communicate with the subcustodian. Which method is used depends to an extent on whether the subcustodian is a branch of the global custodian or a third party:

- If there is an own-branch relationship and both global custodian and subcustodian share the same systems technology, then trade instructions are transmitted through this medium.
- If the subcustodian is a third party or an own branch without a common technology, then instructions will be translated into a suitable message format and transmitted electronically through a communication network known as SWIFT.
- Tested telex.

The methods by which subcustodians communicate with the settlement agents and CSDs are dependent on local market practices. There are a number of issues which affect the ability of an investor to achieve timely settlement of overseas securities trades. Following the initiatives by G30, International Securities Services Association (ISSA) and other industry participants, global settlement practices are improving and time scales shrinking. There is a danger that if the lines of communication between investor and global custodian, global custodian and subcustodian, and subcustodian and local market fail to meet the new settlement standards, then settlement performance will be compromised.

With the final objective of a global convention of $T + 3$ and then a reduction to $T + 1$ for the equity settlement period, there is the problem of initiating a settlement instruction early enough to allow the global custodian to pass on the instruction to the subcustodian and from there to the local market. The global custodian receives the investor's instruction and ensures that it is valid before passing it on to the subcustodian. If this involves transferring the information from one system to another by a process of rekeying the data, then the risk of error and delay is high. Consequently, there is little time to correct any errors before settlement due date.

The solution is based on the ability of the investor to prepare and transmit a data file of information (i.e., the settlement instructions) to the local market without the need for either the global custodian or subcustodian to rekey the data into another format. This is known as 'straight through' information processing and requires common technology standards at every stage along the communication chain. The global custodian is able to offer settlement activity reports to the investor in either hardcopy form or by data transmitted electronically to the investor's PC link. Electronic reporting provides the investor with the opportunity to extract only the information that is required. This is achieved by transferring the data from the custodian's *Securities Movement and*

Control (*SMAC*) system into the investor's proprietary computer system.

Through the use of spreadsheet software, the investor is able to sort the information in any order – e.g., all trades on a particular settlement date, all trades in a particular security number, etc.

It is important to note that custody is an integral part of the investment process and a high level of confidence in the security of safe custody is indispensable in meeting the investor protection objectives of:

- preventing misuse of investors' assets;
- safeguarding ownership rights.

For registered securities, the name of the investor is shown on the face of the certificate and reflected on the issuing company's register of shareholders. Private investors who do not use the services of a custodian for safekeeping purposes may have their holdings registered in their own names. Whilst this has the advantage that the beneficial owner can be readily identifiable (i.e., name on register), it does cause administrative problems for custodians who are appointed to look after the shareholdings of many investors.

For example, all dividends, corporate actions, company announcements, etc. will be sent directly to the shareholders' addresses, and not to the custodian. The custodian will arrange for its clients' registrable investments to be registered in the name of a nominee company established by it specifically for that purpose. Whether

Table 6.1 Register details.

Whose name is on company register?	Legal ownership held by	Ownership held by
Investor	Investor	Investor
Nominee	Nominee	Investor

the shares are registered in the name of the investor or the nominee, making changes on the company share register can be a time-consuming process, especially in a certificated environment. Re-registration can take anything from a week up to several months to complete, depending on the particular country. It is important to differentiate between legal ownership and beneficial ownership. Whoever's name is on the register has legal ownership of the securities. In the case of a nominee's name, the beneficial owner is the underlying investor, as shown in Table 6.1.

For book-entry securities, there are no certificates; these will be reflected by entries on a ledger statement.

The nominee company becomes the legal owner of the investments and its name appears on the issuing company's register of shareholders. Beneficial ownership is implied in this situation and it is the custodian's responsibility to maintain accurate records of the underlying beneficial owners. There are two different approaches to the management of nominee holdings, both of which provide a secure and effective custody environment. This can only occur so long as proper and continuous controls are operated by the custodian. Under the pooled

nominee system or 'omnibus system' as it is often referred to – where all investors' holdings are registered in
the same name (e.g., ABC Nominees Ltd) – the entries on
the share register and the certificates do not identify the
actual beneficial owners.

What are the advantages of pooling?

- Administration is simplified and risk of clerical error
  reduced.
- The settlement process is made easier as any certifi-
  cate(s) may be delivered from the pool so long as the
  total does not exceed the number of shares actually
  held for the shareholder at the time of delivery.
- There is only one holding for the custodian to reconcile in respect of each issue (although there must be
  a subsequent reconciliation of this holding to the
  records of the underlying investors).
- It reduces the number of names that need to be maintained by the registrar on the company register.
- It provides anonymity for the investors except in cases
  where disclosure is required in accordance with the
  Companies Act 1985 s. 212.

What, then, are the disadvantages of pooling?

- Although it is prohibited, there is the risk that a
  custodian with poor controls might use the shares of
  one investor to settle trades of another when there are
  delays in the settlement system.
- It is difficult to establish beneficial ownership in the
  absence of comprehensive and up-to-date records.

- More time is required to allocate dividends, corporate actions, proxy voting, etc. to individual investors.

We can also use *individual designation* or *segregation*. Under a system of individual designation within a nominee name, individual beneficial owners are identified by the addition of a designation. This designation, which can be a unique reference rather than a name, will also be reflected in the issuing company's register.

What are the advantages of individual designation?

- Beneficial owners are more easily identifiable from the company register and the share certificates.
- Reconciliation of shareholdings to investors' balances is more straightforward.
- Time spent allocating dividends, etc. is reduced.
- The risk of using the balance of one investor to settle the trades of another is reduced.
- Individual designation will facilitate the process of establishing claims for securities in a default situation.

What, then, are the disadvantages of individual designation?

- There is the risk that the holdings of one investor might be incorrectly designated under the designation of another investor.
- It might be unsuitable for a custodian with many holdings over a wide client base. This would make the administration of such a client base difficult to manage and costly to operate.

We have discussed already the importance of the reconciliation process. Securities reconciliation is a control
that seeks to establish that balances of assets beneficially
owned by one party agree with the balances in the same
assets held on behalf of the beneficial owner by another
party. The Rules require that all safe custody holdings of
investments must be reconciled at least twice during
a period of 12 months at intervals of approximately
6 months. The Financial Services Authority (FSA) in the
UK allows reconciliation on a rolling basis rather than at
two points in time. In this case there are extra conditions
which must be satisfied including:

- confirmation from an auditor that there are adequate
  internal controls;
- additional records reflecting clients' entitlements
  from an issuer's perspective.

Positions which do not agree, or reconcile, are queried in
order to establish the reasons why; these can range from
clerical error, unsettled trades and unauthorised use/
fraudulent misappropriation of the assets. Global custodians and their investors reconcile their positions by
electronically matching their respective securities balances, outstanding trades and corporate action events
and, in so doing, produce an exception report highlighting
only those securities which require remedial action.

Both investor and global custodian require asset listings
which can be available in hardcopy format or from the
custodian's software. The information on the asset listings usually indicates:

- investor account identification;
- security name;
- security identification number;
- quantity of securities (ledger and settled balances, outstanding receipts/deliveries, balances);
- name of depository in which security is held;
- valuation in currency of security;
- valuation in base currency of investor.

We know that 'corporate actions' is a collective term used to describe the entitlements of any securities holder. We also know that they can be divided into those which require no action from the investor (e.g., a bonus issue) and those which do call for the investor to make a decision (e.g., a rights issue). What are the issues and implications in respect of custody arrangements and what does the operations manager and his team need to understand about this? For the global custodian, as for the operations manager in the firm or client using the custodian, there are a number of issues to take into consideration when dealing with events that require the investor either to make a decision or take no action at all. Timing is a big issue. Disregarding the risk factors, a trade that fails to settle on time will eventually settle. There might very well be penalty interest to pay and possible delays in other related trades; the trade nevertheless still stands. The overriding factor in those cases which require a proactive approach in order to benefit from the corporate action is for all parties in the information chain to deliver instructions before the deadline expires. A missed corporate action is irretrievable and internal controls must be able to recognise this possibility. It is important to record details of corporate actions in the ledgers on the correct date to ensure that the fund is priced correctly.

We have already discussed the source of information, and managers must recognise that this is therefore important in the context of time and procedures. The prime source of information covering registered securities is the issuing company or its agent. The global custodian has to rely on the subcustodian network to gather this information and pass it on with a minimum of delay and translated preferably into English.

Other sources of information are the numerous information vendors, such as Reuters, *International Securities Market Association* (*ISMA*) updates and the financial press. However, these secondary sources become primary sources for bearer securities where the issuing companies are unable to communicate directly with their shareholders and bond holders. The quality of information can be poor with two or more providers giving different versions of the 'same' data, language problems and time delays being the main problems experienced. The amount of benefit due to an investor is determined by reference to the quantity of shares each investor holds on a record date. This record date is announced by the issuing company. The local market will establish a date (the *ex date*) which is used to determine whether the buyer or seller of shares is entitled to receive the benefit.

A problem arises when a purchaser who has bought shares before the ex date (i.e., is entitled to receive the benefit) does not have his name placed on the register

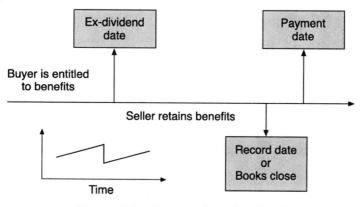

Figure 6.2 Cum and ex-dividend.
Source: the *dsc*.portfolio.

before the record date (see Figure 6.2). As the registrar is unable to recognise the new shareholder, the benefit is given to the previous shareholder (the seller), even though he is not entitled to it.

The global custodian must make sure that entitlements are received in a timely basis to avoid lost opportunities in trading. There should therefore be a mechanism in place to ensure that the correct entitlements are received and, if not, claimed from the seller.

It is the global custodian's duty to provide as much information as possible to enable the client to make the necessary decisions, to ensure that the information is accurate and to allow enough time for the client's instructions, where appropriate, to be relayed back to the company. As there is a variety of information types, it has not been easy for the global custodians to translate this into electronic message formats for the client. Instead, information on corporate actions has tended in the past to be sent by telex and mail. This situation is changing as the quality of information from the overseas markets improves.

The investor will be given a deadline before which to convey any instructions to the global custodian and for the global custodian to pass them on to the local market.

This can cause a problem for the investor who might want to delay his decision until the last possible moment, which will be the deadline stated in the local market rather than the global custodian's. In this case the investor's settlement department and the global custodian have to delay sending their respective instructions until the very last moment and, in so doing, risk missing the deadline.

The investor must accept full responsibility for a missed event if instructions are sent after the custodian's deadline. Global custodians must ensure that clients' instructions are passed on to the local market and also that the benefit is received in good time. Where appropriate, market claims must be made.

An ISSA working party at the 6th Symposium in May 1992 recommended:

That standard messages be used and standard time frames be developed for various corporate actions. Distinctions need to be made between those requiring timely reaction by the client and those which involve a simple notification and no response.

That the information must be provided electronically as well in hard copy form. A central body, either public or private and accessible to domestic and international bodies, must be designated as the official carrier of the data in each market.

That international issues should be communicated in English as well as the local language.

Despite the above recommendation, when it comes to things like proxy voting, with communication in a foreign language, possibly across different time zones, there is a danger that companies are not able to inform their shareholders in time to cast their votes or react to news about corporate actions concerning their securities.

For global custodians to act efficiently and effectively on behalf of their investing clients, timely information has to be received from the companies. It is necessary for the custodians to have highly skilled staff in order to:

- decipher and translate lengthy technical information; and
- reorganise it in such a way that the client can make a timely and informed decision on the options available.

To ensure that all clients' decisions are transmitted to the company, custodian banks' staff must:

- be aware of the deadlines given by the company;
- inform the clients of these deadlines;
- ensure that missing client instructions are chased up before the deadline; and

- know the length of time it takes to send instructions to the company by:
  - SWIFT;
  - telex/facsimile;
  - mail.

It is not difficult to see that – with the advent of widespread foreign share ownership and cross-border settlement – it would be an advantage if there were:

- greater uniformity of information dissemination;
- standardised timeframes;
- reliable information databases with easy global access.

These databases and the data communication networks connecting them to the information suppliers and users would be well suited to serve cross-border proxy voting.

It is now universally accepted that all shareholders should have an opportunity to exercise their voting rights, even though many of them may not actually wish to cast their votes. Indeed, there are some countries which are now beginning to encourage a more proactive participation by shareholders in the affairs of companies.

Proxy voting is not normally a widely debated issue, and only in isolated cases (where, for example, there is an outside attempt to gain control of a company) does the subject get coverage in the press.

As a result of increased shareholdings by large institutional investors, investment and pension fund managers have shown a new interest in exercising their voting rights.

This is partly in response to expectations expressed by the various regulatory bodies and partly an apparent underlying desire to influence a company's business or information policy. Large cross-border investments are reinforcing this trend, and there is a call for a mechanism that will permit the exercise of voting rights across borders with the same ease as found in the investor's home country.

Let us consider the problems for non-resident investors. Whilst the interest shown by the investors is both positive and appreciated by the companies, it is rarely possible for the foreign investors themselves to attend shareholders' meetings in person, due to the distances and costs involved. Procedures vary greatly from country to country because:

- there are different laws and traditions;
- there are different types of securities.

By the very nature of the instrument, companies do not know the names of shareholders whose certificates are in bearer form. These holders can only be contacted:

- via the media; and
- by custodians who research relevant information.

Registered shareholders usually have to be advised by mail via the registrars and, if applicable, by the relevant nominee companies. In a number of countries there are equity-type instruments or shares which:

- prohibit non-resident investors from voting;
- carry no voting rights (e.g., preference shares – these will only carry voting rights if the company has failed to pay its preference dividend);
- have a split voting structure (e.g., companies such as Great Universal Stores plc with both voting shares and non-voting 'A' shares listed on the London Stock Exchange).
- use different languages;
- have different time zones; and
- have formal requirements – e.g., a printed proxy statement.

Investors now are opposed to the issue of equity without votes, or with restricted votes, in the belief that all shareholders who bear the same level of risk should have an equal voice in the management of the business.

As a consequence, and with few exceptions, custodian banks do not advise their clients of forthcoming general meetings abroad. Therefore, the holdings of non-resident investors are as a rule not represented at these meetings, unless standing proxy instructions are permitted and have actually been given. In the long term, this may prove harmful to the functioning of the democratic principles in a free market economy. The system should enable all shareholders, whether domestic or foreign, to vote if they should want to.

Furthermore, the cost of voting should be kept low and preferably absorbed by the issuing companies.

Of crucial importance in custody is cash management, as the movement of securities, and in particular the settlement of securities trades, is linked to the movement of the corresponding countervalue of cash. Cash must be found to cover purchases; proceeds of sales and income payments must be re-invested in some way or another.

The prediction of cash requirements (funding requirements) and the movement of cash itself is known as 'cash management'. The performance of an investor's portfolio is made up of:

- profit (or loss) on trading activity; and
- yield of the portfolio through receipt of income.

If little attention is paid to cash management, then – together with poor settlement performance – the overall performance of the securities portfolio will be affected.

The problems that would be created should a global custodian fall into receivership should be considered. It has been established that the ways in which clients' non-cash assets are held by global custodians are sufficient for the liquidator to identify separately those assets which are beneficially owned by the clients, and those which belong to the global custodian. The position for cash assets is not so secure; owners of cash are considered by the liquidator to be unsecured creditors in the accounts of the bank (deposit taker, borrower or global custodian). It is, therefore, wise to deposit cash only with those organisations which are able to honour debts and repay loans as and when they fall due. An indication of this ability is provided by *credit rating* companies, such as Moody's, Standard & Poor's and Fitch IBCA. These organisations constantly monitor the banks and will upgrade or downgrade the rating to reflect the changed situation. A bank with a rating of AAA is considered better able to honour all debts whilst a bank with a rating of B is considered to be rather more risky.

Investors can reduce this risk by, for example:

- implementing in-house rules that might allow exposure limits of say $10 million with an AAA-rated bank down to $5 million with an A-rated bank, and no exposure allowed to banks with a B rating or lower; and
- making sure that the cash assets are placed with a number of highly rated banks.

While this will help to reduce the levels of risk, there is a price to be paid in terms of requiring more sophisticated cash monitoring systems and the extra expense associated with transferring cash around the banking system.

The global custodians are aware of the problems involved and constantly seek new ways to keep the client's cash-related business in house.

Clients whose business generates cash in (mainly) one currency and who wish to enter into cross-border trading might prefer to operate with cash accounts in a single currency. They will arrange for all purchase costs, sale proceeds and income receipts to be exchanged – a foreign exchange (*Forex*) trade – into their base currency as and when the need arises.

For the investor, the advantages are:

- the exposure to adverse foreign exchange rate movements is removed once the Forex trade has been executed;
- with only one currency, the funding requirement calculations are simplified;
- the investor is free to obtain the most advantageous exchange rates from the Forex market place;
- cash reconciliation and control processes are more straightforward.

The disadvantages are:

- there will be extra Forex trading charges to consider over and above the securities trading commissions;
- the securities trade settlements will no longer be on a Delivery Versus Payment (*DVP*) basis, as the currency movements will take place independently from the securities movements. The risk of non-performance of the trade as a whole is greater than it would be for a DVP settlement;
- for Forex trades dealt with counterparties other than the global custodian, the investor must give settlement instructions for the cash side in addition to instructions for the securities.

For the global custodian, the implications are:

- the relationship is not one of global custodianship as defined by ISSA;
- all income receipts are exchanged into the base currency;
- the global custodian will not necessarily be responsible for exchanging the purchase and sale amounts, as the investor will look around the Forex market for the best Forex rates;
- the global custodian will continue to settle trades in the relevant currency on a DVP basis (where applicable);
- the global custodian is under no obligation to offer CSDA, as the transfer of securities occurs independently from the movement of the client's cash.

On the other hand, a client may require multi-currency accounts. Multi-currency banking will suit those investors whose ordinary business activities generate cash flows in foreign currencies and/or who prefer to settle the securities trades on a DVP basis in the foreign currency. The cash funding requirements will be undertaken as a separate process.

For the investor, the advantages are:

- the securities trades benefit from DVP settlement;
- the investor is able to take advantage of the global custodian's CSDA settlement service;
- there are more options available in terms of subsequent use of the foreign currency balances.

The disadvantages are the increased control and administrative burden as a result of operating many different currency accounts.

For the global custodian, the implications are:

- a more rounded custody and banking service can be provided to the client; and
- the need to exchange all income into the base currency is removed, thus reducing the number of relatively small value Forex trades that must be executed.

Investors who actively manage their cash balances wish to reduce or eliminate the time that uninvested or uncommitted cash balances remain in non-interest bearing accounts. Cash balances will be transferred to deposit accounts or other financial products. Although this achieves the objective, it increases the administrative burden and becomes expensive to operate. The global custodians now provide interest on various currency accounts and thus help to cut down the number of cash movements across the accounts. The global custodian may offer to transfer automatically (or 'sweep') uninvested and uncommitted balances overnight from non-interest bearing accounts into interest bearing deposit accounts or *Short Term Investment Funds* (*STIFs*). This ensures that cash balances are being used in a more efficient manner.

Global custodians hold accounts in the same currency and/or multi-currency accounts for their clients. For interest calculations only the custodians can pool the balances by currency into one larger balance in order to attract a higher rate of interest or reduce the effect of some accounts being overdrawn. Global custodians are also able to offer a wide range of banking services including:

- Funds transmission systems that enable the client to transfer electronically funds covering clean payments – i.e., those not directly connected to a securities trade.
- Treasury services that provide dealing facilities to purchase and sell foreign currency, place funds on deposit and draw down funds on loan.
- Screen-based dealing systems that some global custodians have now made available which allow clients to execute their smaller Forex deals without reference to a bank dealer. Clients are able to accept or reject the rates offered on the screen and, should the rate be acceptable, the transaction is immediately confirmed.

Withholding Tax (*WHT*) occurs when cash benefits paid by companies to their shareholders in the form of dividends are subject to local tax. This WHT is deducted at source with the shareholder receiving the net amount.

The rate of WHT is determined by the tax authorities of the country in which the company is based. With the increase in cross-border investment activity, investors are subject to different tax regimes. Tax reclaims must be made in the issuer's country of origin and they will be submitted by the global custodian on behalf of the client.

There is no standard global approach to tax reclamation in terms of the timing of claims and repayment. In 1990,

ISSA Recommendation 5 (*www.issanet.org*) addressed this problem by seeking to obtain treaty benefits in an efficient manner by recommending that:

1. Treaty rates should be applied at source.
2. Documentation should be streamlined and standardised.
3. Details of beneficial ownership should be given on an exceptional basis only.
4. Processing should take place through one agency per country.

Efforts to improve the situation have been made by the global custodians at the highest levels in the problem countries. Unfortunately, progress is sometimes slow in spite of the industry's efforts, as the issue of tax can only be resolved at an international, governmental level.

The problem for non-resident investors is that the net income is additionally subject to further taxation in their own country – i.e., the income is double-taxed. Most governments have recognised this issue as being unfair and allow most or all of the WHT to be reclaimed by entering into a *Double Taxation Agreement (DTA)* with other like-minded governments. Governments enter into these agreements with other countries in order to:

- prevent income being taxed twice; *and*
- render reciprocal assistance to prevent tax evasion.

WHT reclamation works along one of the following bases:

- certain classes of income are made taxable only in one of the countries that is party to a DTA – e.g., in the country of the tax payer's residence;
- income is taxable in both countries, but (in the case of UK residents) the overseas tax is allowable as a credit against UK tax.

Additionally, global custodians offer investment accounting services – i.e., the provision of a full range of reports which may include fully accrued, multi-currency valuations, performance measurement, investment analysis – at both detailed and summary levels. Reports may apply to a single portfolio or a consolidation of a number of portfolios.

The cash management for principal dealers' positions is also crucial and will be managed in various ways including treasury functions within the bank. A whole range of reporting of asset positions, funding requirements, credit lines, etc. needs to be managed efficiently and yet, as we have already seen, this relies on efficient settlement and information about settlement (on time, delayed, etc.) as well as timely instructions to move cash in and out of accounts and liaison with custodians or other parties.

Another important service involves pricing and valuation reporting. Prices of individual securities are obtained from a variety of external price feeds, such as Reuters or Bloomberg, and allow the calculation of market value. From this, investors' portfolios can be valued both in the currency of the security and the base currency of the investor. It is important that the pricing of securities is carried out accurately and at timely intervals so the fund's *Net Asset Value (NAV)* calculations can be performed. An incorrectly priced security will lead to an erroneous NAV, with the consequence that compensation might have to be paid to unitholders of the funds.

Funds and investors will wish to constantly analyse the performance of the investments. Using pricing information the investments can be analysed in a variety of ways:

- by instrument type – i.e., equities, corporate bonds, international bonds, government bonds, convertible bonds, derivatives and cash, and cash equivalents;
- by industrial sector;
- against a benchmark index;
- by geographical location;
- as a percentage of the portfolio that each security or its type, industrial sector and geographical location represents;
- by a sensitivity analysis showing how changes in securities or country allocations affect the return on the portfolio.

The information provided allows the investor to evaluate the value of the securities by stock selection, markets and currencies. There are a number of external performance measurement companies who collect relevant data from investors or global custodians in order to determine how investor types compare with each other or against industry-recognised indices. This is relevant, for example, for marketing purposes when fund managers hoping to win new business will state that they have outperformed the relevant index by, say, 2% when the average has been 1%.

As the investment performance of a security includes the income received and income due, it is important to be able to track the investment income. This is especially important for debt securities for which income (interest) accrues on a daily basis until the payment is made, usually annually or biannually depending on the security type and domicile. Equally, Forex creates a possible cost or gain to the portfolio. The risk of Forex exposure needs to be managed, and therefore the Forex reporting for a fund is vitally important.

Forex transactions should be related back to the underlying securities trades or income receipts. Historical exchange rates and interest rates should be reported to allow the investor to check the actual rates obtained against the market closing rates.

There are also requirements for consolidated reporting. Investors might use two or more fund managers, because each has a particular specialist investment skill. If the fund managers use their own global custodian, the investors have the problem of consolidating a range of reports from the fund managers and their global custodians into one combined set of reports. To save the investors' time and effort in making the consolidation, one global custodian acts as recipient for the reports generated by the other global custodians and prepares the consolidated set of reports.

For dealers' positions, *Mark to Market* (*MTM*) reports are generated for comparison and reconciliation with dealers' profit/loss records. MTM is the revaluation of positions against a price representative of the current market. The price can be generated and published by an exchange or can be generated from a pricing model.

Custody is integral to the whole clearing and settlement process and will form an important part of each organisation's overall procedures for their business. As such, operations managers must ensure that they understand the role of the custodian and how the custodians impact on their particular firm. Likewise, staff should be fully conversant with the services and structure of custodians, so that they are aware of crucial issues like timings, instruction formats, etc.

Box 6.1 Work session.

Consider the various operational issues and problems that the manager in a custodian faces. Compare these with the problems that the manager in a client of the custodian might face and how the custodian has influenced this by either creating the problem or helping to address it.

Part of custody is the comprehensive use of technology, and in Chapter 7 we look at this important subject and how it affects operations in today's markets.

Chapter

7

....

TECHNOLOGY

Nothing has changed so much in the financial services industry as technology. A relatively short time ago most processes – and particularly those in operations – were manual and paper-intensive. It is still true today of some processes and certainly in some countries, but in general terms the use of technology has automated not just operations processes, but trading, payments, and the passing of messages and instructions as well.

This move towards greater reliance on technology is not without its problems. Issues like reliability, security and capability are usually all significant for organisations. So, too, is cost and support, for – as we saw in Chapter 4 on Concepts of Risk – system risk is a key one in the industry. However, today most people working in operations are at least in possession of some IT skills although true understanding of the systems being used may not be great.

So, what are the technology issues for operations managers?

Well, the last point in the previous paragraph is one. Just what do we know about the systems being used? What is the scope of the system to meet the operational needs? Are procedures driven by systems or do systems fit in with the procedures? Next to people, systems and technology in general can be the weakest part of any operations function, and here we are not just talking about performance but about total collapse of the operational process.

Far too many operations teams operate on systems that

are apparently unreliable and incapable of handling the products being traded or systems that are 'adapted' to handle activity they were never designed for. The cause is usually lack of investment or poor operations and/or technology management, or both. The cause of technology problems can be many and often includes corporate policy or lack of it, failure of operations managers and teams to understand the technology issues and failure of technology personnel to understand operations functions and needs. So, one blames the other and *vice versa* and the end result is more problems and greater risk.

The reality, of course, is that technology is expected to provide the answer to everything when, in fact, the systems are only as good as the input into their design from operations. Here lies the operations manager's real challenge: understand the technology needs for the procedures and processes and then manage the development of those systems within the IT area.

Of course, there are many different ways in which systems are operated. They may be one or a combination of the following:

- systems developed and supported in-house by the IT team;
- systems bought in from an external supplier and supported in-house by the IT team;
- systems bought in from an external supplier and supported externally by the supplier.

In some larger organisations, the in-house IT team may not be employed by the company. Mostly for reasons of the enormous costs associated with IT, technology development and support may be outsourced to a specialist company.

Managing the IT relationship is crucial. Key projects like straight-through-processing (*STP*) and automating key processes – like trade input, reconciliation and client services – are critical to the business. Design, choice, implementation and post-implementation are critical stages, and the operations manager must be certain that the result will be right. There will be pressure from the team, from clients and also from senior management to get the 'solution' implemented, and yet rushing in new systems or even system enhancements rarely proves beneficial. Technology is power, and yet so often it is power that is not realised because of relationship issues, resistance to change, politics, budget, lack of knowledge of the system and a tendency to blame systems for what is actually nothing to do with the system.

You will gather that the operations manager must be realistic when it comes to technology, recognising its benefits, seeing the need to ensure that sufficient knowledge about technology and the specific systems used are available in the team and to the team. The relationship between IT and operations will be either a formidable asset to the business or a potential disaster; it's up to the IT and operations managers to make it the former. This can be achieved by establishing operations representatives with responsibility to liaise with IT and to provide the business reasons for issues. At the same time, they receive the technology viewpoint and relay that to the operations teams in terms they will understand. In many organisations this works well, in others it doesn't and it shows!

The use of technology in driving the industry forward is immense. Without it, book-entry transfer would not be possible, so dematerialised settlement would be difficult to have. The volume and diversity of business would in turn be impossible to handle and the globalisation of the industry would never have happened.

STP is a key project for most organisations and obviously relies heavily on technology, and yet its successful implementation is also dependent on operations teams changing their skill sets and working practices to embrace technology. Managing this process is also a key responsibility for the operations manager.

Internet and intranet facilities are changing the whole face of clearing and settlement, leading the way in offering standard delivery mechanisms and links between customers and brokers and custodians' own networks.

The introduction of *Real Time Gross Settlement* (*RTGS*) and *Continuous Linked Settlement* (*CLS*) require connectivity and two-way access to data.

Technology also embraces most of the key functions associated with operations including:

- record keeping;
- accounts;
- valuations;

- position reports;
- netting;
- profit/loss calculation;
- client service delivery (Internet/intranet data access, etc.);
- margin calculations (derivatives);
- trade confirmations;
- messages;
- settlement instructions;
- payment instructions;
- management information;
- static data;
- risk management (limits, etc.);
- reconciliation.

The effectiveness of the procedures and controls applied by the manager will determine the efficiency of the operations team. In turn, the systems used for each of these processes need to be able to deliver the performance the operations manager needs.

Industry-wide technology is also crucial to the overall clearing and settlement process. The impact of the G30/ ISSA Recommendations on standard messaging formats and the use of international securities identification numbering (*ISIN*) allow transactions to be universally recognised and the details to be matched. Thus, we use unique identifying numbering systems – such as CUSIP (US), SEDOL (UK), etc. – for securities.

The SWIFT system of electronic communication with standard *message types* (*MTs*) for various cash and securities transactions – developed by the *Society for World-wide Interbank Financial Telecommunications* – is one of the most reliable systems around and handles millions of messages between all the major players in the markets. Organisations like ISMA have reporting systems (TRAX).

Treasury operations teams rely heavily on systems capabilities for information on funding requirements, positions and cash movement. Various systems are utilised in different jurisdictions. So, we have the *Trans-European Automated Real-time Gross settlement Express Transfer (TARGET)* system that handles the settlement of cross-border payments of the euro. Other systems utilised include the *Clearing House Interbank Payment System* (CHIPS) in the US and *Clearing House Automated Payment System* (CHAPS) in the UK. Most people are familiar with another payment system widely used – BACS – and there are other retail funds transfer systems that are not typically used in the wholesale markets.

The whole process of fund management requires a range of critically important reporting and valuation processes enabling investors and trustees to track the performance of the fund and to see the value and price at which they can buy or sell the shares or units. The accuracy of the valuations is vital, and therefore the source of the information is also vital. High-quality pricing data available online and in real time applied to accurate records of the assets in the fund are needed to complete the *Net Asset Value (NAV)* calculations on which prices are based. For all types of funds – from unit trusts to hedge funds – any significant errors and the regulators will take action. For instance, a mispricing of a unit trust can require compensation to be paid by the manager to the investor and must be reported to the Trustee and the regulator. Reporting to customers is also subject to regulatory requirements including content, frequency, etc.

Another important technology issue the operations manager needs to be aware of is the use of technology in enterprise-wide risk information systems. Risk data are managed in organisations through systems that receive the data from the business areas and then process that data through, for instance, an Interface Layer to a Data Integration Engine and onward into a Data Warehouse from which key risk reports, exposure monitoring and integrated reporting is made.

The operations manager will be involved in both the input of data from their area and the receipt of data from the Data Warehouse in terms of management information (*MI*).

In output terms the use of MI by the manager is important as part of the ongoing performance measurement process. Reconciliation breaks, interest claims, volumes, error rates, etc. are all fundamental indicators of performance. As far as input is concerned, well we have already stressed that the quality of data out of operations and into the enterprise-wide systems is paramount. 'Rubbish in = rubbish out' may be an old expression, but it is nevertheless true. Today, the inability to maintain accurate records has significant regulatory and, in an increasingly competitive environment, business implications.

Technology risk also needs to be considered. Access to systems is obviously vital for operations personnel, and yet any tampering with data in the system can create massive problems. Creating procedures that segregate people with access to parameters and static data in the systems from those using the systems helps to control the risk. The maintenance of static data is crucial. The system output is driven from static data on:

- products;
- clients;
- calculations (formulas, prices, interest rates, exchange rates);
- standard settlement instructions (SSIs);
- limits;
- charges, fees and commissions;
- maturity, expiry and termination;
- corporate actions.

Data control sections in organisations are often established to oversee static data, procedures and elements of risk control. This is logical given the importance of data and technology in the operations environment.

The operations manager, therefore, has many technology issues to consider. Technology is driving the industry forward, and the competition in the industry at all levels and in all fields makes effective use of technology critically important. Many of the day-to-day problems that arise in operations are or tend to be blamed on IT, so clearly the operations manager must be able to assess the true situation. Many routine and essential functions require systems to have good static data, so this is another area of immense importance. Processes – like netting, margining and real-time settlement – that are becoming more and more standard in all types of securities and derivatives clearing and settlement need system capabilities within the users to make them effective. Understanding the requirements and delivering the in-house solution is the manager's objective.

We cannot leave the technology chapter without returning to the developments going on in the industry today. The impact of Internet and intranet facilities from a trading point of view – where, for instance, an increase in private client business was seen after brokers began offering Internet dealing – has been significant and will grow in significance in the global environment, opening up markets and increasing cross-border business. Also, the so-called 'added value' services that can be provided to clients using the available technology is changing the role of the broker, bank, custodian, creating the need for massive investment in systems or a strategic withdrawal from the operational function – in other words, outsourcing core clearing and settlement.

Examples where this is found include fund administration services, centralised clearing of derivatives and the concepts of prime brokerage. Operations outsourcing and insourcing will, I suspect, be a significant issue in the markets for some time. Outsourcing does not mean an end to the operations function in the outsourcer, but it certainly changes the role. Likewise, the insourcing company has taken on a massive workload and responsibility where the performance is subject to *Service Level Agreements*, and the technology capability and investment needed to ensure that performance is significant.

Technology is changing operations and, as it does so, the operations manager must also change the procedures and the role of the people to meet the new world – whatever it may be.

Chapter

8

REGULATION AND COMPLIANCE

E verybody from banks and brokers to fund managers and global custodians and their clients must operate within the general laws of the countries in which they are based, as well as complying with any regulatory obligations. We could fill a whole book on regulation in the UK, let alone globally, and then be faced with the fact that change is happening in regulation as elsewhere in the industry. Keeping up to date with the regulations and their impact and complying with them is not always easy.

For some organisations – like a global custodian – this can become a complicated exercise when entering into legal agreements with subcustodians based in different jurisdictions. Equally, there are issues for brokers and banks operating for clients where assets and money must be kept separate from firms' money and assets. Operations staff are in the front line, as they are dealing with the flow of assets and money that must be safeguarded and treated as per the rules and regulations of the jurisdiction concerned.

Not only must the rules and regulations (as laid down by the country concerned) be adhered to, but so must the rules and regulations of the exchanges and clearing houses involved in the various processes. The regulatory environments need to be understood by operations teams, even though compliance departments will specialise in the regulatory requirements.

Let us review the regulatory structures in the UK and US, starting with the UK where there has been significant changes. The main regulator of the securities industry is the Financial Services Authority (*FSA*) – formerly the Securities and Investment Board (*SIB*) – which operates under the Financial Services Act 1986 (*FSA 86*) and the Financial Services and Markets Act 2000.

The changes to the UK regulatory structure have taken place in stages. The UK structure consisted of 10 Principles laid down by the FSA, 40 Core Rules and a system of Self-Regulatory Organisations (*SROs*) and Recognised Public Bodies. These organisations were required to implement the Principles and Core Rules set out in their own rule books, which had been drawn up to meet the specific needs of its members.

There were three SROs in the UK:

- Securities & Futures Authority (*SFA*);
- Investment Management Regulatory Organisation (*IMRO*);
- Personal Investment Authority (*PIA*).

Further change took place with the introduction of the Financial Services and Markets Act 2000, which created a single regulator in the UK, the FSA.

The FSA has acquired the regulatory and registration functions which were formerly carried out by the SROs and other regulatory bodies (as detailed in Table 8.1).

FSMA 2000 and Statutory Instruments give powers to and impose obligations on the FSA, which in turn creates rules and monitors behaviour of the regulated entities.

Table 8.1 Regulatory organisations now directly under the regulation of the Financial Services Authority.

Regulator	Regulated organisations
Building Societies Commission (BSC)	Building societies
Friendly Societies Commission (FSC)	Friendly societies
Insurance Directorate (ID) of the Department of Trade and Industry	Insurance companies
Investment Management Regulatory Organisation (IMRO)	Investment management
Personal Investment Authority (PIA)	Retail investment business
Registry of Friendly Societies (RFS)	Credit unions' supervision (and the registration and public records of building societies, friendly societies, industrial and provident societies, and other mutual societies)
Securities and Futures Authority (SFA)	Securities and derivatives business
Securities and Investments Board (SIB)	Investment business (including responsibility for supervising exchanges and clearing houses)
Supervision and Surveillance (S&S) Division of the Bank of England	Banking supervision (including the wholesale money market regimes)

The Act legislates in relation to regulated activities and Section 22 describes these as being a range of specified activities in connection with a range of specified investments. These are:

1. Deposits.
2. Contracts of insurance.
3. Shares.
4. Bonds.
5. Instruments giving entitlements to investments (e.g., warrants).
6. Certificates representing securities (e.g., Depositary Receipts).
7. Units in collective investment schemes.
8. Rights under a stakeholder pension scheme.
9. Options.
10. Futures.
11. Contracts for differences.
12. Lloyds syndicate capacity and syndicate membership.
13. Funeral plan contracts.
14. Regulated mortgage contracts.

Clearly, the power of the FSA is extensive, and regulated activities include dealing as a principal or agent, managing investments, establishing and running collective investment schemes or stakeholder pension schemes, deposit taking and custody.

The FSA has developed a set of 11 FSA Principles (Box 8.1), a set of Conduct of Business Rules and lists recognised exchanges and clearing houses as well. It is imperative

---

Box 8.1   The 11 FSA Principles.

---

1. *Integrity* – a firm must conduct its business with integrity.
2. *Skill, care and diligence* – a firm must conduct its business with due skill, care and diligence.
3. *Management and control* – a firm must take reasonable care to organise and control its affairs responsibly and effectively, with adequate risk management systems.
4. *Financial prudence* – a firm must maintain adequate financial resources.
5. *Market conduct* – a firm must observe proper standards of market conduct.
6. *Customers' interests* – a firm must pay due regard to the interests of its customers and treat them fairly.
7. *Communications with clients* – a firm must pay due regard to the information needs of its clients and communicate information to them in a way that is clear, fair and not misleading.
8. *Conflicts of interest* – a firm must manage conflicts of interest fairly, both between itself and its customers and between a customer and another client.
9. *Customers: relationships of trust* – a firm must take reasonable care to ensure the suitability of its advice and discretionary decisions for any customer who is entitled to rely upon its judgement.
10. *Clients' assets* – a firm must arrange adequate protection for clients' assets when it is responsible for them.
11. *Relations with regulators* – a firm must deal with its regulators in an open and cooperative way, and must disclose to the FSA appropriately anything relating to the firm of which the FSA would reasonably expect notice.

Source: *FSA Handbook.*

that these are fully understood by the operations manager and that the appropriate procedures and controls exist within the operations area to address the issues that arise. There are so many key issues that affect the operations teams. It is not possible to cover the role of the FSA in great detail in this book. Readers who wish to know more about the UK regulatory environment and anyone taking Securities Institute examinations are urged to visit the FSA website – *www.fsa.gov.uk* – or alternatively purchase a copy of the *FSA Regulatory Environment IAQ Workbook* (available from the Securities Institute).

Operations managers must liaise closely with the compliance department over what is required to comply with the rules and regulations.

Another important key piece of regulation is the *Investment Services Directive (ISD)*, which sets out the criteria for firms from EU member states involved in the provision of certain types of financial services. A key element of the ISD is the provision of the single passport allowing a firm to carry on business throughout the *European Economic Area (EEA)* with a single authorisation. The ISD defines the investments for which the passport applies and, consequently, a firm may be involved in investment activity that is defined under FSA, but not ISD, and other business that is defined under both. The *Second Banking Co-ordination Directive (2BCD)* affords a similar passport system for credit institutions – i.e., banks.

Regulation in other major jurisdictions varies from that in the UK. In the United States, the *Securities and Exchange Commission (SEC)* and the *Commodity Futures Trading Commission* are key regulators with commissioners appointed by the President. In Japan the *Financial*

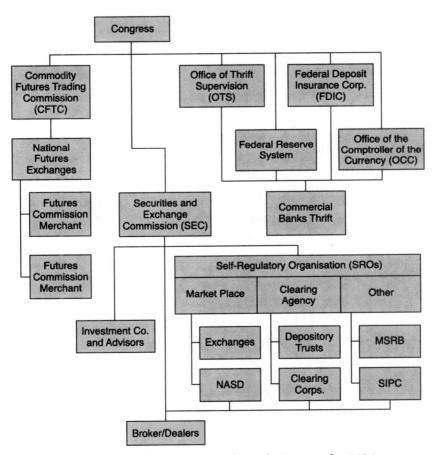

Figure 8.1   The structure of regulation in the USA.

Source: ISSA Handbook (visit www.issanet.org)

Services Agency and the *Ministry of Finance* oversee the regulation of markets and participants. From the operations manager's point of view, understanding the relevant regulation in each jurisdiction is crucial and – as we have noted here – there needs to be close liaison with the compliance department. Figure 8.1 shows the structure of regulation in the US.

The strength of regulation is by no means standard

around the world and operations managers need to be aware of this, particularly where assets and cash are being held or moved. It is important for the reader of the book to research these international regulators, particularly those relevant to their firm's business, and to make comparison between the regulatory structure and workings. However, in general terms there are some key issues for the operations manager to address. These would include:

- reporting requirements;
- client money and assets;
- money laundering;
- insider dealing.

The reporting requirements will range from activity reporting to large positions. The inference for the manager here is, therefore, that the record keeping function must be accurate, any amendments need to be made and, if necessary, the reporting also amended. Late reporting or failure to report amended trades can have significant repercussions.

With client money and assets, the requirements to adequately safeguard and segregate the assets is crucial. Calculating client money requirements and making shortfalls from own funds means that the manager must ensure that procedures and controls are effective and that one client's assets are never used to cover another client's shortfall, or for principal activity. In the global context this will include ensuring that any assets or money held overseas is subject to the protection required or – if this is not possible – that the client is aware that the protection afforded is not to the standard of that in the UK.

Money laundering and insider dealing are serious issues, indeed criminal offences in some jurisdictions like the UK. More importantly, each employee has the responsibility – particularly under the money laundering rules – to report suspicious activity or simply their concerns that something may be suspicious. The operations manager must make sure that at all times the team is aware of its collective and individual responsibility, and the business must make sure that each employee is aware of how money laundering-type and insider dealing-type situations can occur. The name of the firm's *Money Laundering Reporting Officer* (*MLRO*) must also be known to all employees.

Basel II, Sarbanes–Oxley and UCITS Directive

Operations managers are affected by the regulations related to Basel II, Sarbanes–Oxley and the EU Undertakings for Collective Investment in Transferable Securities (*UCITS*) Directive. It is therefore important for the manager and supervisors to familiarise themselves with these regulations and to make sure that they are aware of the current situation and any changes. Brief details and an overview of each is provided in the appendices at the back of the book.

Box 8.2 Work session.

Compare the regulatory structure in the US, UK, Europe and Japan and note the key differences and the impact on the operations team.

Look at regulation in other markets like Australia, South Africa and China. What are the additional issues, if any, that arise and then consider two emerging markets and again consider what operational issues arise?

Chapter

9

....

CLIENT SERVICES

In a highly competitive industry the provision of high-quality client services and customer relationship management is critical to all organisations.

There is choice in almost every field, and with electronic processes switching counterparts is nothing like as difficult as in previous times.

Users or clients are also becoming more and more sophisticated in their use of the markets, so expect better and more comprehensive services from their counterparts.

Everyone from systems suppliers to brokers to custodians is monitored for service levels, reliability, costs and value for money.

The key issues in respect of customer relationships include:

- the approach to client service and establishing a customer-orientated culture;
- the understanding of the client's organisational and business structure;
- the risk impact of providing added value client services;
- measuring client risk;
- introducing controls and procedures to ensure performance standards;
- providing a competitive edge to the business;
- dealing with complaints.

These issues are of great importance. The ability of a business to retain and gain clients relies heavily on all aspects of customer relationship. The service provided out of the operations area will be judged by the client as part of the overall service provided by the organisation.

Managing and supervising customer relationships successfully revolves around:

- choice of personnel;
- definition of the client service function;
- structure of the client service team or group;
- adequate training in key relationship skills;
- understanding of the client's business;
- policy and procedures for identifying and dealing with problems;
- relationship management policy.

Without the above it will be impossible for the manager/ supervisor to monitor the service levels provided to meet client requirements. As a result, relationship management will be more difficult than it should be and there will be a real chance that the relationship may deteriorate and ultimately the client will move away. Figure 9.1 shows a generic relationship between a fund manager and a derivatives clearing broker and illustrates the complexity, in terms of roles, responsibilities and potential problems areas.

Providing a high-quality client service is a full-time role for a dedicated team of people. It is not therefore something that can be provided without a clearly defined policy and an adequate budget.

The customer relationship policy of the organisation must encompass both front office and operations such that the client is aware only of the 'company' service.

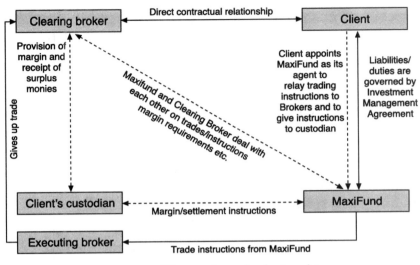

Figure 9.1 Illustration of relationships.

High degrees of personal and business skills are therefore required in the team.

This chapter will help to develop an understanding of the complex and crucial role of relationship management.

The approach to customer relationships and the 'client culture'

Box 9.1 Definition of 'client culture'.

A culture within and across an organisation that places the relationship with a client as the key to growth and profitability of the organisation, and one which is totally supported, resourced, implemented and managed by senior personnel in all areas of the business.

Both the approach to customer relationships and the establishing of a client culture are driven by market considerations as well as corporate policy. High on the agenda of business managers is the need for either market share or premier revenue generation from the client base. Both have fundamentally different implications for the way in which the client facing policy will be formulated. We must also add to this equation the market-driven and dictated 'customer service' issues and whether or not a particular business sector is service- or profit-driven. Today, operational areas are just as much likely to be structured as revenue generators as service/administration providers. At one end of the scale, there are organisations that have operations-based client teams contributing significant revenue to the business by selling services and products independently from the sales teams. At the other end, client teams operating in 'traditional' structures are providing the support and service levels that contribute to the company's core product. One might think there would be a significant variance to the approach to the relationships from two very different setups, and yet in reality there will be little, if any, difference.

Customer business is won or lost for many reasons. A company failing to provide the client with the service they want and expect will lose that client whether or not they are revenue- or cost-based as a team. It is the service, not the structure, that is important, and service depends on the culture possessed by the team. Most managers and supervisors would consider themselves customer-orientated. How can it be otherwise, when their function is to head up a team that serves others. However, what we think and what the customer thinks are potentially two very different viewpoints.

Understanding the client, its business, its structure, its people and its objectives are vitally important. So, too, is the recognition that the client needs to believe that the service being provided is:

- as much for their benefit as the supplier's;
- is supported by personnel that understand the client's profile;
- is able to offer innovative solutions to problems;
- can be expanded and adapted to meet the growth in the client's business;
- is 'tailored' for the client.

Whether the client is in-house or external, the above are all true. There is often a misconception about the importance of treating in-house relationships on the same basis as external client relationships. In many cases the principal activity is not only significant, it is also dependent on an efficient post-transaction process to prevent unnecessary additional costs that will impact on profitability. There should be a clear policy that in-house 'clients' receive a service in exactly the same way as an external client would expect to do so. It is not acceptable to treat the in-house client as 'tame' and therefore provide a substandard service. If there is any reluctance to accept this viewpoint it may be worth reminding people that outsourcing is a very real option in today's markets!

So, the client culture needs to be established as:

- a business objective for the organisation as a whole;
- a function staffed by individuals that fully understand the concepts of and are totally focused on client service;
- managed by an innovative and industry-aware group;
- led by key managers interacting across the company.

Client satisfaction and support can be lost in a matter of months, even when the relationship has been in existence for many years. Managing the relationship and service successfully is therefore crucial.

Box 9.2   Work session.

Marks & Spencer and Sainsburys are two examples where client loyalty has been lost at some point. What are the causes of the problems they have faced and what are the main issues in these two cases that can be applied to client service in the financial services industry?

We need to be able to define the service and establish relationships so that our personnel with direct client contact and, most importantly, the rest of the operations team understand the business need. It begs the question, then: What is considered as 'client service'?

One approach is to develop a service that can be a uniform product based on the basic settlement function that is 'tweaked' to suit different types of client. This is reasonable as there are certain standard or core processes that will take place and there are common added value products – like prime brokerage, fund administration and global clearing – or specific services – like valuations, average pricing and single currency settlement. System-supported services are important to many clients, but not so important to smaller clients with regard to, say, help and advice on new products, valuations and even regulatory issues. This is where tweaking comes into play.

So, client service could be said to be: *A standard settlement relationship that is enhanced by the provision of additional services that benefit the client.*

Managing the relationship and service successfully is therefore crucial. Relationships in any walk of life revolve around two key factors, *trust* and *compatibility*. There is no change to this when we look at the relationship between a bank or broker or custodian and their clients. The fundamental issues are about a belief that the relationship is mutually beneficial, is wanted and will be viewed as a long-term relationship.

The latter is very important. Today, with so many system-related issues and straight through processing high on the agenda, clients are seeking a counterpart that they will have a significant dependency on in terms of these system-related services. It may therefore be tempting for a broker to believe that the client is 'locked in' by the provision of technology-related services. However, that would be a mistake. Clients will move if the relationship sours, whatever the cost in terms of finance and disruption. The need to establish a monitoring process for the relationship for signs of problems is also a key element of managing the relationship. For instance, a problem may be occurring only occasionally and yet is having an unseen, dramatic and damaging effect. For example, a client is being inconvenienced and is losing confidence in their broker/bank as the counterpart. As we know, in such a situation it is not inconceivable that the client may gradually move their business elsewhere and the counterparty may never be aware that it is the operations teams performance that is to blame.

Without adequate monitoring of performance and the relationship, there is undoubtedly a strong probability that clients will be lost when it could and should have been avoided. The key issue is to develop the relationship in terms of both the team concept and the corporate concept. Clearly, day-to-day activities will be part of the relationship and it is here that the client culture we looked at earlier will be crucial. The minor issues and problems that may occur are being dealt with by contacts in both parties' operations. The way in which the operations area is structured will determine who is dealing with the client on the daily and ongoing basis.

So, what are the main considerations for the manager?

- Structure of the operations team.
- Who has responsibility for day-to-day client contact?
- How is performance monitored?
- What are the escalation procedures for problems?
- Establishing a client liaison programme.

- Interaction and co-operation with the front-office client team.
- Identifying industry issues affecting or likely to affect the client.
- Training the client facing and support teams in product awareness.
- Analysing the competition.
- Constantly reviewing, developing and refining the client service product.

Each of these issues is very much interlinked and forms the core subjects for customer relationship building and maintenance. We should consider them in turn.

Structure of client services within the operations team

Operations teams will all be different and, yet, will all be performing largely the same functions. The client facing team may be an actual team of people dedicated to the provision of client service. Equally, it could be part of a middle office concept or designated people within a general settlements/clearing team.

Responsibility

In most cases a client is looking for designated contacts at different levels (see Figure 9.2). Daily contact is likely to be provided from a client team with a designated representative or account manager at the next level.

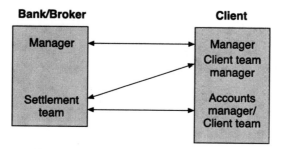

Figure 9.2   An illustration of the communication lines between a client (a) and a broker (b).

Overseeing the whole client team may be a supervisor and team manager reporting to the operations manager.

It is important that the day-to-day communication is separated from the senior management contact such that the people doing the processes deal with the majority of issues and problems. There can be a temptation, in the marketing of services, for more senior staff to offer to be the contact, a form of assurance of how important the client is viewed. Clearly, this can be flattering for the client but is almost certainly going to be the beginning of a nightmare situation whereby every issue, however minor, is automatically routed to the manager or accounts manager. There is a need for the responsibilities of each team member to be defined and for the contacts and their responsibilities to be explained to the client. This is important for external relationships, but applies as well to the internal client. Clearly, the client must not feel that the door is closed to them at any level, but equally there has to be a logical order to the relationship. This may be included as part of a service level agreement, if used.

Establishing the roles and responsibilities of the personnel on both sides of the relationship is fundamental to a workable and successful arrangement.

Measuring performance

The combination of basic settlement processes and added value services makes measuring performance a complex exercise. As far as the basic settlement processes are concerned, performance is being monitored through workflow analysis. Our own benchmarking will provide the information that will highlight any potential problems the client might have experienced as a result. The unknown is what the client has perceived as a problem or what has occurred, but, for whatever reason, it is not identified in monitoring/benchmarking. It is important that within the client culture there is recognition of the need to understand the client's business. Only by doing this will the client facing team be able to appreciate what may be a potential problem for the client, but is of no consequence to the broker. Another important factor in managing the relationship is to encourage open and frank discussion at all levels. Surprisingly, clients may not voice concerns as one might imagine. Therefore, whilst the feedback from the team members and accounts managers is essential, it is still also imperative that the senior managers periodically meet with their counterparts at the client and encourage discussion of any concerns, etc. Performance measurement and benchmarking is therefore a combination of:

- management information generated by workflow analysis;
- feedback from the client team;
- feedback from periodic senior manager/client liaison meetings;
- internal feedback across the organisation.

The collation of the information, assessment and action must take place on a regular, possibly daily, basis and must be discussed with other client facing areas in the organisation. It is doubtful if many clients have only a single relationship with the organisation, and to ignore the relationships with other non-derivative areas is fool-hardy to say the least. We stated earlier that the client would look at the whole relationship with the counter-part, quite likely on a global basis, so feedback must be on a similar basis. It is important from a risk management point of view to share information and compare situations with respect to a counterpart. It is just as important to do so from a client service viewpoint because, as we have already noted, client service and customer relationship management is a team effort.

Escalation procedures

It is vital that the manager establishes a procedure whereby all issues are reported and documented and that appropriate action is signed off. This may well be by maintaining a 'client log'. Issues cover such things as:

- complaints;
- errors;
- failure to meet benchmark standard.

Action will range from written communication through to arranging a client meeting if the issue is serious. There may equally be a 'no action' decision. By establishing the 'client log' as a discipline in the team, the manager has every chance to pre-empt and prevent problems as well as providing a proactive management and response to the client in the event of a problem or failure to meet standard levels.

'Client logs' must be completed daily and record 'no issues' as well as matters that require logging. It is important to set this 'no issues' reporting as it can be used as a high-profile means to measure performance.

Client liaison programmes

The important question here is what are the liaison meetings to achieve?

Box 9.3 Work session.

Consider the following statements:

- liaison meetings are only needed when a problem has occurred;
- liaison meetings are to allow a preamble before some kind of corporate entertaining;
- liaison meetings are to enable the broker to make a presentation on the developments to the services;
- liaison meetings are an informal opportunity to discuss issues.

Decide which of these statements you most agree with and then prepare an Objective List (internal use) and an Agenda (to be sent to the client) for such a meeting.

Front-office client team

Any client liaison programme will need to be worked out with reference to internal co-operation and relationship with the sales desk. Simple co-ordination of client meetings and information can be supplemented by regular meetings to discuss the client's activities, feedback, etc. The successful development of the relationship with the client is conditional on the development of the relationship between operations and the sales desk team internally.

Industry issues

Understanding the client's business, as we have stressed before, is essential to providing the kind of service the client will benefit from and appreciate.

The manager needs to create the environment where awareness of developments in the industry (in particular, those that will have a significant impact on the client base) is obtainable.

This can be achieved through:

- giving access to industry journals and websites of relevant organisations – such as the Association of British Insurers, Association of Unit Trust and Investment Funds (*AUTIF*), etc.;
- being members of industry associations;

- nominating people for membership of committees and working parties.

The ability of team members at all levels to discuss business issues with clients counts towards creating the desired professional image.

Training the team

There is a constant need for training in client teams.

This training encompasses not only relevant business skills but personal skills – such as languages – as well. Part of the manager's role will be to establish co-ordinated, structured training programmes for client facing teams.

Analysing the competition

Clients will inevitably make comparisons between the services available from brokers. They will analyse the latest developments in technology-based services, costs, innovative services like OTC pricing, clearing, etc.

The manager must be prepared to establish a process to provide continuous monitoring of the market place, both domestically and internationally.

This monitoring will feed into the ongoing development of the services.

Developing the service

There can be a danger that a client team is set up with adequate resources, good levels of activity from quality clients and suitable procedures, but without adequate planning. As a result, business expands, clients increase in number and demands, and the service is under pressure. This leads to problems, reputation damage and, ultimately, loss of business. This is perhaps an obvious observation, and yet it can happen quickly if there is no planning and development of the service by the manager. This planning can be achieved by creating a business plan for the service encompassing:

- products to be offered;
- products to be developed;
- personnel development;
- technology development;
- client business awareness;
- relationship management;
- performance measurement.

Such plans should cover the short-, medium- and long-term and should not be a 'wish list', but a carefully thought out plan including costs, revenue and risk management analysis.

Box 9.4 Work session.

Consider what would be needed from operations to support a Prime Brokerage product and also what a user of the product would expect from the Prime Broker.

What are the potential problems in customer relationships?

There are numerous potential problems ranging from minor issues to full-blown complaints. Identifying and dealing with each is the key to successful relationship management.

If we assume that problems will fall into various categories, we might come up with a matrix like the one in Table 9.1.

Any of the above can be minor or major issues and can occur because of either the broker or the client, or both. It may also be the fault of an agent (internal/external) – such as custodians, clearing agents, executing brokers, etc.

Table 9.1 An illustration of the types of problems that can occur between a client and a broker and why they might occur.

Category	Probable source or cause
Incorrect data	System problems, human error
Delayed data	System problems
Late settlement	Incorrect instructions
Missed corporate actions	Human error
Failure to respond to query	Human error
Argument over process or procedure	Personality clash
Interest claim	Delayed settlement/incorrect data
Problems with 'give-ups'	Poor communication/human error

Clearly, the 'give-up' process offers scope for problems, so does the potential for a personality clash, although in the latter case active management of the client team should avoid an account manager being unsuited to the client.

Communication is often at the heart of many problems. It may be internal or external, or both, where the breakdown occurs.

Either way it needs to be stressed to the team that communication is vitally important to the efficient operation of the service.

The timing of any response is also vital. It is quite possible to pre-empt an issue becoming a problem simply by advising the client if, say, a system problem is likely to delay data.

Managing risk within the customer relationship

Whilst the provision of a high-quality client service is the objective of the team, doing so in a controlled manner is the overriding goal.

It is not good enough to take decisions on matters with a view to not upsetting the client. Avoiding unnecessary and contentious actions is fine only if there is no inherent risk and, where there may be a risk, that action is cleared at the highest level.

The manager has the responsibility for maintaining a good working relationship with the client in an environment that reflects the regulatory requirements and risk parameters of the organisation.

Offering client services like global clearing is exposing the organisation to certain risks over and above that for its normal business.

It is important to accept that client business is a counter-part risk and the added value services offered as part of the client package are increasing that risk.

The controls and procedures put in place by the manager to protect the organisation from such risk must form the basis of the customer relationship. Only in very exceptional cases or where there is realistically little or no risk in waiving a control can such a decision be acceptable.

A client pressurising the broker to waive those controls in any other circumstance is unacceptable, whoever that client may be. Likewise, client service personnel cannot have the authority to waive controls and the manager should only authorise such a decision after first clearing it with the group risk managers.

If enforcing the procedure means that a client moves elsewhere, then that is a risk the manager must take after fully consulting with the client, the sales desk and the risk manager. Consider the following potential situations:

1. Client fails to pay a derivative margin call on due day and due day + 1, citing problems at the custodian, but says they will definitely settle tomorrow.

2. Client fails to sign and return swap confirmation sent out 10 days ago.

3. Client needs to withdraw a maturing Treasury Bill which is collateral for a stock borrowing and promises to replace it with a new one next day.

4. Client cannot provide the booking for a contingent trade in UK equities and US equities as the fund managers have not completed the order.

Box 9.5 Work session.

Consider the implications of the above situations and decide on the course of action you, as the manager, would take.

Client visits

We looked earlier at the client liaison visit and the objectives such a visit should have. Other important issues surround communication with the sales desk and other client groups within the organisation over planned visits. It hardly inspires a positive image when the client receives two visits, sales desk and operations, on the same day from the same counterpart. This is particularly the case if the two teams are not aware that each other are making the visit.

In this chapter we have looked at an overview of customer relationships, a key area of the operations manager's role. Successfully managing this area will depend on the choice of people, the policy on service products and support, and the constant monitoring of performance, industry initiatives and developments, and changes to the business profiles of individual clients.

Years of building reputation and creditability can be destroyed in a very short space of time. The managers must convey this to ALL the team and make it especially clear to the client services team that they are nothing without the support and skills of the rest of the team. Likewise, a super support team are wasted if the client service team cannot retain and gain new clients. Building a successful customer-orientated operations team takes patience and often considerable tact. It needs to be managed and developed with drive and innovation allied to discipline and attention to detail. Over-selling the services will lead to problems; under-resourcing the structure will also cause problems. Failure to have adequate procedures and controls and to oversee relationship management will be disastrous.

Chapter

10

....

OPERATIONS IN THE FUTURE

Nothing stays the same for long. It is a fact all of us in the financial services industry know to be very true, especially so over the last 20 years or so. We have already seen in the previous chapters just how much change is currently happening and, indeed, some of the change that will happen in the future.

As we move towards more automation in the markets, centralised clearing and dematerialisation in the clearing processes, so the straight-through processing (STP) projects will become complete. These STP projects will deliver greater capacity, which will be filled by new products and increased use of existing products.

Probably the biggest challenge the operations manager faces moving forward, however, is the conversion of teams, processes and procedures from various levels of paper and manual processes to more client-focused and risk management functions. Overcoming the natural resistance to change is going to be a significant challenge, particularly as there will be no 'big bang' change, but rather a change over time.

As the operations function becomes more professional and more high profile in its contribution to successful businesses, demands for greater and more diverse skills will arise. The manager needs to focus today on what will be needed in the future. Training and re-training individuals and teams to meet new requirements will obviously be a large part of the manager's role.

As regulatory environments evolve, other challenges will occur both in terms of ensuring that the operations function is complying with the environment, but also in the need to maintain the levels of competency laid down.

The ever-increasing competitiveness in the industry will also create challenges. As less paper and faster settlement become the norm, so the ability to provide new, innovative and reliable client services products from operations, to supplement the products offered from the front office, will become absolutely critical.

Systems as always will be central to the whole operations environment, and STP projects, Internet/intranet settlement and client services facilities will be at the heart of the future operations setup.

As the industry moves forward, the increasing demands for high-skilled teams, ever-more sophisticated systems to support increased volumes in diverse products and more complex client services products will lead to reviews of the merits of insourcing and outsourcing. The custody industry has seen changes in the past caused by reassessment of viability as costs increased and revenue was squeezed. Many organisations opted to close their custody operations, and it is likely that similar decisions will be taken by banks and fund management companies in the future.

We know that operational risk is now a significant subject in the industry. The importance of the subject will not diminish, especially in the light of the terrible events on the 11th September 2001 that not only so graphically illustrated the need for disaster recovery sites, but also showed just what a valuable commodity people are. In fact, risk and the people management process are the challenges of the future in a changing world full of uncertainty. This includes recognising the value of everyone in the process chain in terms of not only their qualities that may be lost, but also in the immense ability of people to overcome a setback, however big, and win through because of sheer willpower, pride and skills. Harnessing the talents of people and developing people will become a greater part of the operations manager's brief in years to come. More sophisticated use of more complex and varied products – coupled with shortening settlement cycles, STP, more demanding regulatory environments and greater emphasis on the delivery and use of client service products – will create demands on people and systems, the like of which we do not currently see.

Today, there are many demands on individuals, systems and managers. At present, the problems and challenges stem from the evolution of clearing and settlement, an evolution that is neither consistent nor complete in many parts of the industry and certainly not world-wide.

The GSCS Benchmarks[1] show us that standards are rising, but that there is still a gulf between different countries, markets and products. Centralising clearing will undoubtedly address this, but that will not happen uniformly whilst politics and vested interests are at work. The next 10 years will see central counterparty clearing for all major products traded on-exchange and

---

[1] GSCS publishes a range of benchmarks covering custody, settlement, specialised risk, etc. – see *www.gscsbenchmarks.com*

for many over-the-counter products as well. The greater, independent risk management afforded by the use of a central counterparty will need to be mirrored by enhanced risk management in the banks, brokers and institutional clients. Private client business, either in the private banking/broking fields or through the Internet shops, will no doubt continue to grow. Operational risk capital will occupy thoughts, minds and not a little money, and faster settlement, seamless delivery of information, less time to analyse and resolve errors, highly competitive and pressurised environments will all be there for the manager to manage.

With so much change, much of it to the fundamental structures of the markets, it will probably be the pace of that change that will present the greatest challenge for the operations manager. If we consider how London has relatively rapidly moved from a large, domestic-run market to one that is now dominated by foreign banks, we can understand why it is argued in some quarters that the markets themselves may move out of the UK. On the plus side for London is of course the huge pool of expertise here, plus the fact that many of the 'foreign' owners are, in fact, American and the infrastructure including language suits them. However, business is global and if the operations arms of foreign banks are to have any significant role in London rather than, say, Frankfurt, operations teams have to be developed that are versatile, innovative, highly trained and delivering a consistently high standard. The need to be cost-effective goes without saying.

The challenge for the future, then, is managing rapid change and re-training and equipping operations teams. The market downturn through the latter part of 2000 has not helped the case for high expenditure to develop and deliver the operations teams of tomorrow. Managers may be used to tight budgets, but in this case they must fight the finance director by developing coherent and cost-effective policies and business plans to take operations to the next stage.

Within those business plans must be the way in which operations delivers critical input to the business.

This can be illustrated by focusing on key issues such as:

- capital for operational risk;
- delivery of client added value services;
- increased risk management role.

Outsourcing is an inevitable option for senior management in most organisations, but equally insourcing can be a counter-option.

Other key factors will be those that all managers and supervisors have faced before, such as managing expectations, balancing skill sets, responding to business flows and forging relationships with counterparties.

The future, like the present, will be a huge challenge, but then again professionals relish challenge.

Appendix

A

UCITS III: INTRODUCTION

Source: Ernst & Young

The objective of the original Undertakings for Collective Investment in Transferable Securities (*UCITS*) directive, which was adopted in 1985 ('1985 Directive' – visit *www.bis.org*), was to allow for open-ended funds investing in transferable securities to be subject to the same regulation in every Member State. It was hoped that once such legislative uniformity was established throughout Europe, funds authorised in one Member State could be sold to the public in each Member State without further authorisation, thereby furthering the EU's goal of a single market for financial services in Europe.

The reality differed somewhat from the expectation due primarily to individual marketing rules in each Member State that created obstacles to cross-border marketing of UCITS. In addition, the limited definition of permitted investments for UCITS weakened the marketing possibilities of a UCITS. Accordingly, in the early 1990s and in recognition of the weaknesses of the 1985 Directive, proposals were developed to amend the 1985 Directive and more successfully achieve the harmonisation of laws throughout Europe. These discussions, although leading to a draft UCITS II directive, were subsequently abandoned as being too ambitious when the Council of Ministers could not reach a common position.

In July 1998, the EU Commission published a new proposal, which was drafted in two parts (a product proposal and a service provider proposal), which sought to amend the 1985 Directive.

These proposals were finally adopted in December 2001 and are generally referred to as UCITS III. UCITS III consists of the following two directives (the 'Directives'):

- Directive 2001/107/EC of the European Parliament and of the Council (the 'Management Directive'); and
- Directive 2001/108/EC of the European Parliament and of the Council (the 'Product Directive').

The *Management Directive* seeks to give management companies a 'European passport' to operate throughout the EU and widens the activities which they are allowed to undertake. It also introduces the concept of a simplified prospectus, which is intended to provide more accessible, comprehensive information in a simplified format to assist the cross-border marketing of UCITS throughout Europe.

The primary aim of the *Product Directive* is to remove barriers to the cross-border marketing of units of collective investment funds by allowing funds to invest in a wider range of financial instruments. Under the new Directive, it is possible to establish money market funds, derivatives funds, index-tracking funds and funds of funds as UCITS.

The ultimate success of UCITS III will depend on the way in which each Member State implements the Directives. Many Member States have already begun to incorporate the new Directives into their domestic legislation,[1]

---

[1] For more information on the status of implementation of UCITS III in individual Member States, please contact your local Ernst & Young office for a copy of *UCITS III: Status of Implementation* or visit their website, *www.ey.com*, where the information is updated on a regular basis in line with developments in Member States.

ahead of the deadline of August 2003. Few, however, have issued guidelines on the practical application of the more complex aspects of the Directives, such as the risk management reporting requirements in relation to derivatives (Product Directive) and the substance and 'passportability' of management companies (Management Directive).

This appendix is intended as a reference document for fund promoters, highlighting both the challenges and the opportunities which UCITS III presents.

Some of the issues discussed are complex in nature and are set out in general terms for guidance purposes only.

The Product Directive expands the range and type of financial instruments permitted under the 1985 Directive to include the following:

- transferable securities and money market instruments;
- bank deposits;
- units of other investment funds;
- financial derivative instruments;
- index tracking funds.

In addition, the definition of 'transferable securities' has been amended and is now defined as:

- shares in companies and other securities equivalent to shares in companies;
- bonds and other forms of securitised debt; and
- any other negotiable securities which carry the right

to acquire any such transferable securities by subscription or exchange.

This definition does not include techniques and instruments used for efficient portfolio management.

AGGREGATE LIMITS

The Product Directive applies individual investment restriction limits to each financial instrument. These individual investment restriction limits are subject to overall combined limits of 20% and 35% of the Net Asset Value (*NAV*) of a UCITS Fund.

A UCITS Fund is permitted to invest an overall combined limit of 35% of its assets in the following investments:

- transferable securities and money market instruments;
- deposits; and/or
- derivative instruments

issued by, or made with, the same body.

A maximum limit of 20% of the NAV of a UCITS Fund applies to the following investments:

- transferable securities and money market instruments;
- deposits; and/or
- exposures arising from OTC derivative transactions

issued by, or made with, the same body.

In summary, the 20% limit applies to combined investments including OTC derivatives whilst the 35% limit is an overall limit that refers to derivatives traded on a regulated market, as well as OTC derivatives.

Group companies are regarded as single issuers for the purposes of calculating individual and aggregate restriction limits.

TRANSFERABLE SECURITIES AND MONEY MARKET INSTRUMENTS

Money market instruments are described in the Product Directive as instruments normally dealt in on the money market that are liquid and have a value that can be accurately determined at any time:

- a UCITS may invest a maximum of 5% of its assets in transferable securities and money market instruments issued by a single issuer. Member States may increase this limit to 10%, but the total value of positions in excess of 5% must not exceed 40% of NAV;
- Member States may permit a UCITS to invest a maximum of 35% of its assets in transferable securities and money market instruments issued or guaranteed by an EU Member State or its local authorities, by a non-Member State or by public international bodies to which one or more Member States belong.

Subject to certain conditions a UCITS may invest up to

100% of its net assets in different transferable securities and money market instruments issued or guaranteed by any Member State, its local authorities, non-Member State or public international body, of which one or more Member States are members.

Where money market instruments are not traded on a regulated market, investment is only permitted if the issuer is regulated and provided that the money market instruments are:

- issued or guaranteed by a central, regional or local authority or central bank of a Member State;
- issued by an undertaking, any securities of which are dealt in on a regulated market;
- issued or guaranteed by an establishment subject to prudential supervision in accordance with criteria defined by the European Union;
- issued by other bodies belonging to the categories approved by the UCITS' competent authority.

BANK DEPOSITS

Deposits with credit institutions are permitted provided the credit institution has its registered office in an EU Member State or, if located in a non-Member State, it is subject to equivalent prudential rules of an EU Member State. The deposits must be repayable on demand or have the right to be withdrawn and may have a maturity of up to 12 months.

Not more than 20% of the UCITS' investments in deposits may be placed with the same credit institution (including the UCITS' custodian).

FINANCIAL DERIVATIVES INSTRUMENTS

Under the 1985 Directive, UCITS were permitted to invest in derivatives for the purposes of efficient portfolio management only.

The Product Directive still permits UCITS to invest in derivatives for efficient portfolio management. However, the Product Directive extends the nature of the investments to include financial derivative instruments including equivalent cash-settled instruments dealt in on a regulated market and/or over-the-counter derivatives ('OTC derivatives').

The conditions and limits set out in the Product Directive for derivatives must apply even where derivatives are used for efficient portfolio management or are embedded in transferable securities or money market instruments.

The conditions set out in the Product Directive in relation to the calculation of the exposure of derivative instruments include the following:

- the global exposure relating to the derivative instruments must not exceed the total NAV of the UCITS Fund;
- the exposure must be calculated taking into account

the current value of the underlying assets, the counter-party risk, future market movements and the time available to liquidate the positions; and

- in the case of OTC derivatives, the exposure to a single counterparty must not exceed 10% of NAV if the counterparty is an EU credit institution or equivalent, or 5% of NAV in other cases.

For OTC derivative transactions, the counterparties must be subject to prudential supervision, the OTC derivatives must be subject to reliable and verifiable valuation on a daily basis and must be capable of being closed out at any time.

The permitted underlying investments of OTC deriva-tives include financial indices, interest rates, foreign ex-change rates or currencies in which the UCITS Fund may invest according to its constitutional documents. The selection of financial indices as underlying investments for OTC derivatives is a management technique. How-ever, competent authorities may require the assets underlying the financial indices to be assets that a UCITS Fund may directly invest in pursuant to the Product Directive.

Special risk management reporting to the competent authority is required in relation to investment in deriva-tives. A UCITS must demonstrate that it has appropriate risk management controls and valuation procedures in place. The risk management processes to be applied are not, however, laid down in the Directive and will, there-fore, be determined by Member States on an individual basis. It should be noted that where financial derivatives do not form the main part of a fund's investments but are, rather, employed for the purposes of efficient portfolio management, these risk management procedures will still apply and will override any previous rules for derivatives used for efficient portfolio management.

It should also be noted that short sales continue to be prohibited as investments for UCITS Funds.

FUNDS OF FUNDS

Under the Product Directive, a fund of funds can now qualify for UCITS status subject to the following conditions:

- a fund of funds, established as a UCITS, is permitted to invest up to 10% of its NAV in a single UCITS or equivalent, provided the equivalent structure is subject to risk diversification, leverage and regulatory controls similar to that of a UCITS. Member States are permitted under the Product Directive to increase this 10% limit to 20%;
- total investment in funds other than UCITS must not exceed 30% of the NAV of the fund;
- a UCITS may not acquire more than 25% of the units of any single UCITS; and
- a UCITS fund of funds may not invest in an underlying fund if that underlying fund is permitted to invest more than 10% of its NAV in other funds of funds.

INDEX TRACKING FUNDS

In the case of funds, the aim of which is to replicate an index, an investment limit of 20% of the NAV of the UCITS Fund applies where the investment consists of shares and/or debt securities issued by the same body. This limit may be increased by Member States to 35% where it is justified by exceptional market conditions. The index must be sufficiently diversified, represent an adequate benchmark and be published in an appropriate manner.

It is the responsibility of each Member State to assess the suitability of a particular index as the basis for a UCITS.

USE OF SUBSIDIARIES

The Product Directive provides that a UCITS may have a subsidiary for the purposes of management, advice or marketing, with regard to the repurchase of units, in the country where the subsidiary is located. Although there is some uncertainty as to whether certain existing subsidiary structures will be permitted in the future, it seems clear that the Product Directive removes the opportunity which was previously available for a UCITS to establish a subsidiary company in a non-EU jurisdiction for the purposes of efficient portfolio management, including access to tax treaties.

The purpose of the Management Directive is threefold. Firstly, it seeks to widen the scope of activities that may be undertaken by management companies; secondly, it seeks to strengthen the availability of an EU 'passport' for such companies to operate throughout the EU; and, thirdly, it introduces a requirement for a simplified prospectus, which is intended to provide more accessible, comprehensive information to investors as a means of enhancing marketing opportunities for UCITS.

PERMITTED ACTIVITIES OF MANAGEMENT COMPANIES

The Management Directive extends the permitted activities of management companies to make it consistent with the Investment Services Directive, to include the management of UCITS, investment funds other than UCITS, managed accounts (including private pension funds) and non-core activities such as custody, administration, investment advice and transfer agency services.

EU PASSPORT FOR MANAGEMENT COMPANIES

The Management Directive establishes a passport which will enable a management company to carry on activities in Member States other than the country in which the management company is established. It should be noted, however, that a UCITS will be deemed to be situated in the Member State in which its management company has its registered office. The passport is designed to operate on the basis that, once a management company is authorised in its home state, that authorisation extends to all

Member States, subject to compliance with host state notifications.

Amendments to the rules on delegation should also be noted. Although a management company may delegate some of its functions, they must not do so to the extent that it becomes a 'letterbox' entity. Management companies should, therefore, put in place measures to monitor the relevant activities of any entity to which functions have been delegated and ensure that the entity is qualified and capable of performing the duties that have been delegated to it, so as to maintain the level of 'control' and 'supervision' that is required to be demonstrated by every management company. It should be noted, therefore, that the ultimate responsibility will remain with the management company. What constitutes substance, control and supervision may, however, differ between Member States.

SIMPLIFIED PROSPECTUS

The Management Directive also introduces the concept of a simplified prospectus, which must be investor friendly whilst at the same time include all relevant information to enable investors to make an informed judgement. The investor must always be offered a copy of the simplified prospectus prior to the conclusion of the sale of units. In addition, the simplified prospectus should include a statement informing the investor that more detailed information on the UCITS is contained in the full prospectus, a copy of which must be made available free of charge.

The Directive identifies the key information for the simplified prospectus to be as follows:

- country of registration of the UCITS and identity of the management company, service providers, auditors and fund promoter;
- investment objective and policy, risk warnings and investor profile;
- tax regime, commissions and fees and expenses;
- subscription/redemption/conversion details, distribution policy and availability of NAV per share details; and
- name of Regulator and where the prospectus and fund reports may be obtained.

Arguably, the greatest advantage of the simplified prospectus is that it will remove any opportunity for Member States to impose further documentation requirements on funds wishing to market their shares throughout other Member States.

CAPITAL ADEQUACY REQUIREMENTS

The Management Directive introduces capital adequacy requirements for the management companies of UCITS.

A management company must now have an initial share capital of at least €125,000.

Where the management company's assets under management exceed €250 million it must provide additional own funds at a rate of 0.02% of the amount of the excess. The aggregate of initial capital and own funds to be maintained by a management company is subject to a maximum of €10 million and a minimum of a quarter of the preceding year's fixed overheads (i.e., 13 weeks' expenditure).

An investment company that does not designate a management company to be responsible for the management of the investment company will have a capital adequacy requirement of €300,000. Such an investment company is managed by its board of directors, but the UCITS management passport will not apply.

FURTHER INVESTOR PROTECTION MEASURES

In addition to the measures outlined above, the Management Directive also requires that a comprehensive risk management process is established, whereby the management company may monitor and calculate the overall risk of the fund's positions at any time.

Reporting requirements have also been extended. The management company must report regularly to the regulator on the individual portfolios which it manages, the types of derivatives used, their underlying risks, the quantitative limits and the methods established to estimate the risks associated with those instruments.

Appendix

B

EXTRACTS FROM SARBANES–OXLEY ACT OF 2002

Source: American Institute of Certified Public Accountants

Section 3: Commission Rules and Enforcement

A violation of Rules of the Public Company Accounting Oversight Board ('Board') is treated as a violation of the 1934 Act, giving rise to the same penalties that may be imposed for violations of that Act.

Section 101: Establishment; Board Membership

The Board will have five financially-literate members, appointed for 5-year terms. Two of the members must be, or have been, certified public accountants, and the remaining three must not be, and cannot have been, CPAs. The Chair may be held by one of the CPA members, provided that he or she has not been engaged as a practicing CPA for 5 years.

The Board's members will serve on a full-time basis.

No member may, concurrent with service on the Board, 'share in any of the profits of, or receive payments from, a public accounting firm,' other than 'fixed continuing payments,' such as retirement payments.

Members of the Board are appointed by the Commission, 'after consultation with' the Chairman of the Federal Reserve Board and the Secretary of the Treasury.

Members may be removed by the Commission 'for good cause.'

Section 103: Auditing, Quality Control, and Independence Standards and Rules

The Board shall:

(1) register public accounting firms;
(2) establish, or adopt, by rule, 'auditing, quality control, ethics, independence, and other standards relating to the preparation of audit reports for issuers';
(3) conduct inspections of accounting firms;
(4) conduct investigations and disciplinary proceedings, and impose appropriate sanctions;
(5) perform such other duties or functions as necessary or appropriate;
(6) enforce compliance with the Act, the rules of the Board, professional standards, and the securities laws relating to the preparation and issuance of audit reports and the obligations and liabilities of accountants with respect thereto;
(7) set the budget and manage the operations of the Board and the staff of the Board.

Auditing standards. The Board would be required to 'cooperate on an on-going basis' with designated professional groups of accountants and any advisory groups convened in connection with standard-setting, and although the Board can 'to the extent that it determines appropriate' adopt standards proposed by those groups, the Board will have authority to amend, modify, repeal, and reject any standards suggested by the groups. The Board must report on its standard-setting activity to the Commission on an annual basis.

The Board must require registered public accounting firms to 'prepare, and maintain for a period of not less than 7 years, audit work papers, and other information related to any audit report, in sufficient detail to support the conclusions reached in such report.'

The Board must require a 2nd partner review and approval of audit reports and registered accounting firms must adopt quality control standards.

The Board must adopt an audit standard to implement the internal control review required by section 404(b). This standard must require the auditor evaluate whether the internal control structure and procedures include records that accurately and fairly reflect the transactions of the issuer, provide reasonable assurance that the transactions are recorded in a manner that will permit the preparation of financial statements in accordance with GAAP, and a description of any material weaknesses in the internal controls.

Section 109(d): Funding; Annual Accounting Support Fee for the Board

In order to audit a public company, a public accounting firm must register with the Board. The Board shall collect 'a registration fee' and 'an annual fee' from each registered public accounting firm, in amounts that are 'sufficient' to recover the costs of processing and reviewing applications and annual reports.

The Board shall also establish by rule a reasonable 'annual accounting support fee' as may be necessary or appropriate to maintain the Board. This fee will be assessed on issuers only.

Section 104: Inspections of Registered Public Accounting Firms

Annual quality reviews (inspections) must be conducted for firms that audit more than 100 issues, all others must be conducted every 3 years. The SEC and/or the Board may order a special inspection of any firm at any time.

Section 105(d): Investigations and Disciplinary Proceedings; Reporting of Sanctions

All documents and information prepared or received by the Board shall be 'confidential and privileged as an evidentiary matter (and shall not be subject to civil discovery or other legal process) in any proceeding in any Federal or State court or administrative agency, ... unless and until presented in connection with a public proceeding or [otherwise] released' in connection with a disciplinary action. However, all such documents and information can be made available to the SEC, the US Attorney General, and other federal and appropriate state agencies.

Disciplinary hearings will be closed unless the Board orders that they be public, for good cause, and with the consent of the parties.

Sanctions can be imposed by the Board on a firm if it fails to reasonably supervise any associated person with regard to auditing or quality control standards, or otherwise.

No sanctions report will be made available to the public unless and until stays pending appeal have been lifted.

Section 106: Foreign Public Accounting Firms

The bill would subject foreign accounting firms who audit a US company to registrations with the Board. This would include foreign firms that perform some audit work, such as in a foreign subsidiary of a US company, that is relied on by the primary auditor.

Section 107(d): Censure of the Board and Other Sanctions

The SEC shall have 'oversight and enforcement authority over the Board.' The SEC can, by rule or order, give the Board additional responsibilities. The SEC may require the Board to keep certain records, and it has the power to inspect the Board itself, in the same manner as it can with regard to SROs such as the NASD.

The Board, in its rulemaking process, is to be treated 'as if the Board were a "registered securities association"' – that is, a self-regulatory organization. The Board is required to file proposed rules and proposed rule changes with the SEC. The SEC may approve, reject, or amend such rules.

The Board must notify the SEC of pending investigations involving potential violations of the securities laws, and coordinate its investigation with the SEC Division of Enforcement as necessary to protect an ongoing SEC investigation.

The SEC may, by order, 'censure or impose limitations upon the activities, functions, and operations of the Board' if it finds that the Board has violated the Act or the securities laws, or if the Board has failed to ensure the compliance of accounting firms with applicable rules without reasonable justification.

Section 107(c): Commission Review of Disciplinary Action Taken by the Board

The Board must notify the SEC when it imposes 'any final sanction' on any accounting firm or associated person. The Board's findings and sanctions are subject to review by the SEC.

The SEC may enhance, modify, cancel, reduce, or require remission of such a sanction.

Section 108: Accounting Standards

The SEC is authorized to 'recognize, as "generally accepted" ... any accounting principles' that are established by a standard-setting body that meets the bill's criteria, which include requirements that the body:

(1) be a private entity;
(2) be governed by a board of trustees (or equivalent body), the majority of whom are not or have not been associated persons with a public accounting firm for the past 2 years;
(3) be funded in a manner similar to the Board;

(4) have adopted procedures to ensure prompt consideration of changes to accounting principles by a majority
vote;

(5) consider, when adopting standards, the need to keep
them current and the extent to which international
convergence of standards is necessary or appropriate.

Section 201: Services outside the Scope of Practice of Auditors; Prohibited Activities

It shall be 'unlawful' for a registered public accounting
firm to provide any non-audit service to an issuer con-
temporaneously with the audit, including:

(1) bookkeeping or other services related to the accounting records or financial statements of the audit client;

(2) financial information systems design and implementation;

(3) appraisal or valuation services, fairness opinions, or
contribution-in-kind reports;

(4) actuarial services;

(5) internal audit outsourcing services;

(6) management functions or human resources;

(7) broker or dealer, investment adviser, or investment
banking services;

(8) legal services and expert services unrelated to the
audit;

(9) any other service that the Board determines, by regulation, is impermissible.

The Board may, on a case-by-case basis, exempt from
these prohibitions any person, issuer, public accounting

firm, or transaction, subject to review by the Commission.

It will not be unlawful to provide other non-audit services if they are pre-approved by the audit committee in the following manner. The bill allows an accounting firm to 'engage in any non-audit service, including tax services,' that is not listed above, only if the activity is pre-approved by the audit committee of the issuer. The audit committee will disclose to investors in periodic reports its decision to pre-approve non-audit services. Statutory insurance company regulatory audits are treated as an audit service, and thus do not require pre-approval.

The pre-approval requirement is waived with respect to the provision of non-audit services for an issuer if the aggregate amount of all such non-audit services provided to the issuer constitutes less than 5% of the total amount of revenues paid by the issuer to its auditor (calculated on the basis of revenues paid by the issuer during the fiscal year when the non-audit services are performed), such services were not recognized by the issuer at the time of the engagement to be non-audit services; and such services are promptly brought to the attention of the audit committee and approved prior to completion of the audit.

The authority to pre-approve services can be delegated to one or more members of the audit committee, but any decision by the delegate must be presented to the full audit committee.

Section 203: Audit Partner Rotation

The lead audit or coordinating partner and the reviewing partner must leave the audit process by rotation every 5 years.

Section 204: Auditor Reports to Audit Committees

The accounting firm must report to the audit committee all 'critical accounting policies and practices to be used, all alternative treatments of financial information within [GAAP] that have been discussed with management, ramifications of the use of such alternative disclosures and treatments, and the treatment preferred' by the firm.

Section 206: Conflicts of Interest

The CEO, Controller, CFO, Chief Accounting Officer or person in an equivalent position cannot have been employed by the company's audit firm during the 1-year period preceding the audit.

Section 207: Study of Mandatory Rotation of Registered Public Accountants

The GAO will do a study on the potential effects of requiring the mandatory rotation of audit firms.

Section 209: Consideration by Appropriate State Regulatory Authorities

State regulators are directed to make an independent determination as to whether the Board's standards shall be applied to small and mid-size non-registered accounting firms.

Section 301: Public Company Audit Committees

Each member of the audit committee shall be a member of the board of directors of the issuer, and shall otherwise be independent.

'Independent' is defined as not receiving, other than for service on the board, any consulting, advisory, or other compensatory fee from the issuer, and as not being an affiliated person of the issuer, or any subsidiary thereof.

The SEC may make exemptions for certain individuals on a case-by-case basis.

The audit committee of an issuer shall be directly responsible for the appointment, compensation, and oversight of the work of any registered public accounting firm employed by that issuer.

The audit committee shall establish procedures for the 'receipt, retention, and treatment of complaints' received by the issuer regarding accounting, internal controls, and auditing.

Each audit committee shall have the authority to engage independent counsel or other advisors, as it determines necessary to carry out its duties.

Each issuer shall provide appropriate funding to the audit committee.

Section 302: Corporate Responsibility for Financial Reports

The CEO and CFO of each issuer shall prepare a statement to accompany the audit report to certify the 'appropriateness of the financial statements and disclosures contained in the periodic report, and that those financial statements and disclosures fairly present, in all material respects, the operations and financial condition of the issuer.' A violation of this section must be knowing and intentional to give rise to liability.

Section 303: Improper Influence on Conduct of Audits

It shall be unlawful for any officer or director of an issuer to take any action to fraudulently influence, coerce, manipulate, or mislead any auditor engaged in the performance of an audit for the purpose of rendering the financial statements materially misleading.

Section 305: Officer and Director Bars and Penalties; Equitable Relief

If an issuer is required to prepare a restatement due to 'material noncompliance' with financial reporting requirements, the CEO and CFO shall 'reimburse the issuer for any bonus or other incentive-based or equity-based compensation received' during the 12 months following the issuance or filing of the non-compliant document and 'any profits realized from the sale of securities of the issuer' during that period.

In any action brought by the SEC for violation of the

securities laws, federal courts are authorized to 'grant any equitable relief that may be appropriate or necessary for the benefit of investors.'

Section 305: Officer and Director Bars and Penalties

The SEC may issue an order to prohibit, conditionally or unconditionally, permanently or temporarily, any person who has violated section 10(b) of the 1934 Act from acting as an officer or director of an issuer if the SEC has found that such person's conduct 'demonstrates unfitness' to serve as an officer or director of any such issuer.

Section 306: Insider Trades during Pension Fund Blackout Periods Prohibited

Prohibits the purchase or sale of stock by officers and directors and other insiders during blackout periods. Any profits resulting from sales in violation of this section 'shall inure to and be recoverable by the issuer.' If the issuer fails to bring suit or prosecute diligently, a suit to recover such profit may be instituted by 'the owner of any security of the issuer.'

Section 401(a): Disclosures in Periodic Reports; Disclosures Required

Each financial report that is required to be prepared in accordance with GAAP shall 'reflect all material correcting adjustments ... that have been identified by a registered accounting firm ...'

'Each annual and quarterly financial report ... shall disclose all material off-balance sheet transactions' and 'other relationships' with 'unconsolidated entities' that may have a material current or future effect on the financial condition of the issuer.

The SEC shall issue rules providing that pro forma financial information must be presented so as not to 'contain an untrue statement' or omit to state a material fact necessary in order to make the pro forma financial information not misleading.

Section 401 (c): Study and Report on Special Purpose Entities

The SEC shall study off-balance sheet disclosures to determine (a) extent of off-balance sheet transactions (including assets, liabilities, leases, losses and the use of special purpose entities); and (b) whether generally accepted accounting rules result in financial statements of issuers reflecting the economics of such off-balance sheet transactions to investors in a transparent fashion and make a report containing recommendations to the Congress.

Section 402(a): Prohibition on Personal Loans to Executives

Generally, it will be unlawful for an issuer to extend credit to any director or executive officer. Consumer credit companies may make home improvement and consumer credit loans and issue credit cards to its directors and executive officers if it is done in the ordinary course of business on the same terms and conditions made to the general public.

Section 403: Disclosures of Transactions Involving Management and Principal Stockholders

Directors, officers, and 10% owners must report designated transactions by the end of the second business day following the day on which the transaction was executed.

Section 404: Management Assessment of Internal Controls

Requires each annual report of an issuer to contain an 'internal control report', which shall:

(1) state the responsibility of management for establishing and maintaining an adequate internal control structure and procedures for financial reporting; and
(2) contain an assessment, as of the end of the issuer's fiscal year, of the effectiveness of the internal control structure and procedures of the issuer for financial reporting.

Each issuer's auditor shall attest to, and report on, the assessment made by the management of the issuer. An attestation made under this section shall be in accordance with standards for attestation engagements issued or adopted by the Board. An attestation engagement shall not be the subject of a separate engagement.

The language in the report of the Committee which accompanies the bill to explain the legislative intent states, '... the Committee does not intend that the auditor's evaluation be the subject of a separate engagement or the basis for increased charges or fees.'

Directs the SEC to require each issuer to disclose whether it has adopted a code of ethics for its senior financial officers and the contents of that code.

Directs the SEC to revise its regulations concerning prompt disclosure on Form 8-K to require immediate disclosure 'of any change in, or waiver of,' an issuer's code of ethics.

Section 407: Disclosure of Audit Committee Financial Expert

The SEC shall issue rules to require issuers to disclose whether at least one member of its audit committee is a 'financial expert.'

Section 409: Real Time Disclosure

Issuers must disclose information on material changes in the financial condition or operations of the issuer on a rapid and current basis.

Section 501: Treatment of Securities Analysts by Registered Securities Associations

National Securities Exchanges and registered securities associations must adopt conflict of interest rules for research analysts who recommend equities in research reports.

Section 601: SEC Resources and Authority

SEC appropriations for 2003 are increased to $776 million. $98 million of the funds shall be used to hire an additional 200 employees to provide enhanced oversight of auditors and audit services required by the Federal securities laws.

Section 602(a): Appearance and Practice before the Commission

The SEC may censure any person, or temporarily bar or deny any person the right to appear or practice before the SEC if the person does not possess the requisite qualifications to represent others, lacks character or integrity, or has willfully violated Federal securities laws.

Section 602(c): Study and Report

The SEC is to conduct a study of 'securities professionals' (public accountants, public accounting firms, investment bankers, investment advisors, brokers, dealers, attorneys) who have been found to have aided and abetted a violation of Federal securities laws.

Section 602(d): Rules of Professional Responsibility for Attorneys

The SEC shall establish rules setting minimum standards for professional conduct for attorneys practicing before it.

Section 701: GAO Study and Report regarding Consolidation of Public Accounting Firms

The GAO shall conduct a study regarding the consolidation of public accounting firms since 1989, including the present and future impact of the consolidation, and the solutions to any problems discovered.

Title VIII: Corporate and Criminal Fraud Accountability Act of 2002

It is a felony to 'knowingly' destroy or create documents to 'impede, obstruct or influence' any existing or contemplated Federal investigation.

Auditors are required to maintain 'all audit or review work papers' for 5 years.

The statute of limitations on securities fraud claims is extended to the earlier of 5 years from the fraud, or 2 years after the fraud was discovered, from 3 years and 1 year, respectively.

Employees of issuers and accounting firms are extended 'whistleblower protection' that would prohibit the employer from taking certain actions against employees who lawfully disclose private employer information to, among others, parties in a judicial proceeding involving a fraud claim. Whistleblowers are also granted a remedy of special damages and attorney's fees.

A new crime for securities fraud that has penalties of fines and up to 10 years imprisonment.

Title IX: White Collar Crime Penalty Enhancements

Maximum penalty for mail and wire fraud increased from 5 to 10 years.

Creates a crime for tampering with a record or otherwise impeding any official proceeding.

SEC given authority to seek court freeze of extraordinary payments to directors, officers, partners, controlling persons, agents of employees.

US Sentencing Commission to review sentencing guidelines for securities and accounting fraud.

The SEC may prohibit anyone convicted of securities fraud from being an officer or director of any publicly traded company.

Financial statements filed with the SEC must be certified by the CEO and CFO. The certification must state that the financial statements and disclosures fully comply with provisions of the Securities Exchange Act and that they fairly present, in all material respects, the operations and financial condition of the issuer. Maximum penalties for willful and knowing violations of this section are a fine of not more than $500,000 and/or imprisonment of up to 5 years.

Section 1001: Sense of Congress regarding Corporate Tax Returns

It is the sense of Congress that the Federal income tax return of a corporation should be signed by the CEO of such corporation.

Section 1102: Tampering with a Record or Otherwise Impeding an Official Proceeding

Makes it a crime for any person to corruptly alter, destroy, mutilate, or conceal any document with the intent to impair the object's integrity or availability for use in an official proceeding or to otherwise obstruct, influence or impede any official proceeding is liable for up to 20 years in prison and a fine.

Section 1103: Temporary Freeze Authority

The SEC is authorized to freeze the payment of an extraordinary payment to any director, officer, partner, controlling person, agent, or employee of a company during an investigation of possible violations of securities laws.

Section 1105: SEC Authority to Prohibit Persons from Serving as Officers or Directors

The SEC may prohibit a person from serving as an officer or director of a public company if the person has committed securities fraud.

Appendix

C

....

THE G30 TWENTY RECOMMENDATIONS

Source: Group of 30 (*G30*)

CREATING A STRENGTHENED, INTEROPERABLE GLOBAL NETWORK

1. Eliminate paper and automate communication, data capture, and enrichment.
2. Harmonize messaging standards and communication protocols.
3. Develop and implement reference data standards.
4. Synchronize timing between different clearing and settlement systems and associated payment and foreign-exchange systems.
5. Automate and standardize institutional tradematching.
6. Expand the use of central counterparties.
7. Permit securities lending and borrowing to expedite settlement.
8. Automate and standardize asset servicing processes, including corporate actions, tax relief arrangements, and restrictions on foreign ownership.

MITIGATING RISK

9. Ensure the financial integrity of providers of clearing and settlement services.
10. Reinforce the risk management practices of users of clearing and settlement service providers.
11. Ensure final, simultaneous transfer and availability of assets.
12. Ensure effective business continuity and disaster recovery planning.

13. Address the possibility of failure of a systemically important institution.
14. Strengthen assessment of the enforceability of contracts.
15. Advance legal certainty over rights to securities, cash, or collateral.
16. Recognize and support improved valuation and closeout netting arrangements.

IMPROVING GOVERNANCE

17. Ensure appointment of appropriately experienced and senior board members.
18. Promote fair access to securities clearing and settlement networks.
19. Ensure equitable and effective attention to stakeholder interests.
20. Encourage consistent regulation and oversight of securities clearing and settlement service providers.

Appendix

D

....

SOUND PRACTICES FOR THE MANAGEMENT AND SUPERVISION OF OPERATIONAL RISK

(February 2003)

Source: Basel Committee on Banking Supervision, Bank for International Settlements

Introduction

1.   The following paper outlines a set of principles that provide a framework for the effective management and supervision of operational risk, for use by banks and supervisory authorities when evaluating operational risk management policies and practices.

2.   The Basel Committee on Banking Supervision (the Committee) recognises that the exact approach for operational risk management chosen by an individual bank will depend on a range of factors, including its size and sophistication and the nature and complexity of its activities. However, despite these differences, clear strategies and oversight by the board of directors and senior management, a strong operational risk culture[1] and internal control culture (including, among other things, clear lines of responsibility and segregation of duties), effective internal reporting, and contingency planning are all crucial elements of an effective operational risk management framework for banks of any size and scope. The Committee therefore believes that the principles outlined in this paper establish sound practices relevant to all banks. The Committee's previous paper *A Framework for Internal Control Systems in Banking Organisations* (September 1998 – visit *www.bis.org*) underpins its current work in the field of operational risk.

---

[1] *Internal operational risk culture* is taken to mean the combined set of individual and corporate values, attitudes, competencies and behaviour that determine a firm's commitment to and style of operational risk management.

Background

3. Deregulation and globalisation of financial services, together with the growing sophistication of financial technology, are making the activities of banks and thus their risk profiles (i.e., the level of risk across a firm's activities and/or risk categories) more complex. Developing banking practices suggest that risks other than credit, interest rate and market risk can be substantial. Examples of these new and growing risks faced by banks include:

- If not properly controlled, the greater use of more highly automated technology has the potential to transform risks from manual processing errors to system failure risks, as greater reliance is placed on globally integrated systems.
- Growth of e-commerce brings with it potential risks (e.g., internal and external fraud and system security issues) that are not yet fully understood.
- Large-scale acquisitions, mergers, de-mergers and consolidations test the viability of new or newly integrated systems.
- The emergence of banks acting as large-volume service providers creates the need for continual maintenance of high-grade internal controls and back-up systems.
- Banks may engage in risk mitigation techniques (e.g., collateral, credit derivatives, netting arrangements and asset securitisations) to optimise their exposure to market risk and credit risk, but which in turn may produce other forms of risk (e.g., legal risk); and

- Growing use of outsourcing arrangements and the participation in clearing and settlement systems can mitigate some risks but can also present significant other risks to banks.

4.   The diverse set of risks listed above can be grouped under the heading of 'operational risk', which the Committee has defined as 'the risk of loss resulting from inadequate or failed internal processes, people and systems or from external events'.[2] The definition includes legal risk but excludes strategic and reputational risk.

5.   The Committee recognises that operational risk is a term that has a variety of meanings within the banking industry, and therefore for internal purposes (including in the application of the Sound Practices paper), banks may choose to adopt their own definitions of operational risk. Whatever the exact definition, a clear understanding by banks of what is meant by operational risk is critical to the effective management and control of this risk category. It is also important that the definition considers the full range of material operational risks facing the bank and captures the most significant causes of severe operational losses. Operational risk event types that the Committee – in co-operation with the industry – has identified

---

[2] This definition was adopted from the industry as part of the Committee's work in developing a minimum regulatory capital charge for operational risk. While this paper is not a formal part of the capital framework, the Committee nevertheless expects that the basic elements of a sound operational risk management framework set out in this paper will inform supervisory expectations when reviewing bank capital adequacy – for example, within the supervisory review process.

as having the potential to result in substantial losses include:

- Internal fraud. For example, intentional misreporting of positions, employee theft, and insider trading on an employee's own account.
- External fraud. For example, robbery, forgery, cheque kiting, and damage from computer hacking.
- Employment practices and workplace safety. For example, workers' compensation claims, violation of employee health and safety rules, organised labour activities, discrimination claims, and general liability.
- Clients, products and business practices. For example, fiduciary breaches, misuse of confidential customer information, improper trading activities on the bank's account, money laundering, and sale of unauthorised products.
- Damage to physical assets. For example, terrorism, vandalism, earthquakes, fires and floods.
- Business disruption and system failures. For example, hardware and software failures, telecommunication problems, and utility outages.
- Execution, delivery and process management. For example, data entry errors, collateral management failures, incomplete legal documentation, unapproved access given to client accounts, non-client counterparty misperformance, and vendor disputes.

Industry trends and practices

6.   In its work on the supervision of operational risks, the Committee has aimed to develop a greater understanding

of current industry trends and practices for managing operational risk. These efforts have involved numerous meetings with banking organisations, surveys of industry practice, and analyses of the results. Based on these efforts, the Committee believes that it has a good understanding of the banking industry's current range of practices, as well as the industry's efforts to develop methods for managing operational risks.

7.   The Committee recognises that management of specific operational risks is not a new practice; it has always been important for banks to try to prevent fraud, maintain the integrity of internal controls, reduce errors in transaction processing, and so on. However, what is relatively new is the view of operational risk management as a comprehensive practice comparable to the management of credit and market risk in principle, if not always in form. The trends cited in the introduction to this paper, combined with a growing number of high-profile operational loss events worldwide, have led banks and supervisors to increasingly view operational risk management as an inclusive discipline, as has already been the case in many other industries.

8.   In the past, banks relied almost exclusively upon internal control mechanisms within business lines, supplemented by the audit function, to manage operational risk. While these remain important, recently there has been an emergence of specific structures and processes aimed at managing operational risk. In this regard, an increasing number of organisations have concluded that an operational risk management programme pro-

vides for bank safety and soundness, and are therefore making progress in addressing operational risk as a distinct class of risk similar to their treatment of credit and market risk. The Committee believes that an active exchange of ideas between the supervisors and industry is key to ongoing development of appropriate guidance for managing exposures related to operational risk.

9.   This paper is organised along the following lines: developing an appropriate risk management environment; risk management: identification, assessment, monitoring and control/mitigation; the role of supervisors; and the role of disclosure.

Sound practices

10.   In developing these sound practices, the Committee has drawn upon its existing work on the management of other significant banking risks, such as credit risk, interest rate risk and liquidity risk, and the Committee believes that similar rigour should be applied to the management of operational risk. Nevertheless, it is clear that operational risk differs from other banking risks in that it is typically not directly taken in return for an expected reward, but exists in the natural course of corporate activity, and that this affects the risk management process.[3] At the same time, failure to properly

---

[3] However, the Committee recognises that in some business lines with minimal credit or market risk (e.g., asset management, and payment and settlement), the decision to incur operational risk, or compete based on the ability to manage and effectively price this risk, is an integral part of a bank's risk/reward calculus.

manage operational risk can result in a misstatement of an institution's risk profile and expose the institution to significant losses. Reflecting the different nature of operational risk, for the purposes of this paper, 'management' of operational risk is taken to mean the 'identification, assessment, monitoring and control/mitigation' of risk. This definition contrasts with the one used by the Committee in previous risk management papers of the 'identification, measurement, monitoring and control' of risk. In common with its work on other banking risks, the Committee has structured this sound practice paper around a number of principles. These are:

Developing an Appropriate Risk Management Environment

Principle 1: The board of directors[4] should be aware of the major aspects of the bank's operational risks as a distinct risk category that should be managed, and it should approve and periodically review the bank's operational risk management framework. The framework should provide a firm-wide definition of operational risk and lay down the principles of how operational risk is to be identified, assessed, monitored, and controlled/mitigated.

---

[4] This paper refers to a management structure composed of a board of directors and senior management. The Committee is aware that there are significant differences in legislative and regulatory frameworks across countries as regards the functions of the board of directors and senior management. In some countries, the board has the main, if not exclusive, function of supervising the executive body (senior management, general management) so as to ensure that the latter fulfils its tasks. For this reason, in some cases, it is known as a supervisory board. This means that the board has no executive functions. In other countries, the board has a broader competence in that it lays down the general framework for the management of the bank. Owing to these differences, the terms 'board of directors' and 'senior management' are used in this paper not to identify legal constructs but rather to label two decision-making functions within a bank.

Principle 2: The board of directors should ensure that the bank's operational risk management framework is subject to effective and comprehensive internal audit by operationally independent, appropriately trained and competent staff. The internal audit function should not be directly responsible for operational risk management.

Principle 3: Senior management should have responsibility for implementing the operational risk management framework approved by the board of directors. The framework should be consistently implemented throughout the whole banking organisation, and all levels of staff should understand their responsibilities with respect to operational risk management. Senior management should also have responsibility for developing policies, processes and procedures for managing operational risk in all of the bank's material products, activities, processes and systems.

Risk Management: Identification, Assessment, Monitoring, and Mitigation/Control

Principle 4: Banks should identify and assess the operational risk inherent in all material products, activities, processes and systems. Banks should also ensure that before new products, activities, processes and systems are introduced or undertaken, the operational risk inherent in them is subject to adequate assessment procedures.

Principle 5: Banks should implement a process to regularly monitor operational risk profiles and material exposures to losses. There should be regular reporting of pertinent information to senior management and the board of directors that supports the proactive management of operational risk.

Principle 6: Banks should have policies, processes and procedures to control and/or mitigate material operational risks. Banks should periodically review their risk limitation and control strategies and should adjust their operational risk profile accordingly using appropriate strategies, in light of their overall risk appetite and profile.

Principle 7: Banks should have in place contingency and business continuity plans to ensure their ability to operate on an ongoing basis and limit losses in the event of severe business disruption.

Role of Supervisors

Principle 8: Banking supervisors should require that all banks, regardless of size, have an effective framework in place to identify, assess, monitor and control/mitigate material operational risks as part of an overall approach to risk management.

Principle 9: Supervisors should conduct, directly or indirectly, regular independent evaluation of a bank's policies, procedures and practices related to operational risks. Supervisors should ensure that there are appropriate mechanisms in place which allow them to remain apprised of developments at banks.

Role of Disclosure

Principle 10: Banks should make sufficient public disclosure to allow market participants to assess their approach to operational risk management.

Developing an appropriate risk management environment

11. Failure to understand and manage operational risk, which is present in virtually all bank transactions and activities, may greatly increase the likelihood that some risks will go unrecognised and uncontrolled. Both the board and senior management are responsible for creating an organisational culture that places high priority on effective operational risk management and adherence

to sound operating controls. Operational risk management is most effective where a bank's culture emphasises high standards of ethical behaviour at all levels of the bank. The board and senior management should promote an organisational culture which establishes through both actions and words the expectations of integrity for all employees in conducting the business of the bank.

> **Principle 1**: The board of directors should be aware of the major aspects of the bank's operational risks as a distinct risk category that should be managed, and it should approve and periodically review the bank's operational risk management framework. The framework should provide a firm-wide definition of operational risk and lay down the principles of how operational risk is to be identified, assessed, monitored, and controlled/mitigated.

12. The board of directors should approve the implementation of a firm-wide framework to explicitly manage operational risk as a distinct risk to the bank's safety and soundness. The board should provide senior management with clear guidance and direction regarding the principles underlying the framework and approve the corresponding policies developed by senior management.

13. An operational risk framework should be based on an appropriate definition of operational risk which clearly articulates what constitutes operational risk in that bank. The framework should cover the bank's appetite and tolerance for operational risk, as specified through the policies for managing this risk and the bank's prioritisation of operational risk management activities, including the extent of, and manner in which, operational risk is transferred outside the bank. It should

also include policies outlining the bank's approach to identifying, assessing, monitoring and controlling/ mitigating the risk. The degree of formality and sophistication of the bank's operational risk management framework should be commensurate with the bank's risk profile.

14.   The board is responsible for establishing a management structure capable of implementing the firm's operational risk management framework. Since a significant aspect of managing operational risk relates to the establishment of strong internal controls, it is particularly important that the board establishes clear lines of management responsibility, accountability and reporting. In addition, there should be separation of responsibilities and reporting lines between operational risk control functions, business lines and support functions in order to avoid conflicts of interest. The framework should also articulate the key processes the firm needs to have in place to manage operational risk.

15.   The board should review the framework regularly to ensure that the bank is managing the operational risks arising from external market changes and other environmental factors, as well as those operational risks associated with new products, activities or systems. This review process should also aim to assess industry best practice in operational risk management appropriate for the bank's activities, systems and processes. If necessary, the board should ensure that the operational risk management framework is revised in light of this analysis, so

that material operational risks are captured within the framework.

> **Principle 2**: The board of directors should ensure that the bank's operational risk management framework is subject to effective and comprehensive internal audit by operationally independent, appropriately trained and competent staff. The internal audit function should not be directly responsible for operational risk management.

16.   Banks should have in place adequate internal audit coverage to verify that operating policies and procedures have been implemented effectively.[5] The board (either directly or indirectly through its audit committee) should ensure that the scope and frequency of the audit programme is appropriate to the risk exposures. Audit should periodically validate that the firm's operational risk management framework is being implemented effectively across the firm.

17.   To the extent that the audit function is involved in oversight of the operational risk management framework, the board should ensure that the independence of the audit function is maintained. This independence may be compromised if the audit function is directly involved in the operational risk management process. The audit function may provide valuable input to those responsible for operational risk management, but should not itself have direct operational risk management

---

[5] The Committee's paper, *Internal Audit in Banks and the Supervisor's Relationship with Auditors* (August 2001) describes the role of internal and external audit.

responsibilities. In practice, the Committee recognises that the audit function at some banks (particularly smaller banks) may have initial responsibility for developing an operational risk management programme. Where this is the case, banks should see that responsibility for day-to-day operational risk management is transferred elsewhere in a timely manner.

Principle 3: Senior management should have responsibility for implementing the operational risk management framework approved by the board of directors. The framework should be consistently implemented throughout the whole banking organisation, and all levels of staff should understand their responsibilities with respect to operational risk management. Senior management should also have responsibility for developing policies, processes and procedures for managing operational risk in all of the bank's material products, activities, processes and systems.

18.   Management should translate the operational risk management framework established by the board of directors into specific policies, processes and procedures that can be implemented and verified within the different business units. While each level of management is responsible for the appropriateness and effectiveness of policies, processes, procedures and controls within its purview, senior management should clearly assign authority, responsibility and reporting relationships to encourage and maintain this accountability, and ensure that the necessary resources are available to manage operational risk effectively. Moreover, senior management should assess the appropriateness of the manage-

ment oversight process in light of the risks inherent in a business unit's policy.

19. Senior management should ensure that bank activities are conducted by qualified staff with the necessary experience, technical capabilities and access to resources, and that staff responsible for monitoring and enforcing compliance with the institution's risk policy have authority independent from the units they oversee. Management should ensure that the bank's operational risk management policy has been clearly communicated to staff at all levels in units that incur material operational risks.

20. Senior management should ensure that staff responsible for managing operational risk communicate effectively with staff responsible for managing credit, market, and other risks, as well as with those in the firm who are responsible for the procurement of external services such as insurance purchasing and outsourcing agreements. Failure to do so could result in significant gaps or overlaps in a bank's overall risk management programme.

21. Senior management should also ensure that the bank's remuneration policies are consistent with its appetite for risk. Remuneration policies which reward staff that deviate from policies (e.g., by exceeding established limits) weaken the bank's risk management processes.

22. Particular attention should be given to the quality of documentation controls and to transaction-handling practices. Policies, processes and procedures related to

advanced technologies supporting high transactions volumes, in particular, should be well documented and disseminated to all relevant personnel.

Risk Management: Identification, Assessment, Monitoring and Mitigation/Control

Principle 4: Banks should identify and assess the operational risk inherent in all material products, activities, processes and systems. Banks should also ensure that before new products, activities, processes and systems are introduced or undertaken, the operational risk inherent in them is subject to adequate assessment procedures.

23.   Risk identification is paramount for the subsequent development of a viable operational risk monitoring and control system. Effective risk identification considers both internal factors (such as the bank's structure, the nature of the bank's activities, the quality of the bank's human resources, organisational changes and employee turnover) and external factors (such as changes in the industry and technological advances) that could adversely affect the achievement of the bank's objectives.

24.   In addition to identifying the most potentially adverse risks, banks should assess their vulnerability to these risks. Effective risk assessment allows the bank to better understand its risk profile and most effectively target risk management resources.

25.   Amongst the possible tools used by banks for identifying and assessing operational risk are:

● Self- or Risk Assessment: a bank assesses its operations and activities against a menu of potential operational risk vulnerabilities. This process is internally driven and often incorporates checklists and/or workshops to identify the strengths and weaknesses of the operational risk environment. Scorecards, for example, provide a means of translating qualitative assessments into quantitative metrics that give a relative ranking of different types of operational risk exposures. Some scores may relate to risks unique to a specific business line while others may rank risks that cut across business lines. Scores may address inherent risks, as well as the controls to mitigate them. In addition, scorecards may be used by banks to allocate economic capital to business lines in relation to performance in managing and controlling various aspects of operational risk.

- Risk Mapping: in this process, various business units, organisational functions or process flows are mapped by risk type. This exercise can reveal areas of weakness and help prioritise subsequent management action.

- Risk Indicators: risk indicators are statistics and/or metrics, often financial, which can provide insight into a bank's risk position. These indicators tend to be reviewed on a periodic basis (such as monthly or quarterly) to alert banks to changes that may be indicative of risk concerns. Such indicators may include the number of failed trades, staff turnover rates and the frequency and/or severity of errors and omissions.

- Measurement: some firms have begun to quantify their exposure to operational risk using a variety of approaches. For example, data on a bank's historical loss experience could provide meaningful information for assessing the bank's exposure to operational risk and developing a policy to mitigate/control the risk. An effective way of making good use of this information is to establish a framework for systematically tracking and recording the frequency, severity and other relevant information on individual loss events. Some firms have also combined internal loss data with external loss data, scenario analyses, and risk assessment factors.

Principle 5: Banks should implement a process to regularly monitor operational risk profiles and material exposures to losses. There should be regular reporting of pertinent information to senior management and the board of directors that supports the proactive management of operational risk.

26.   An effective monitoring process is essential for adequately managing operational risk. Regular monitoring activities can offer the advantage of quickly detecting and correcting deficiencies in the policies, processes and procedures for managing operational risk. Promptly detecting and addressing these deficiencies can substantially reduce the potential frequency and/or severity of a loss event.

27.   In addition to monitoring operational loss events, banks should identify appropriate indicators that provide early warning of an increased risk of future losses. Such indicators (often referred to as key risk indicators or early warning indicators) should be forward-looking and could reflect potential sources of operational risk such as rapid growth, the introduction of new products, employee

turnover, transaction breaks, system downtime, and so on. When thresholds are directly linked to these indicators an effective monitoring process can help identify key material risks in a transparent manner and enable the bank to act upon these risks appropriately.

28.   The frequency of monitoring should reflect the risks involved and the frequency and nature of changes in the operating environment. Monitoring should be an integrated part of a bank's activities. The results of these monitoring activities should be included in regular management and board reports, as should compliance reviews performed by the internal audit and/or risk management functions. Reports generated by (and/or for) supervisory authorities may also inform this monitoring and should likewise be reported internally to senior management and the board, where appropriate.

29.   Senior management should receive regular reports from appropriate areas such as business units, group functions, the operational risk management office and internal audit. The operational risk reports should contain internal financial, operational, and compliance data, as well as external market information about events and conditions that are relevant to decision making. Reports should be distributed to appropriate levels of management and to areas of the bank on which areas of concern may have an impact. Reports should fully reflect any identified problem areas and should motivate timely corrective action on outstanding issues. To ensure the usefulness and reliability of these risk and audit reports, management should regularly verify the timeliness,

accuracy, and relevance of reporting systems and internal controls in general. Management may also use reports prepared by external sources (auditors, supervisors) to assess the usefulness and reliability of internal reports. Reports should be analysed with a view to improving existing risk management performance as well as developing new risk management policies, procedures and practices.

30. In general, the board of directors should receive sufficient higher-level information to enable them to understand the bank's overall operational risk profile and focus on the material and strategic implications for the business.

Principle 6: Banks should have policies, processes and procedures to control and/or mitigate material operational risks. Banks should periodically review their risk limitation and control strategies and should adjust their operational risk profile accordingly using appropriate strategies, in light of their overall risk appetite and profile.

31. Control activities are designed to address the operational risks that a bank has identified.[6] For all material operational risks that have been identified, the bank should decide whether to use appropriate procedures to control and/or mitigate the risks, or bear the risks. For those risks that cannot be controlled, the bank should decide whether to accept these risks, reduce the level of

---

[6] For more detail, see the *Framework for Internal Control Systems in Banking Organisations*, Basel Committee on Banking Supervision, September 1998 at *www.bis.org*).

business activity involved, or withdraw from this activity completely. Control processes and procedures should be established and banks should have a system in place for ensuring compliance with a documented set of internal policies concerning the risk management system. Principle elements of this could include, for example:

- top-level reviews of the bank's progress towards the stated objectives;
- checking for compliance with management controls;
- policies, processes and procedures concerning the review, treatment and resolution of non-compliance issues; and
- a system of documented approvals and authorisations to ensure accountability to an appropriate level of management.

32. Although a framework of formal, written policies and procedures is critical, it needs to be reinforced through a strong control culture that promotes sound risk management practices. Both the board of directors and senior management are responsible for establishing a strong internal control culture in which control activities are an integral part of the regular activities of a bank. Controls that are an integral part of the regular activities enable quick responses to changing conditions and avoid unnecessary costs.

33. An effective internal control system also requires that there be appropriate segregation of duties and that personnel are not assigned responsibilities which may create a conflict of interest. Assigning such conflicting

duties to individuals, or a team, may enable them to conceal losses, errors or inappropriate actions. Therefore, areas of potential conflicts of interest should be identified, minimised, and subject to careful independent monitoring and review.

34.　In addition to segregation of duties, banks should ensure that other internal practices are in place as appropriate to control operational risk. Examples of these include:

- close monitoring of adherence to assigned risk limits or thresholds;
- maintaining safeguards for access to, and use of, bank assets and records;
- ensuring that staff have appropriate expertise and training;
- identifying business lines or products where returns appear to be out of line with reasonable expectations (e.g., where a supposedly low risk, low margin trading activity generates high returns that could call into question whether such returns have been achieved as a result of an internal control breach); and
- regular verification and reconciliation of transactions and accounts.

Failure to implement such practices has resulted in significant operational losses for some banks in recent years.

35.　Operational risk can be more pronounced where banks engage in new activities or develop new products (particularly where these activities or products are not consistent with the bank's core business strategies), enter unfamiliar markets, and/or engage in businesses that are geographically distant from the head office. Moreover, in many such instances, firms do not ensure that the risk management control infrastructure keeps pace with the growth in the business activity. A number of the most sizeable and highest-profile losses in recent years have taken place where one or more of these conditions existed. Therefore, it is incumbent upon banks to ensure that special attention is paid to internal control activities where such conditions exist.

36. Some significant operational risks have low probabilities but potentially very large financial impact. Moreover, not all risk events can be controlled (e.g., natural disasters). Risk mitigation tools or programmes can be used to reduce the exposure to, or frequency and/or severity of, such events. For example, insurance policies, particularly those with prompt and certain pay-out features, can be used to externalise the risk of 'low frequency, high severity' losses which may occur as a result of events such as third-party claims resulting from errors and omissions, physical loss of securities, employee or third-party fraud, and natural disasters.

37. However, banks should view risk mitigation tools as complementary to, rather than a replacement for, thorough internal operational risk control. Having mechanisms in place to quickly recognise and rectify legitimate operational risk errors can greatly reduce exposures. Careful consideration also needs to be given to the extent to which risk mitigation tools such as insurance truly

reduce risk, or transfer the risk to another business sector or area, or even create a new risk (e.g., legal or counter-party risk).

38.   Investments in appropriate processing technology and information technology security are also important for risk mitigation. However, banks should be aware that increased automation could transform high-frequency, low-severity losses into low-frequency, high-severity losses. The latter may be associated with loss or extended disruption of services caused by internal factors or by factors beyond the bank's immediate control (e.g., external events). Such problems may cause serious diffi-culties for banks and could jeopardise an institution's ability to conduct key business activities. As discussed below in Principle 7, banks should establish disaster recovery and business continuity plans that address this risk.

39.   Banks should also establish policies for managing the risks associated with outsourcing activities. Out-sourcing of activities can reduce the institution's risk profile by transferring activities to others with greater expertise and scale to manage the risks associated with specialised business activities. However, a bank's use of third parties does not diminish the responsibility of the board of directors and management to ensure that the third-party activity is conducted in a safe and sound manner and in compliance with applicable laws. Out-sourcing arrangements should be based on robust con-tracts and/or service level agreements that ensure a clear allocation of responsibilities between external service

providers and the outsourcing bank. Furthermore, banks need to manage residual risks associated with outsourcing arrangements, including disruption of services.

40.   Depending on the scale and nature of the activity, banks should understand the potential impact on their operations and their customers of any potential deficiencies in services provided by vendors and other third-party or intra-group service providers, including both operational breakdowns and the potential business failure or default of the external parties. The board and management should ensure that the expectations and obligations of each party are clearly defined, understood and enforceable. The extent of the external party's liability and financial ability to compensate the bank for errors, negligence, and other operational failures should be explicitly considered as part of the risk assessment. Banks should carry out an initial due diligence test and monitor the activities of third-party providers, especially those lacking experience of the banking industry's regulated environment, and review this process (including re-evaluations of due diligence) on a regular basis. For critical activities, the bank may need to consider contingency plans, including the availability of alternative external parties and the costs and resources required to switch external parties, potentially on very short notice.

41.   In some instances, banks may decide to either retain a certain level of operational risk or self-insure against that risk. Where this is the case and the risk is material, the decision to retain or self-insure the risk should be

transparent within the organisation and should be consistent with the bank's overall business strategy and appetite for risk.

> **Principle 7**: Banks should have in place contingency and business continuity plans to ensure their ability to operate on an ongoing basis and limit losses in the event of severe business disruption.

42.   For reasons that may be beyond a bank's control, a severe event may result in the inability of the bank to fulfil some or all of its business obligations, particularly where the bank's physical, telecommunication, or information technology infrastructures have been damaged or made inaccessible. This can, in turn, result in significant financial losses to the bank, as well as broader disruptions to the financial system through channels such as the payments system. This potential requires that banks establish disaster recovery and business continuity plans that take into account different types of plausible scenarios to which the bank may be vulnerable, commensurate with the size and complexity of the bank's operations.

43.   Banks should identify critical business processes, including those where there is dependence on external vendors or other third parties, for which rapid resumption of service would be most essential. For these processes, banks should identify alternative mechanisms for resuming service in the event of an outage. Particular attention should be paid to the ability to restore electronic or physical records that are necessary for business resumption. Where such records are backed up at an off-site facility, or where a bank's operations must be relocated

to a new site, care should be taken that these sites are at an adequate distance from the impacted operations to minimise the risk that both primary and back-up records and facilities will be unavailable simultaneously.

44. Banks should periodically review their disaster recovery and business continuity plans so that they are consistent with the bank's current operations and business strategies. Moreover, these plans should be tested periodically to ensure that the bank would be able to execute the plans in the unlikely event of a severe business disruption.

Role of Supervisors

Principle 8: Banking supervisors should require that all banks, regardless of size, have an effective framework in place to identify, assess, monitor and control/mitigate material operational risks as part of an overall approach to risk management.

45. Supervisors should require banks to develop operational risk management frameworks consistent with the guidance in this paper and commensurate with their size, complexity, and risk profiles. To the extent that operational risks pose a threat to banks' safety and soundness, supervisors have a responsibility to encourage banks to develop and use better techniques in managing those risks.

Principle 9: Supervisors should conduct, directly or indirectly, regular independent evaluation of a bank's policies, procedures and practices related to operational risks. Supervisors should ensure that there are appropriate mechanisms in place which allow them to remain apprised of developments at banks.

46. Examples of what an independent evaluation of operational risk by supervisors should review include the following:

- the effectiveness of the bank's risk management process and overall control environment with respect to operational risk;
- the bank's methods for monitoring and reporting its operational risk profile, including data on operational losses and other indicators of potential operational risk;
- the bank's procedures for the timely and effective resolution of operational risk events and vulnerabilities;
- the bank's process of internal controls, reviews and audit to ensure the integrity of the overall operational risk management process;
- the effectiveness of the bank's operational risk mitigation efforts, such as the use of insurance;
- the quality and comprehensiveness of the bank's disaster recovery and business continuity plans; and
- the bank's process for assessing overall capital adequacy for operational risk in relation to its risk profile and, if appropriate, its internal capital targets.

47. Supervisors should also seek to ensure that, where banks are part of a financial group, there are procedures in place to ensure that operational risk is managed in an appropriate and integrated manner across the group. In performing this assessment, co-operation and exchange of information with other supervisors, in accordance with established procedures, may be necessary. Some

supervisors may choose to use external auditors in these assessment processes.

48. Deficiencies identified during the supervisory review may be addressed through a range of actions. Supervisors should use the tools most suited to the particular circumstances of the bank and its operating environment. In order that supervisors receive current information on operational risk, they may wish to establish reporting mechanisms, directly with banks and external auditors (for example, internal bank management reports on operational risk could be made routinely available to supervisors).

49. Given the general recognition that comprehensive operational risk management processes are still in development at many banks, supervisors should take an active role in encouraging ongoing internal development efforts by monitoring and evaluating a bank's recent improvements and plans for prospective developments. These efforts can then be compared with those of other banks to provide the bank with useful feedback on the status of its own work. Further, to the extent that there are identified reasons why certain development efforts have proven ineffective, such information could be provided in general terms to assist in the planning process. In addition, supervisors should focus on the extent to which a bank has integrated the operational risk management process throughout its organisation to ensure effective business line management of operational risk, to provide clear lines of communication and responsibility, and to encourage active self-assessment of existing

practices and consideration of possible risk mitigation enhancements.

Role of Disclosure
Principle 10: Banks should make sufficient public disclosure to allow market participants to assess their approach to operational risk management.

50. The Committee believes that the timely and frequent public disclosure of relevant information by banks can lead to enhanced market discipline and, therefore, more effective risk management. The amount of disclosure should be commensurate with the size, risk profile and complexity of a bank's operations.

51. The area of operational risk disclosure is not yet well established, primarily because banks are still in the process of developing operational risk assessment techniques. However, the Committee believes that a bank should disclose its operational risk management framework in a manner that will allow investors and counterparties to determine whether a bank effectively identifies, assesses, monitors and controls/mitigates operational risk.

GLOSSARY

. . . .

30/360 Also 360/360 or 30(E)/360. A day/year count convention assuming 30 days in each calendar month and a 'year' of 360 days; adjusted in America for certain periods ending on 31st day of the month (and then sometimes known as 30(A)/360).

AAA The highest credit rating for a company or asset – the risk of default is negligible.

Accrued interest Interest due on a bond or other fixed income security that must be paid by the buyer of a security to its seller. Usual compensation: coupon rate of interest times elapsed days from prior interest payment date (i.e., coupon date) up to but not including settlement date.

Actual settlement date Date the transaction effectively settles in the clearing house (exchange of securities eventually against cash).

Add-on In capital adequacy calculations, the extra capital required to allow for the possibility of a deal moving into profit before a mark-to-market calculation is next made.

Affirmation Affirmation refers to the counterparty's agreement with the terms of the trade as communicated.

Agent One who executes orders for or otherwise acts on behalf of another (the principal) and is subject to its control and authority. The agent takes no financial risk and may receive a fee or commission.

Alternative Investment Market (AIM) Second tier of market run by the London Stock Exchange.

American Depository Receipt (ADR) Document giving the owner rights to UK shares. They are effectively bearer documents.

American-style option The holder of the long position can choose to exercise the position into the underlying instrument until the expiry day.

AMEX American Stock Exchange.

Amortisation Accounting procedure that gradually reduces the cost value of a limited life asset or intangible asset through periodic charges to income. The purpose of amortisation is to reflect the resale or redemption value. Amortisation also refers to the reduction of debt by regular payments of interest and principal to pay off a loan by maturity.

Ask price Price at which a market maker will sell stock. Also known as the **Offer price**.

Asset allocation The use of derivatives by a fund manager, to immediately gain or reduce exposure to different markets.

Asset-backed securities Debt obligations that pay principal and interest, principal only or interests only, deferred interest and negative interest using a combination of factors and rate multipliers. The issues are serviced by multiple vendors that supply the necessary data to make the corresponding payments.

Assets Everything of value that is owned or is due: fixed assets (cash, buildings and machinery) and intangible assets (patents and goodwill).

Assignment The process by which the holder of a short option position is matched against a holder of a similar long option position who has exercised his right.

ASX Australian Stock Exchange.

Authentication agent A bank putting a signature on each physical bond to certify its genuineness prior to the distribution of the definitive bonds on the market.

Authorisation Status required by the Financial Services and Markets Act 2000 for any firm that wants to conduct investment business.

Authorised unit trust Unit trust which meets the requirements of the Financial Services Authority to allow it to be freely marketable.

Bank commercial Organisation that takes deposits and makes loans.

Bank merchant Organisation that specialises in advising on take-overs and corporate finance activities.

Bank of England The UK's central bank which undertakes policy decided by the Treasury and determines interest rates.

Bankers' acceptance Short-term negotiable discount note, drawn on and accepted by banks which are obliged to pay the face value amount at maturity.

Bargain Another word for a transaction or deal. It does not imply that a particularly favourable price was obtained.

Base currency Currency chosen for reporting purposes.

Basis (gross) The difference between the relevant cash instrument price and the futures price. Often used in the context of hedging the cash instrument.

Basis (value or net) The difference between the gross basis and the carry.

Basis point (b.p.) A change in the interest rate of one-hundredth of 1% (0.01%). One basis point is written as 0.01 when 1.0 represents 1%.

Basis risk The risk that the price or rate of one instrument or position might not move exactly in line with the price or rate of another instrument or position which is being used to hedge it.

BBA British Bankers' Association.

Bear Investor who believes prices will fall.

Bearer document Documents which state on them that the person in physical possession (the bearer) is the owner.

Benchmark bond The most recently issued and most liquid government bond.

Beneficial owner The underlying owner of a security who has paid for the stock and is entitled to the benefits of ownership.

Bid The price or yield at which a purchaser is willing to buy a given security. To quote a price or yield at which a purchaser is able to buy a given security.

Bilateral netting A netting system in which all trades executed on the same date in the same security between the same counterparties are grouped and netted to one final delivery versus payment. *See* **Netting**.

Bill of exchange A money market instrument.

BIS Bank for International Settlements.

Block trade A purchase or sale of a large number of shares or dollar value of bonds, normally much more than what constitutes a round lot in the market in question.

Bond A certificate of debt, generally long-term, under the terms of which an issuer contracts, *inter alia*, to pay the holder a fixed principal amount on a stated future date and, usually, a series of interest payments during its life.

Bonus issue A free issue of shares to a company's existing shareholders. No money changes hands and the share price falls *pro rata*. It is a cosmetic exercise to make the shares more marketable. Also known as a **Capitalisation** or **Scrip** issue.

Book-entry transfer System of recording ownership of securities by computer where the owners do not receive a certificate. Records are kept (and altered) centrally in 'the book'.

Break A term used for any out-of-balance condition. A money break means that debits and credits are not equal. A trade break means that some information such as that from a contra broker is missing to complete that trade.

Bretton Woods Agreement An agreement that set a system of exchange rate stability after World War II, with all member currencies having a par value pegged to the US$, allowing a 1% variance. This was agreed by major economists from 44 countries. The International Monetary Fund and the World Bank were agreed to be set up at this conference.

Broker/Dealer Any member firm of the Stock Exchange except those specialists that are gilt-edged market makers and inter-dealer brokers.

Broken date A maturity date other than the standard ones normally quoted.

Broken period A period other than the standard ones normally quoted.

Broking The activity of representing a client as agent and charging commission for doing so.

Bull Investor who believes prices will rise.

Buying in The action taken by a broker failing to receive delivery of securities from a counterparty on settlement date to purchase these securities in the open market.

CASCADE Name of the settlement system used by Clearstream for German equity settlement.

Calendar spread The simultaneous purchase (or sale) of a futures or option contract for one date and the sale (or purchase) of a similar futures contract for a different date. *See* **Spread**.

Call option An option that gives the seller the right, but not the obligation, to buy a specified quantity of the underlying asset at a fixed price, on or before a specified date. The buyer of a call option has the obligation (because they have bought the right) to make delivery of the underlying asset if the option is exercised by the seller.

Call spread The purchase of a call option coupled with the sale of another call option at a different strike, expecting a limited rise or fall in the value of the underlying.

Callable bond A bond that the issuer has the right to redeem prior to maturity by paying some specified call price.

Capital adequacy Requirement for firms conducting investment business to have sufficient funds.

Capital markets A term used to describe the means by which large amounts of money (capital) are raised by companies, governments and other organisations for long-term use and the subsequent trading of the instruments issued in recognition of such capital.

Capitalisation issue *See* **Bonus issue**.

Cash market A term used to describe the market where the cash asset trades, or the underlying market when talking about derivatives.

Cash sale A transaction on the floor of the stock exchange which calls for delivery of the securities that same day. In 'regular way' trades, the seller delivers securities on the fifth business day.

Cash settlement In the money market a transaction is said to be 'made for cash settlement' if the securities purchased are delivered against payment on the same day the trade is made.

CBOT Chicago Board of Trade.

CEDCOM Communication system operated by Clearstream.

Central securities depository An organisation which holds securities in either immobilised or dematerialised form thereby enabling transactions to be processed by book-entry transfer. Also provides securities administration services.

Certificate of deposit A money market instrument.

CFTC The Commodities and Futures Trading Commission (US).

CHAPS Clearing House Automated Payment System – clearing system for sterling and euro payments between banks.

Cheapest to deliver The cash security that provides the lowest cost (largest profit) to the arbitrage trader; the cheapest to deliver instrument is used to price the futures contract.

CHIPS Clearing House Interbank Payments System – clearing system for US dollar payments between banks in New York.

Clean price The total price of a bond less accrued interest.

Clearance The process of determining accountability for the exchange of money and securities between counterparties to a trade: clearance creates statements of obligation for securities and/or funds due.

Clearance broker A broker who will handle the settlement of securities-related transactions for himself or another broker. Sometimes, small brokerage firms may not clear for themselves and therefore employ the services of an outside clearing broker.

Clearing The centralised process whereby transacted business is recorded and positions are maintained.

Clearing organisation The clearing organisation acts as the guarantor of the performance and settlement of contracts that are traded on an exchange.

Clearstream Central securities depository and clearing house based in Luxembourg and Frankfurt.

Close-ended Organisations such as companies which are a certain size as determined by their share capital.

Closing day In a new bond issue, the day when securities are delivered against payment by syndicate members participating in the offering.

Closing trade A bought or sold trade which is used to partly offset an open position, to reduce it or to fully offset it and close it.

CME Chicago Mercantile Exchange.

CMO Central Moneymarkets Office – clearing house and depository for UK money markets.

Collateral An acceptable asset used to cover a margin requirement.

Commercial paper A money market instrument.

Commodity futures These comprise five main categories: agriculturals (e.g., wheat and potatoes); softs (e.g., coffee and cocoa); precious metals (e.g., gold and silver); non-ferrous metals (e.g., copper and lead); and energies (e.g., oil and gas).

Common stock Securities which represent ownership in a corporation. The two most important common stockholder rights are the voting right and dividend right. Common stockholder's claims on corporate assets are subordinate to those of bond holders, preferred stockholders and general creditors.

Compliance officer Person appointed within an authorised firm to be responsible for ensuring compliance with the rules.

Compound interest Interest calculated on the assumption that interest amounts will be received periodically and can be re-invested (usually at the same rate).

Conduct of business rules Rules required by FSA 1986 to dictate how firms conduct their business. They deal mainly with the relationship between firm and client.

Confirm An agreement for each individual **Over-the-counter** transaction which has specific terms.

Continuous net settlement Extends multilateral netting to handle failed trades brought forward. *See* **Multilateral netting**.

Contract The standard unit of trading for futures and options. It is also commonly referred to as a **Lot**.

Contract for difference Contract designed to make a profit or avoid a loss by reference to movements in the price of an item. The underlying item cannot change hands.

Contract note Legal documentation sent by securities house to clients providing details of a transaction completed on their behalf.

Convertible bond Security (usually a bond or preferred stock) that can be exchanged for other securities, usually common stock of the same issuer, at the option of the holder and under certain conditions.

Core rules Forty rules written by the Financial Services Authority under the three-tier approach, to be universally applicable. Dedesignated in November 1994.

Corporate action One of many possible capital restructuring changes or similar actions taken by the company, which may have an impact on the market price of its securities, and which may require the shareholders to make certain decisions.

Corporate debt securities Bonds or commercial papers issued by private corporations.

Corporate finance General title which covers activities such as raising cash through new issues.

Correlation Refers to the degree to which fluctuations of one variable are similar to those of another.

Cost of carry The net running cost of holding a position (which may be negative) – e.g., the cost of borrowing cash to buy a bond, less the coupon earned on the bond while holding it.

Counterparty A trade can take place between two or more counterparties. Usually, one party to a trade refers to its trading partners as counterparties.

Coupon Generally, the nominal annual rate of interest expressed as a percentage of the principal value. The interest is paid to the holder of a fixed income security by the borrower. The coupon is generally paid annually, semi-annually or, in some cases, quarterly depending on the type of security.

Covered writing The sale of call options but the seller owns the stock which would be required to cover the delivery, if called.

Credit creation Expansion of loans which in turn expands the money supply.

Credit derivatives Credit derivatives have as the underlying asset some kind of credit default. As with all derivatives, the credit derivative is designed to enable the risk related to a credit issue, such as non-payment of an interest coupon on a corporate or sovereign bond, or the non-repayment of a loan, to be transferred.

Credit risk The risk that a borrower, or a counterparty to a deal, or the issuer of a security will default on repayment or not deliver its side of the deal.

CREST The organisation in the UK that holds UK and Irish company share in dematerialised form and clears and settles trades in UK and Irish company shares.

CRESTCo Organisation which owns CREST.

CREST member A participant within CREST who holds stock in stock accounts in CREST and whose name appears on the share register. A member is their own user.

CREST sponsored member A participant within CREST who holds stock in stock accounts in CREST and whose name appears on the share register. Unlike a member, a sponsored member is not their own user. The link to CREST is provided by another user who sponsors the sponsored member.

Cross-border trading Trading which takes place between persons or entities from different countries.

Cum-dividend With dividend.

Currency exposure Currency exposure exists if assets are held or income earned in one currency while liabilities are denominated in another currency. The position is exposed to changes in the relative values of the two currencies such that the cost of the liabilities may be increased or the value of the assets or earning decreased.

Currency futures Contracts calling for delivery of a specific amount of a foreign currency at a specified future date in return for a given amount of, say, US dollars.

CUSIP The Committee on Uniform Securities Identification Procedures, the body which established a consistent securities numbering system in the US.

Custodian Institution holding securities in safekeeping for a client. A custodian also offers different services to its clients (settlement, portfolio services).

Customer-non-private Customer who is assumed to understand the workings of the investment world and therefore receives little protection from the **Conduct of business rules**.

Customer private Customer who is assumed to be financially unsophisticated and therefore receives more protection from the **Conduct of business rules**.

Dealer Individual or firm that acts as principal in all transactions, buying for his own account.

Debenture Another name for a corporate bond – usually secured on assets of the company.

Deferred share A class of share where the holder is only entitled to a dividend if the ordinary shareholders have been paid a specified minimum dividend.

Delivery versus payment Settlement where transfer of the security and payment for that security occur simultaneously.

Delivery The physical movement of the underlying asset on which the derivative is based from seller to buyer.

Dematerialised (form) Circumstances where securities are held in a book-entry transfer system with no certificates.

Depository receipts Certificate issued by a bank in a country to represent shares of a foreign corporation issued in a foreign country. It entitles the holder to dividends and capital gains. They trade and pay dividend in the currency of the country of issuance of the certificate.

Depository Trust Company (DTC) A US central securities depository through which members may arrange deliveries of securities between each other through electronic debit and credit entries without the physical delivery of the securities. DTC is industry-owned, with the New York Stock Exchange as the majority owner. DTC is a member of the Federal Reserve System.

Derivative A financial instrument whose value is dependent upon the value of an underlying asset.

Deutsche Börse The German Stock Exchange.

Direct market participant A broker, broker/dealer or any direct member of an exchange.

Dirty price The total price of a bond including accrued interest.

Disclaimer A notice or statement intending to limit or avoid potential legal liability.

Discount securities Non-interest bearing short-term securities that are issued at discount and redeemed at maturity for full face value.

Diversification Investment strategy of spreading risk by investing the total available in a range of investments.

Dividend Distribution of profits made by a company if it chooses to do so.

Dividend yield The dividend expressed as a percentage of the share price.

D.K. Don't Know. Applies to a securities transaction pending settlement where fundamental data are missing, which prevents the receiving party from accepting delivery.

Domestic bond Bond issued in the country of the issuer and according to the regulations of that country.

Dow Jones Index Main share index used in the USA.

DTC Depository Trust Company – central securities depository for shares in the USA.

Duration A measure of the relative volatility of a bond; it is an approximation for the price change of a bond for a given change in the interest rate. Duration is measured in units of time. It includes the effects of time until maturity, cash flows and the yield to maturity.

Earnings per share (EPS) The total profit of a company divided by the number of shares in issue.

ECB European Central Bank.

ECSDA European Central Securities Depository Association.

EFP Exchange of futures for physical. Common in the energy markets. A physical deal priced on the futures markets.

Elective event Corporate action which requires a choice from the security owner.

Electronic order book The electronic order matching system used as the system for dealing in the shares which comprise the FTSE 100 stock.

Emerging market Non-industrialised country with low or middle per capita income, as published annually by the World Bank, and an undeveloped capital market (i.e., the market represents only a small portion of their GDP).

Equity A common term to describe stocks or shares.

Equity/Stock options Contracts based on individual equities or shares. On exercise of the option the specified amount of shares are exchanged between the buyer and the seller through the clearing organisation.

E-T-D This is the common term used to describe exchange-traded derivatives, which are the standardised products. It also differentiates products which are listed on an exchange as opposed to those offered **Over-the-counter**.

ETF (exchange-traded funds) Passively managed basket of stocks that mirrors a particular index and that can be traded like ordinary shares. They trade intra-day on stock exchanges, like securities, at market-determined prices. In essence, ETFs are index funds that trade like stocks.

EUCLID Communications system operated by Euroclear.

EUREX German–Swiss derivatives exchange created by the merger of the German (DTB) and Swiss (SOFFEX) exchanges.

EURIBOR A measure of the average cost of funds over the whole euro area based on a panel of 57 banks.

Euro The name of the single European currency.

Euro-commercial Unsecured corporate debt with a short maturity structured to appeal to large financial institutions active in the Euro Market.

Eurobond An interest bearing security issued across national borders, usually issued in a currency other than that of the issuer's home country.

Euroclear A book-entry clearing facility for most eurocurrency and foreign securities. It is owned by a large number of banks of North American and European origin and is managed by Morgan Guaranty Trust in Brussels.

Euronext An amalgamation of the Dutch, French and Belgian exchanges.

Euronext.liffe *See* **London International Financial Futures and Options Exchange**.

European-style option An option which can only be exercised on the expiry day.

Exception-based processing Transaction processing where straightforward items are processed automatically, allowing staff to concentrate on the items which are incorrect or not straightforward.

Exchange Market place for trading.

Exchange Delivery Settlement Price (EDSP) The price determined by the exchange for physical delivery of the underlying instrument or cash settlement for derivatives.

Exchange-owned clearing organisation Exchange or member-owned clearing organisations are structured so that the clearing members guarantee each other with the use of a members' default fund and additional funding like insurance, with no independent guarantee.

Exchange rate The rate at which one currency can be exchanged for another.

Ex-date Date on or after which a sale of securities is executed without the right to receive dividends or other entitlements.

Ex-dividend Thirty-seven days before interest payment is due gilt-edged stocks are made 'ex-dividend'. After a stock has become 'ex-dividend', a buyer of stock purchases it without the right to receive the next (pending) interest payment.

Execute and eliminate order Type of order input into the Stock Exchange electronic trading service. The amount that can be tracked immediately against displayed orders is completed, with the remainder being rejected.

Execution The action of trading in the markets.

Exercise The process by which the holder of an option may take up their right to buy or sell the underlying asset.

Exercise price (or **Strike price**) The fixed price, per share or unit, at which an option conveys the right to call (purchase) or put (sell) the underlying shares or units.

Expiry date The last date on which an option holder can exercise their right. After this date an option is deemed to lapse or be abandoned.

Ex-warrants Trading a security so that the buyer will not be entitled to warrants that will be distributed to holders.

Face value The value of a bond, note, mortgage or other security that appears on the face of the issue, unless the value is otherwise specified by the issuing company. Face value is ordinarily the amount the issuing company promises to pay at maturity. Face value is also referred to as **Par value** or **Nominal value**.

Failed transaction A securities transaction that does not settle on time – i.e., the securities and/or cash are not exchanged as agreed on the settlement date.

Fair value For futures, it is the true price not the market price, allowing for the cost of carry. For options, it is the true price not the market price, as calculated using an option pricing model.

Federal Reserve book-entry system Central securities depository for US government securities.

Fill or kill order Type of order input into the Stock Exchange electronic trading service. It is either completed in full against displayed orders or rejected in full.

Final settlement The completion of a transaction when the delivery of all components of a trade is performed.

Financial futures/options contracts 'Financial futures' is a term used to describe futures contracts based on financial instruments like currencies, debt instruments and financial indices.

Financial Services and Markets Act 2000 The legislation that created the single UK regulator, the Financial Services Authority.

Financial Services Authority (FSA)   The agency designated by the Treasury to regulate investment business as required by FSA 1986. It is the main regulator of the financial sector and was formerly called the Securities and Investments Board (SIB). It assumed its full powers on 1st December 2001.

Fiscal agent   A commercial bank appointed by the borrower to undertake certain duties related to the new issue, such as assisting the payment of interest and principal, redeeming bonds or coupons, handling taxes, replacement of lost or damaged securities, destruction of coupons and bonds once payments have been made.

Fiscal years   These run from 6th April to 5th April and are the periods of assessment for both income tax and capital gains tax.

Fit and proper   Under FSA 1986 everyone conducting investment business must be a 'fit and proper person'. The Act does not define the term, a function which is left to the regulator.

Fixed income   Interest on a security which is calculated as a constant specified percentage of the principal amount and paid at the end of specified interest periods, usually annually or semi-annually, until maturity.

Fixed-rate   A borrowing or investment where the interest or coupon paid is fixed throughout the arrangement.

Fixed rate borrowing   A fixed rate borrowing establishing the interest rate that will be paid throughout the life of the loan.

Flat position   A position which has been fully closed out and no liability to make or take delivery exists.

Flat yield (*also called* **Income yield**)   The yield of a bond calculated as:

$$\frac{\text{Annual coupon}}{\text{Current market price}} \times 100\%$$

Floating-rate   A borrowing or investment where the interest or coupon paid changes throughout the arrangement in line with some reference rate such as **LIBOR**.

Floating Rate Note (FRN)   Bond where each interest payment is made at the current or average market levels, often by reference to **LIBOR**.

Foreign bond   Bond issued in a domestic market in the domestic currency and under the domestic rules of issuance by a foreign issuer (e.g., Samurai bonds are bonds issued by issuers of other countries on the Japanese market).

Forex   Abbreviation for foreign exchange (currency trading).

Forward delivery   Transactions which involve a delivery date in the future.

Forward rate agreements (FRAs)   An agreement where the client can fix the rate of interest that will be applied to a notional loan or deposit, drawn or placed on an agreed date in the future, for a specified term.

Forwards   Are very similar to futures contracts but they are not mainly traded on an exchange. They are not marked to market daily but settled only on the delivery date.

FSA   Financial Services Authority.

FTSE 100 index   Main UK share index based on 100 leading shares.

Fund manager   An organisation that invests money on behalf of someone else.

Fungibility   A futures contract with identical administration in more than one financial centre. Trades in various geographical locations can be offset (e.g., bought on the International Petroleum Exchange and sold on SGX).

Futures   An agreement to buy or sell an asset at a certain time in the future for a certain price.

Future value   The amount of money which can be achieved at a given date in the future by investing (or borrowing) a given sum of money now at a given interest rate, assuming compound re-investment (or re-funding) of any interest payments received (or paid) before the end.

Gearing   The characteristic of derivatives which enables a far greater reward for the same, or much smaller initial outlay. It is the ratio of exposure to investment outlay, and is also known as **Leverage**.

General Principles   Ten fundamental principles of behaviour written by the Financial Services Authority to apply to all investment businesses.

Gilt   Domestic, sterling-denominated long-term bond backed by the full faith and credit of the UK and issued by the Treasury.

Gilt Edged Market Makers (GEMMs)   A firm that is a market maker in gilts. Also known as a **Primary dealer**.

Gilt-edged security   UK government borrowing.

Give-up   The process of giving a trade to a third party who will undertake the clearing and settlement of the trade.

Global bond   A (temporary) certificate representing the whole of a bond issue.

Global clearing   The channelling of the settlement of all futures and options trades through a single counterparty or through a number of counterparties geographically located.

Global custodian   Institution that safekeeps, settles and performs processing of income collection, tax reclaim, multicurrency reporting, cash management, foreign exchange, corporate action and proxy monitoring, etc. for clients' securities in all required market places.

Global depository receipt (GDR)   A security representing shares held in custody in the country of issue.

GLOBEX   The overnight trading system operated by Reuters and the Chicago Mercantile Exchange.

Good delivery   Proper delivery of certificates that are negotiable and complete in terms of documentation or information.

Gross   A position which is held with both the bought and sold trades kept open.

Gross domestic product (GDP)   A measure of the country's entire output.

Gross redemption yield (GRY)   The annual return on owning a bond, allowing both for interest and profit on redemption.

Group of 30 (G30)   Private international organisation aiming to deepen understanding of international economic and financial issues.

GSCC Government Securities Clearing Corporation, a clearing organisation for US Treasury securities.

Guaranteed bond Bonds on which the principal or income, or both, are guaranteed by another corporation or parent company in case of default by the issuing corporation.

Haircut The discount applied to the value of collateral used to cover margins.

Hard commodities Commodities such as tin or zinc. Futures on them are traded on the London Metal Exchange.

Hedge ratio Determining the ratio of the futures to the cash position so as to reduce price risk.

Hedging A trading method which is designed to reduce or mitigate risk – e.g., reducing the risk of a cash position in the futures instrument to offset the price movement of the cash asset. A broader definition of hedging includes using futures as a temporary substitute for the cash position.

Holder A person who has bought an open derivatives contract.

Home state regulation Under the Investment Services Directive, an investment business is authorised in the place of its head office and registered office. This home state authorisation entitles it to conduct business in any member state of the EU.

Host state regulation Any European investment business operating outside its home basis is regulated by its host for its conduct of business.

ICOM International Currency Options Market standard documentation for netting foreign exchange option settlements.

Immobilisation The storage of securities certificates in a vault in order to eliminate physical movement of certificates/documents in transfer of ownership.

Implied repo rate The rate of return before financing costs implied by a transaction where a longer-term cash security is purchased and a futures contract is sold (or *vice versa*).

Income yield *See* **Flat yield.**

Independent Clearing Organisation The Independent Organisation is quite separate from the actual members of the exchange, and will guarantee to each member the performance of the contracts by having them registered in the Organisation's name.

Index funds Unit trusts which invest in the constituent parts of an index.

Index-linked bond Bond whose interest payment and redemption value are linked to the retail prices index.

Indirect market participation Non-broker/dealers, such as institutional investors, who are active investors/traders.

Inflation A period of generally rising prices.

Initial margin The deposit which the clearing house calls as protection against a default of a derivatives contract. It is returnable to the clearing member once the position is closed. The level is subject to changes in line with market conditions.

Insider dealing   The criminal offence whereby those with unpublished, price-sensitive information deal, advise others to deal or pass the information on. Maximum penalty is 7 years jail and an unlimited fine.

Institutional investor   An institution which is usually investing money on behalf of others. Examples are mutual funds and pension funds.

Integration   The third stage of money laundering, in which the money is finally integrated into the legitimate economy. *See* **Placement, Layering**.

Interbank market   A market for transactions exclusively or predominantly within the banking system. In most countries, the market for short-term money is an interbank market since banks borrow and lend among one and another in order to balance their books on a daily basis. Non-bank entities may or may not be permitted to participate.

Inter-dealer broker (IDB)   Member of the London Stock Exchange that acts as a link between firms to enable them to trade with each other anonymously.

Interest rate futures   Based on a debt instrument – such as a Government Bond or a Treasury Bill – as the underlying product and require the delivery of a bond or bill to fulfil the contract.

Interest rate swap   An agreement to exchange interest-related payments in the same currency from fixed rate into floating rate (or *vice versa*) or from one type of floating rate to another.

Interim dividend   Dividend paid part way through a year in advance of the final dividend.

International depository receipt (IDR)   Receipt of shares of a foreign corporation held in the vaults of a depository bank. The receipt entitles the holder to all dividends and capital gains. Dividends and capital gains are converted to local currency as part of the service. IDRs allow investors to purchase foreign shares without having to involve themselves in foreign settlements and currency conversion.

International equity   An equity of a company based outside the UK but traded internationally.

International Petroleum Exchange (IPE)   Market for derivatives of petrol and oil products.

International securities identification number (ISIN)   A coding system developed by the International Standards Organisation for identifying securities. ISINs are designated to create one unique worldwide number for any security. It is a 12-digit alphanumeric code.

International Standards Organisation (ISO)   An international federation of organisations of various industries which seeks to set common international standards in a variety of fields.

Interpolation   The estimation of a price or rate, usually for a broken date, from two other rates or prices, each of which is for a date either side of the required date.

Intra-day margin   An extra margin call which the clearing organisation can call during the day when there is a very large movement up or down in the price of the contract.

Investment business Dealing, advising or managing investments. Those doing so need to be authorised.

Investment Services Directive (ISD) EU Directive imposing common standards on investment business.

Investments Items defined in the FSA 1986 to be regulated by it. Includes shares, bonds, options, futures, life assurance and pensions.

Investment trust (company) A company whose sole function is to invest in the shares of other companies.

Invoice amount The amount calculated under the formula specified by the futures exchange which will be paid in settlement of the delivery of the underlying asset.

IOSCO International Organisation of Securities Commissions.

IPMA International Primary Markets Association.

Irredeemable gilt A gilt with no fixed date for redemption. Investors receive interest indefinitely.

ISDA International Swaps and Derivatives Association, previously known as the International Swap Dealers Association. Many market participants use ISDA documentation.

ISMA International Securities Markets Association.

ISSA The International Securities Services Association.

Issue Stocks or bonds sold by a corporation or government entity at a particular time.

Issue price The percentage of principal value at which the price of a new issue of securities is fixed.

Issuer Legal entity that issues and distributes securities.

JASDEC Japan Securities Depository Centre, the central securities depository for Japan.

JSCC Japan Securities Clearing Corporation, the clearing organisation in Japan.

Junk bonds High-risk bonds that have low ratings or are in default.

Last notice day The final day that notification of delivery of a futures contract will be possible. On most exchanges all outstanding short futures contracts will be automatically delivered to open long positions.

Last trading day Often the day preceding last notice day which is the final opportunity for holders of long derivatives positions to trade out of their positions and avoid ultimate delivery.

Layering The second stage of money laundering, in which the money is passed through a series of transactions to obscure its origin. *See* **Placement, Integration**.

LCH London Clearing House.

Lead managers In the eurobond markets the description given to the securities house appointed to handle a new issue.

Leverage The magnification of gains and losses by only paying for part of the underlying value of the instrument or asset; the smaller the amount of funds invested, the greater the leverage. It is also known as **Gearing**.

LIBID   The London interbank bid rate. The rate at which one bank will lend to another.

LIBOR   The London interbank offered rate. It is the rate used when one bank borrows from another bank. It is the benchmark used to price many capital market and derivative transactions.

LIFFE connect   Euronext.liffe electronic dealing system.

Limit order   Type of order input into the Stock Exchange electronic trading service. If not completed immediately the balance is displayed on the screen and forms the order book.

Line order   An order in which a customer sets the maximum price he is willing to pay as a buyer or the minimum price he is willing to accept as a seller.

Linked Forex   When the currency contract is purchased to cover the local cost of a security trade.

Liquidity   A liquid asset is one that can be converted easily and rapidly into cash without a substantial loss of value. In the money market, a security is said to be liquid if the spread between bid and asked price is narrow, and reasonable size can be done at those quotes.

Liquidity risk   The risk that a bank may not be able to close out a position because the market is illiquid.

Listed company   Company which has been admitted to listing on a stock exchange and whose shares can then be dealt on that exchange.

Listing   Status applied for by companies whose securities are then listed on the London Stock Exchange and available to be traded.

Listing rules   Rule book for listed companies which governs their behaviour. Commonly known as the *Yellow Book*.

Lloyds of London   World's largest insurance market.

Loan Stock   *See* **Bonds**.

London interbank offer rate (LIBOR)   Rate at which banks lend to each other which is often used as the benchmark for floating rate loans.

London International Financial Futures and Options Exchange (LIFFE)   Market for trading in bond, interest rate, FTSE 100 index and FTSE Mid 250 index, futures, plus equity options and soft commodity derivatives.

London Metal Exchange (LME)   Market for trading in derivatives of metals such as copper, tin, zinc, etc.

London Stock Exchange (LSE)   Market for trading in securities. Formerly known as the International Stock Exchange of the United Kingdom and Republic of Ireland or *ISE*.

Long coupons   (1) Bonds or notes with a long current maturity. (2) A coupon on which the period is longer than the others or the standard coupon period.

Long-dated   Gilts with more than 15 years until redemption.

Long position   Refers to an investor's account in which he has more shares of a specific security than he needs to meet his settlement obligations. Also, a bought position in a derivative which is held open.

Lot The common term used to describe the standard unit of trading for futures and options. It is also referred to as a **Contract**.

Mandatory event A corporate action which affects the securities without giving any choice to the security holder.

Mandatory quote period Time of day during which market makers in equities are obliged to quote prices under London Stock Exchange rules.

Margin Initial margin is collateral placed by one party with a counterparty or clearing house at the time of a deal, against the possibility that the market price will move against the first party, thereby leaving the counterparty with a credit risk. **Variation margin** is a payment made, or collateral transferred, from one party to the other because the market price of the transaction or of collateral has changed. Variation margin payment is either in effect a settlement of profit/loss (e.g., in the case of a futures contract) or the reduction of credit exposure. In a loan, margin is the extra interest above a benchmark such as **LIBOR** required by a lender to compensate for the credit risk of that particular borrower.

Mark-to-market The process of revaluing an **Over-the-counter** or exchange-traded product each day. It is the difference between the closing price on the previous day against the current closing price. For exchange-traded products this is referred to as **Variation margin**.

Market Description of any organisation or facility through which items are traded. All exchanges are markets.

Market counterparty A person dealing as agent or principal with the broker and involved in the same nature of investment business as the broker. This also includes fellow members of the Securities and Futures Authority or trading members of an investment exchange, for those products only where they are members.

Market forces Supply and demand allowing buyers and sellers to fix the price without external interference.

Market maker A trader who works for an organisation such as an investment bank. They quote bids and offers in the market and are normally under an obligation to make a price in a certain number of contracts. They create liquidity in the contract by offering to buy or sell.

Market price In the case of a security, the market price is usually considered as the last reported price at which the stock or bond has been sold.

Market risk (position risk) The risk that the market value of a position falls.

Market value The price at which a security is trading and could presumably be purchased or sold.

Master agreement This agreement is for **Over-the-counter** transactions and is signed between the client and the broker. It covers the basic terms under which the client and broker wish to transact business. Each individual trade has a separate individual agreement with specific terms known as a **Confirm**.

Matching (comparison)   Another term for comparison (or checking); a matching system to compare trades and ensure that both sides of a trade correspond.

Maturity   The date on which the principal or nominal value of a bond becomes due and payable in full to the holder.

Medium dated   Gilts due to be redeemed within the next 7 to 15 years.

Mergers & acquisitions (M&A)   Divisions of securities houses or merchant banks responsible for advising on take-over activity. Usually work with the corporate finance department and is often kept as a single unit.

Mixed economy   Economy which relies on a mix of market forces and government involvement.

Model Code for Securities Dealing   Part of the *Yellow Book* that relates to directors dealing in their own company's securities. Prohibits them from doing so during the 2 months before results are announced.

Model risk   The risk that the computer model used by a bank for valuation or risk assessment is incorrect or misinterpreted.

Modified following   The convention that if a settlement date in the future falls on a non-business day, the settlement date will be moved to the next following business day, unless this moves it to the next month, in which case the settlement date is moved back to the last previous business day.

MOF   The Ministry of Finance (Japan).

Money market   The market for the purchase and sale of short-term financial instruments. 'Short term' is usually defined as less than 1 year.

Money market fund   An open-end mutual fund which invests in commercial paper, bankers' acceptances, repurchase agreements, government securities, and other highly liquid and safe securities. The fund pays money market rates of interest. Many money market funds are part of fund families; investors can switch their money from one fund to another and back again without charge.

Moody's Investment Service   Located in New York City with its parent, Dun & Bradstreet, Moody's is one of the two most popular bond rating agencies in the US. The other agency is Standard and Poor's.

Mortgage   A form of security on borrowing commonly associated with home borrowing.

Mortgage-backed security   Security backed by an investment company that raises money from shareholders and invests it in stocks, bonds or other instruments (unit trust, investment fund, SICAV, BEVEK).

Multilateral netting   Trade between several counterparties in the same security are netted such that each counterparty makes only one transfer of cash or securities to another party or to a central clearing system. Handles only transactions due for settlement on the same day.

Mutual collateralisation   The deposit of collateral by both counterparties to a transaction.

NASDAQ   National Association of Securities Dealers Automated Quotation system.

Net Asset Value (NAV) In mutual funds, the market value of the fund share. It is common practice for an investment trust to compute its assets daily, or even twice a day, by totalling the closing market value of all securities and assets (i.e., cash) owned. All liabilities are deducted, and the balance is divided by the number of shares outstanding. The resulting figure is the net asset value per share.

Net Present Value (NPV) The net total of several present values (arising from cash flows at different future dates) added together, some of which may be positive and some negative.

Netting Trading partners offset their positions thereby reducing the number of positions for settlement. Netting can be either **Bilateral**, **Multilateral** or **Continuous net settlement**.

New issues Company-raised additional capital by issuing new securities. 'New issue' is the name given to the bonds or stocks offered to investors for the first time.

Nikkei Dow Index Main share index in Japan.

Nil paid rights price Ex-rights price less the subscription price.

Nominal amount Value stated on the face of a security (see **Principal value**, **Par value**). Securities processing: number of securities to deliver/receive.

Nominal value of a bond The value at which the capital, or principal, of a bond will be redeemed by the issuer. See **Par value**.

Nominal value of a share The minimum price at which a share can be issued. See **Par value**.

Nominee An organisation that acts as the named owner of securities on behalf of a different beneficial owner who remains anonymous to the company.

Non-callable Cannot be redeemed by the issuer for a stated period of time from date of issue.

Non-clearing member A member of an exchange who does not undertake to settle their derivatives business. This type of member must appoint a clearing member to register all their trades at the clearing organisation.

Non-competitive bid In an auction, bidding for a specific amount of securities without mentioning a price. Usually, the price paid will be equal to the average of the accepted competitive bids.

Non-cumulative preference share If the company fails to pay a preference dividend the entitlement to the dividend is simply lost. There is no accumulation.

Non-deliverable forward A foreign exchange forward outright where, instead of each party delivering the full amount of currency at settlement, there is a single net cash payment to reflect the change in value between the forward rates transacted and the spot rate two working days before settlement.

Normal market size (NMS) Minimum size in which market makers must quote on the London Stock Exchange.

Nostro A bank's nostro account is its currency account held at another bank.

Nostro reconciliation Checking the entries shown on the bank's nostro account statement with the bank's internal records (the accounting ledgers) to ensure that they correspond exactly.

Note Bonds issued with a relatively short maturity are often called notes.

Notional Contracts for differences require a notional principal amount on which settlement can be calculated.

Novation The process where registered trades are cancelled with the clearing members and substituted by two new ones – one between the clearing house and the clearing member seller, the other between the clearing house and the clearing member buyer.

NSCC National Securities Clearing Corporation, a clearing organisation for US shares.

OASYS Trade confirmation system for US brokers operated by Thomson Financial Services.

OATs *Obligations Assimilables du Trésor*, a 7–10-year French Treasury bond.

Obligation netting An arrangement to transfer only the net amount (of cash or a security) due between two or more parties, rather than transfer all amounts between the parties on a gross basis.

Off-balance sheet A transaction whose principal amount is not shown on the balance sheet because it is a contingent liability or settled as a contract for differences.

Offer for sale Historically, the most popular form of new issue in the UK for companies bringing their securities to the stockmarket for the first time. The company offers its shares to the general public.

Offer price The price at which a trader or market maker is willing to sell a contract. *See also* **Ask price.**

Office of Fair Trading (OFT) Government department which advises the Secretary of State for Trade and Industry on whether or not a proposed take-over should be referred to the Monopolies and Mergers Commission for full investigation.

Offshore Relates to locations outside the controls of domestic monetary, exchange and legislative authorities. Offshore may not necessarily be outside the national boundaries of a country. In some countries, certain banks or other institutions may be granted offshore status and thus be exempt from all or specific controls or legislation.

Omnibus account Account containing the holdings of more than one client.

On-balance sheet A transaction whose principal amount is shown on the balance sheet.

On-line Processing which is executed via an interactive input onto a PC or stationary terminal connected to a processing centre.

Open economy A country where there are no restrictions on trading with other countries.

Open-ended Type of investment such as unit trusts or open-ended investment companies which can expand without limit.

Open-ended investment company (OEIC) New corporate structure introduced in 1997. It is a form of collective investment vehicle.

Open interest The number of contracts both bought and sold which remain open for delivery on an exchange. Important indicator for liquidity.

Open outcry The style of trading whereby traders face each other in a designated area such as a pit and shout or call their respective bids and offers. Hand signals are also used to communicate. It is governed by exchange rules.

Open position The number of contracts which have not been off-set at the clearing organisation by the close of business.

Opening trade A bought or sold trade which is held open to create a position.

Operational risk The risk of losses resulting from inadequate systems and control, human errors or management failings.

Option An option is – in the case of the buyer – the right, but not the obligation, to take (call) or make (put) for delivery of the underlying product and – in the case of the seller – the obligation to make or take delivery of the underlying product.

Option premium The sum of money paid by the buyer for acquiring the right of the option. It is the sum of money received by the seller for incurring the obligation, having sold the rights, of the option. It is the sum of the intrinsic value and the time value.

Optional dividend Dividend that can be paid either in cash or in stock. The shareholders entitled to the dividend make the choice.

Options on futures These have the same characteristics as an option, the difference being that the underlying product is either a long or short futures contract. **Premium** is not exchanged as the contracts are **Marked-to-market** each day.

Order-driven market A stock market where brokers acting on behalf of clients match trades with each other either on the trading floor of the exchange or through a central computer system.

Out-trade A trade which has been incorrectly matched on the floor of an exchange.

Over-subscribed Circumstances where people have applied for more shares than are available in a new issue.

Over-the-counter (OTC) A one-to-one agreement between two counterparties where the specifications of the product are completely flexible and non-standardised.

Overnight money Money placed on the money market for repayment the next day.

Pair off Back-to-back trade between two parties where settlement occurs only by exchanging the cash difference between the two parties.

Panel on Takeovers and Mergers (PTM) A non-statutory body comprising City institutions which regulates take-over activities.

Par value *See* **Nominal value** *and* **Face value**.

Pari passu   Without partiality. Securities that rank *pari passu*, rank equally with each other.

Paying agent   A bank which handles payment of interest and dividends on behalf of the issuer of a security.

Payment date   Date on which a dividend or an interest payment is scheduled to be paid.

Pension fund   Fund set up by a corporation, labour union, governmental entity or other organisation to pay the pension benefits of retired workers. Pension funds invest billions of dollars annually in the securities markets and are therefore major market players.

Perpetual bond   A bond which has no redemption date.

Placement   The first stage of money laundering, in which the money is passed placed in the banking system. *See* **Layering, Integration**.

Placing   Procedure used for new issues where a securities house contracts its own clients to offer them stock. It is almost always used for new issues of eurobonds and for equities on the London Stock Exchange, more so since January 1996 when restrictions on their use were removed.

Plain vanilla or **Vanilla swap**   A swap which has a very basic structure.

Portfolio   List of investments held by an individual or company, or list of loans made by a bank or financial institution.

Power of attorney   The legal authority for one party to sign for and act on behalf of another party.

Preference shares   Shares that have preferential rights to dividends, usually a fixed sum, before dividends are paid out to ordinary shareholders. They usually carry no voting rights. The rights of preference shareholders are established in a company's articles of association and may differ between companies in a variety of ways.

Premium   An option premium is the amount paid up-front by the purchaser of the option to the writer.

Present value   The amount of money which needs to be invested (or borrowed) now at a given interest rate in order to achieve exactly a given cash flow in the future, assuming compound re-investment (or re-funding) of any interest payments received (or paid) before the end. *See* **Future value**.

Pre-settlement   Checks and procedures undertaken immediately after execution of a trade prior to settlement.

Price/earnings ratio   The share price of a company divided by its earnings per share. A high p/e ratio implies that the company is well thought of for its future prospects.

Price (conversion) factor   The price at which a bond would trade, per 1 nominal, to yield the notional coupon of the futures contract on the delivery day (or the first day in the deliverable month if this applies).

Primary dealer   *See* **Gilt-edged market maker**.

Primary market   Market for the placement of new securities such as international, domestic and foreign bond issues. Any subsequent resale or purchase is handled on the secondary market.

Principal-protected product   An investment whose maturity value is guaranteed to be at least the principal amount invested initially.

Principal-to-principal market   A market where the clearing house only recognises the clearing member as one entity, and not the underlying clients of the clearing member.

Principal trading   When a member firm of the London Stock Exchange buys stock from or sells stock to a non-member.

Principal value   That amount inscribed on the face of a security and exclusive of interest or premium. The amount is the one used in the computation of interest due on such a security.

Private customer   An individual person who is not acting in the course of carrying on investment business.

Private placement   Issue of securities that is offered to a limited number of investors.

Privatisation   Process whereby the government puts state-owned industries into the private sector – e.g., water, electricity. Usually involves an offer for sale of its shares.

Project A   The after hours trading system used by the Chicago Board of Trade.

Proprietary trader   A trader who deals for an organisation – such as an investment bank – taking advantage of short-term price movements as well as taking long-term views on whether the market will move up or down.

Prospectus   Offer document detailing the product on offer to investors.

Put option   An option that gives the buyer the right, but not the obligation, to sell a specified quantity of the underlying asset at a fixed price, on or before a specified date. The seller of a put option has the obligation (because they have sold the right) to take delivery of the underlying asset if the option is exercised by the buyer.

Quoted   Colloquial term for a security that is traded on the Stock Exchange.

Quote-driven   Dealing system where some firms accept the responsibility to quote buying and selling prices.

Rating   Evaluation of securities investment and credit risk by rating services – such as Moody's or Standard & Poor's.

RCH   Recognised clearing house under the Financial Services Act.

Real-time gross settlement (RTGS)   Gross settlement system in which trades are settled continuously through the processing day.

Realised profit   Profit which has arisen from a real sale.

Reconciliation   The comparison of a person's records of cash and securities position with records held by another party and the investigation and resolution of any discrepancies between the two sets of records.

Record date   The date on which a securities holder must hold the securities in order to receive an income or entitlement.

Redemption   The purchase and cancellation of outstanding securities through a cash payment to the holder.

Redemption price   A price at which bonds may be redeemed, or called, at the issuer's option, prior to maturity (often with a slight premium).

Registered title   Form of ownership of securities where the owner's name appears on a register maintained by the company.

Registrar of Companies   Government department responsible for keeping records of all companies.

Replacement cost   The **Mark-to-market** loss which would be incurred if it were necessary to undertake a new transaction to replace an existing one, because the existing counterparty defaulted.

Repurchase agreement (repo)   Borrowing funds by providing a government security for collateral and promising to 'repurchase' the security at the end of the agreed-upon time period. The associated interest rate is the 'repo rate'.

Reputational risk   The risk that an organisation's reputation will be damaged.

Reverse repo   Purchase of gilt where the price and date for its re-sale is fixed at the same time.

RIE   Recognised Investment Exchange under the Financial Services Act.

Right of offset   Where positions and cash held by the clearing organisation in different accounts for a member are allowed to be netted.

Rights issue   Offer of shares made to existing shareholders.

Risk warning   Document that must be despatched and signed by private customers before they deal in traded options.

Roll-over   A Libor fixing on a new tranche of loan, or transfer of a futures position to the next delivery month.

Rolling settlement   System used in most countries including the UK. Bargains are settled a set number of days after being transacted.

Round lot   The minimum amount for which dealers' quotes are good.

Safekeeping   Holding of securities on behalf of clients. They are free to sell at any time.

Sale of rights nil paid   The sale of the entitlement to take up a rights issue. *See also* **Nil paid rights price**.

Same day funds   Refers to the availability of funds on the same day as they are deposited.

Scrip dividends   Scrip dividends options provide shareholders with the choice of receiving dividend entitlements in the form of cash, shares or a combination or both. The amount of stocks to be distributed under a scrip option is calculated by dividing the cash dividend amount by the average market price over a recent period of time.

SEATS plus   An order-driven system used on the London Stock Exchange for securities which do not attract at least two firms of market makers and for all **Alternative Investment Market** securities.

Secondary market   Market place for trading in existing securities. The price at which they are trading has no direct effect on the company's fortunes but is a reflection of investors' perceptions of the company.

Securities   Bonds and equities.

Securities house   General term covering any type of organisation involved in securities although usually reserved for the larger firms.

Securities lending   Loan of securities by an investor to another (usually a broker-dealer), normally to cover a short sale.

SEDOL   Stock Exchange Daily Official List, a securities numbering system assigned by the International Stock Exchange in London.

Segregated account   Account in which there are only the holdings of one client.

Segregation of funds   Where the client assets are held separately from those assets belonging to the member firm.

SEQUAL   The checking system used for international equities.

SETS   Stock Exchange electronic trading service, the electronic order book used by the London Stock Exchange.

Settlement   The fulfilment of the contractual commitments of transacted business.

Settlement date   The date on which a trade is cleared by delivery of securities against funds (actual settlement date, contractual settlement date).

17F-5   Legal requirements for world-wide correspondent banks which serve US mutual funds, pension funds and other regulated financial groups.

Share futures   Based on individual shares. Delivery is fulfilled by the payment or receipt of cash against the exchange-calculated delivery settlement price.

Share option   A right sold to an investor conferring the option to buy or sell shares of a particular company at a predetermined price and within a specified time limit.

Short   A sold position in a derivative which is held open.

Short coupons   Bonds or notes with a short current maturity.

Short cover   The purchase of a security that has been previously sold short. The purpose is to return securities that were borrowed to make a delivery.

Short-dated gilt   Gilts due to be redeemed within the next 7 years, according to the London Stock Exchange (*FT* states up to 5 years).

Short sale   The sale of securities not owned by the seller in the expectation that the price of these securities will fall or as part of an arbitrage.

Short selling   Selling stock that you do not own.

Short-term security   Generally, an obligation maturing in less than 1 year.

Soft commodities   Description given to commodities such as sugar, coffee and cocoa, traded through Euronext.liffe since its incorporation of the former London Commodity Exchange (*LCE*).

Sovereign debt securities   Bonds issued by the government of a country.

SPAN   Standardised Portfolio Analysis of Risk, a form of margin calculation for derivatives which is used by various clearing organisations.

Speculator   The speculator is a trader who wants to assume risk for potentially much higher rewards.

Sponsored member   Type of CREST member whose name appears on the register but has no computer link with CREST.

Spot delivery   A delivery or settlement of currencies on the value date, two business days later.

Spot market   Market for immediate as opposed to future delivery. In the spot market for foreign exchange, settlement is two business days ahead.

Spread   The difference between the **Bid** and **Offer** rate. Also describes a trade in more than one delivery month or more than one product. A trading strategy in which a trader buys one instrument and sells another related instrument with a view to profiting from a change in the price difference between the two. A futures spread is the purchase of one futures contract and the sale of another; an option spread is the purchase of one call (or put) and the sale of another.

Stamp duty   Tax on purchase of equities in the UK.

Stamp Duty Reserve Tax (SDRT) (UK)   Tax payable on the purchase of UK equities in uncertified form (i.e., those held within CREST).

Standard settlement instructions   Instructions for settlement with a particular counterparty which are always followed for a particular kind of deal and, once in place, are therefore not repeated at the time of each transaction.

Standing instruction   Default instruction (e.g., provided to an agent processing payments or clearing securities trades), or provided by shareholder on how to vote shares (e.g., vote for all management-recommended candidates).

Stepped   A stepped coupon is one which rises or falls in a pre-determined way over the life of an arrangement.

Stock   In some countries (e.g., the US) the term applies to ordinary share capital of a company. In other countries (e.g., the UK) stock may mean share capital that is issued in variable amounts instead of in fixed specified amounts, or it can describe government loans.

Stock dividend   Dividends paid by a company in stock instead of cash.

Stock Exchange Automated Quotation System (SEAQ)   Electronic screen display system through which market makers in equities display prices at which they are willing to deal.

Stock Exchange Electronic Trading System (SETS)   Share trading system for FTSE 100 stocks and other major shares on the London Stock Exchange.

Stock index futures/options   Based on the value of an underlying stock index – like the FTSE 100 in the UK, the S & P 500 index in the US and the Nikkei 225 and 300 in Japan. Delivery is fulfilled by the payment or receipt of cash against the exchange-calculated delivery settlement price. These are referred to as both indices or indexes.

Stock (or bond) power   A legal document, either on the back of registered stocks and bonds or attached to them, by which the owner assigns his interest in the corporation to a third party, allowing that party the right to substitute another name on the company records instead of the original owner's.

Stock split   When a corporation splits its stock, it divides existing shares into a greater number.

Straight-through-processing   Computer transmission of the details of a trade, without manual intervention, from their original input by the trader to all other relevant areas – position keeping, risk control, accounts, settlement, reconciliation.

Street name   Securities held in street name are held in the name of a broker or another nominee (i.e., a customer).

Strike price   The fixed price, per share or unit, at which an option conveys the right to call (purchase) or put (sell) the underlying shares or units.

Stripped bonds (strips)   Bonds where the rights to the interest payments and eventual repayment of the nominal value have been separated from each other and trade independently. Facility introduced for gilts in December 1997.

Subcustodian   A bank in a foreign country that acts on behalf of the custodian as its custody agent.

Subscription price   Price at which shareholders of a corporation are entitled to purchase common shares in a **Rights issue** or at which subscription warrants are exercisable.

Strike price/rate   The price or rate at which the holder of an option can insist on the underlying transaction being fulfilled. *See also* **Exercise price**.

Strip   The purchase or sale of a series of consecutive interest rate futures contracts or forward rate agreements.

Swap   Arrangement where two borrowers, one of whom has fixed interest and one of whom has floating rate borrowings, swap their commitments with each other. A bank would arrange the swap and charge a fee.

SwapClear   A clearing house and central counterparty for swaps.

SwapsWire   An electronic dealing system for swaps.

SWIFT   Society for Worldwide Interbank Financial Telecommunications, a secure electronic communications network between banks.

Syndicate   A group of bond houses which act together in underwriting and distributing a new securities issue.

TARGET   Trans European Automated Real time Gross settlement Express Transfer, a system linking the real-time gross settlements for euros in the 15 EU countries.

TechMark   Market on the London Stock Exchange for technology-related stocks.

Tender offer   Formal offer to buy made to holders of a particular issue by a third party. Detailed offer is made by public announcement in newspapers and sometimes by personal letter of transmittal to each stockholder.

Thomson Report   An electronic transaction reporting system for international equities on the London Stock Exchange operated by Thomson.

Tick size   The value of a 1-point movement in the contract price of a derivative.

Touch   The best prices available for a stock on the stock market, looking at all market makers.

Trade guarantees Guarantees in place in a market which ensure that all compared or netted trades will be settled as compared regardless of a counterparty default.

Traded option An option which is traded on an exchange.

Trader An individual who buys and sells securities with the objective of making short-term gains.

Trading permits These are issued by exchanges and give the holder the right to have one trader at any one time trading in the contract(s) to which the permit relates.

Transfer agent Agent appointed by a corporation to maintain records of stock and bond owners, to cancel and issue certificates and to resolve problems arising from lost, destroyed or stolen certificates.

Transparency The degree to which a market is characterised by prompt availability of accurate price and volume information which gives participants comfort that the market is fair.

TRAX Trade confirmation system for the euro markets operated by the International Securities Market Association.

Treasury bill Money market instrument issued with a life of less than 1 year issued by the US and UK governments.

Treasury bonds (US) US government bond issued with a 30-year maturity.

Treasury notes (US) US government bond issued with 2-, 3-, 5- and 7-year maturities.

Trustee Appointed to oversee the management of certain funds. They are responsible for ensuring that the fund is managed correctly, that the interests of the investor are protected and that all relevant regulations and legislation are complied with.

Turnaround Securities bought and sold for settlement on the same day.

Two-way price Simultaneous prices in a stock quoted by a market maker, the lower at which he is willing to buy and the higher at which he is willing to sell.

Underlying asset The asset from which the future or option's price is derived.

Underwriters Institutions which agree to take up shares in a new issue if it is undersubscribed. They will charge an underwriting fee.

Unit trust A system whereby money from a number of investors is pooled together and invested collectively on their behalf. Each owns a unit (or number of them) the value of which depends on the value of those items owned by the trust.

Unrealised profit Profit which has not arisen from a sale – an increase in value of an asset.

Value at risk (VaR) The maximum amount which a bank expects to lose, with a given confidence level, over a given time period.

Variation margin The process of revaluing an exchange-traded derivative product each day. It is the difference between the closing price on the previous day against the current closing price. It is physically paid or received each day by the clearing organisation. It is often referred to as **Mark-to-market**.

Volatility The degree of scatter of the underlying price when compared with the mean average rate.

Vostro A vostro account is another bank's account held at our bank in our currency.

Warrants An option which can be listed on an exchange, with a lifetime of generally more than 1 year.

Warrant agent A bank appointed by the issuer as an intermediary between the issuing company and the (physical) warrant holders, interacting when the latter want to exercise the warrants.

Withholding tax In the securities industry, a tax imposed by a government's tax authorities on dividends and interest paid.

Writer A person who has sold an open derivatives contract and is obliged to deliver or take delivery upon notification of exercise from the buyer.

XETRA Dealing system of the Deutsche Börse.

Yankee bond A US dollar bond issued in the US by a non-US corporation.

Yield Internal rate of return expressed as a percentage.

Yield curve For securities that expose the investor to the same credit risk, a graph showing the relationship at a given point in the time between yield and current maturity. Yield curves are typically drawn using yields on governments bonds of various maturities.

Yield to maturity The rate of return yielded by a debt security held to maturity when both interest payments and the investor's capital gain or loss on the security are taken into account.

Zero-coupon bond A bond issued with no coupon but a price substantially below par so that only capital is accrued over the life of the loan, and yield is comparable with coupon bearing instruments.

USEFUL WEBSITES AND SUGGESTED FURTHER READING

· ·

Australian Financial Markets Association	www.afma.com
Australian Stock Exchange	www.asx.com.au
Bank for International Settlement	www.bis.org
Bank of New York	www.fundadmin.com
British Bankers Association	www.bba.org.uk
Chicago Board of Trade	www.cbot.com
Chicago Board Options Exchange	www.cboe.com
Clearnet	www.clearnetsa.com
Clearstream	www.clearstream.com
CLS Bank	www.cls-group.com
Chicago Mercantile Exchange	www.cme.com
Commodities Future Trading Commission	www.cftc.gov
Computer Based Learning Ltd	www.cbl-ltd.co.uk
CRESTCo	www.crestco.co.uk
Depository Trust Company	www.dtc.org
EUREX	www.eurexchange.com
Euroclear	www.euroclear.com

European Central Securities Depositories Association	www.ecsda.com
Financial Services Agency Japan	www.fsa.gov.jp
Financial Services Authority	www.fsa.gov.uk
Futures and Options Association	www.foa.co.uk
Futures Industry Association	www.fiafii.org
G30 Recommendations	http://risk.ifci.ch/
Hong Kong Exchanges and Clearing	www.hkex.com.hk
International Chamber of Commerce	www.iccwbo.org
International Swaps and Derivatives Association	www.isda.org
International Securities Lending Association	www.isla.co.uk
International Securities Markets Association	www.isma.co.uk
International Securities Services Association	www.issanet.org
London Clearing House	www.lch.co.uk
Euronext.liffe	www.euronext.com
London Metal Exchange	www.lme.co.uk
London Stock Exchange	www.londonstockexchange.com
Nasdaq	www.nasdaq.com
New York Stock Exchange	www.nyse.com
Norex Alliance	www.norex.com
Securities Exchange Commission (US)	www.sec.gov
Securities and Investment Institute	www.sii.org.uk
Securities Institute	www.securities-institute.org.uk
Singapore Exchange	www.ses.com.sg
Tokyo Stock Exchange	www.tse.or.jp
virt-x	www.virtx.com

SUGGESTED FURTHER READING

- *Understanding the Financial Markets**
- *Managing Technology in the Operations Function**
- *Clearing, Settlement and Custody**
- *Controls Procedures and Risk**
- *Relationship and Resource Management in Operations**
- *Clearing and Settlement of Derivatives*

Published by Butterworth Heinemann

- *Mastering Treasury Operations*
- *Understanding Foreign Exchange and Currency Options*

Published by FT Prentice Hall

- *Advanced Operations Management,* Second Edition, by David Loader
- *An Introduction to Credit Derivatives,* by David Loader
- *Securities Operations: A Guide to Trade and Position Management,* by Michael Simmons

Published by John Wiley & Sons

visUlearn™ SERIES OF CD-ROMs

- *Equities & Bonds*
- *Derivatives & Commodities*
- *Operations – Clearing, Settlement & Custody*
- *An Overview of the Financial Services Industry*

*Order from *www.dscporfolio.com* or call 0207 403 8383 quoting 'websites/reading' for a major discount.

INDEX